AD

THE YEAR THAT

33

CHANGED THE WORLD

COLIN DURIEZ

IVP Books

An imprint of InterVarsity Press
Downers Grove, Illinois

InterVarsity Press
P.O. Box 1400, Downers Grove, IL 60515-1426
World Wide Web: www.ivpress.com
E-mail: mail@ivpress.com

Published in the United States of America by InterVarsity Press, Downers Grove, Illinois, with permission from Sutton Publishing, Ltd.

InterVarsity Press® is the book-publishing division of InterVarsity Christian Fellowship/USA®, a student movement active on campus at hundreds of universities, colleges and schools of nursing in the United States of America, and a member movement of the International Fellowship of Evangelical Students. For information about local and regional activities, write Public Relations Dept., InterVarsity Christian Fellowship/USA, 6400 Schroeder Rd., P.O. Box 7895, Madison, WI 53707-7895, or visit the IVCF website at <www.intervarsity.org>.

Design: Cindy Kiple
Images: Roz Woodward/Getty Images

ISBN 978-0-8308-3396-2

Printed in Canada ∞

Library of Congress Cataloging-in-Publication Data

Duriez, Colin.
    AD 33 : the year that changed the world / Colin Duriez.
        p. cm.
    Includes bibliographical references (p.   ) and index.
    ISBN-13: 978-0-8308-3396-2 (cloth: alk. paper)
    ISBN-10: 0-8308-3396-X (cloth: alk. paper)
    1. Jesus Christ—Crucifixion. 2. Jesus Christ—Influence. 3.
    Church history—Primitive and early church, ca. 30-600. I. Title.
    II. Title: A.D. 33.
    BT453.D87 2007
    270.1—dc22

                                                                                2006030490

P	18	17	16	15	14	13	12	11	10	9	8	7	6	5	4	3	2	1
Y	22	21	20	19	18	17	16	15	14	13	12	11	10	09	08	07			

CONTENTS

Maps and Plans 7
Preface 19
Prologue: Two Kings, Two Kingdoms 21

1 Papyri and Puzzles 29

THE EAST
2 Tiberius and the Eastern Empire 39

NEAR JERUSALEM
3 The Road of Courage: Jesus of Nazareth, Early Spring A.D. 33 65

ROME
4 Tiberius and the Shadow of Sejanus 73

JERUSALEM
5 Darkness at Noon (March 28-April 3) 85
6 The Glory of the Temple 115
7 Fifty Days: Prelude to Changing the World (April 5-May 23) 124

THE WIDER WORLD
8 The Western Empire 145
9 Past the Boundaries of Empire 154
10 Beyond the Ends of the Earth 162

JERUSALEM
11 Simon Peter: The Birth of the Church (Pentecost, May 24) 169

ROME
12 Agrippina, Sunday, October 18 181

JERUSALEM
13 New Conflict in Jerusalem: Stephen and Saul 193

A WORLD IN THE MAKING
14 What Happened Next? 205

CHRONOLOGY
Dating A.D. 33 219
Chronology of the Period (44 B.C. to A.D. 70) 226
Chronology of A.D. 33 231

Acknowledgments 234
Notes 235
Bibliography 246
Index 252

MAPS AND PLANS

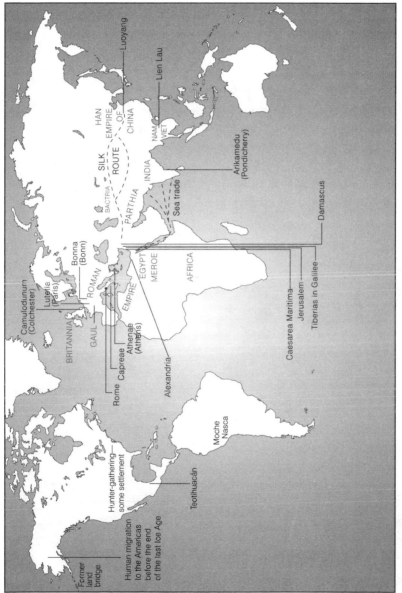

The world in A.D. 33

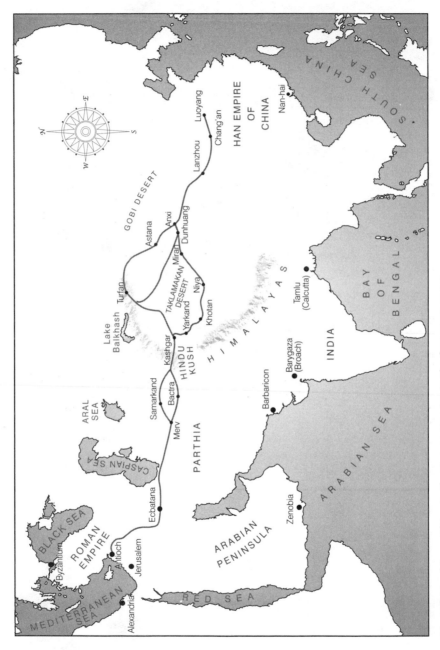

The Silk Road from China to the Roman Empire in the first century A.D.

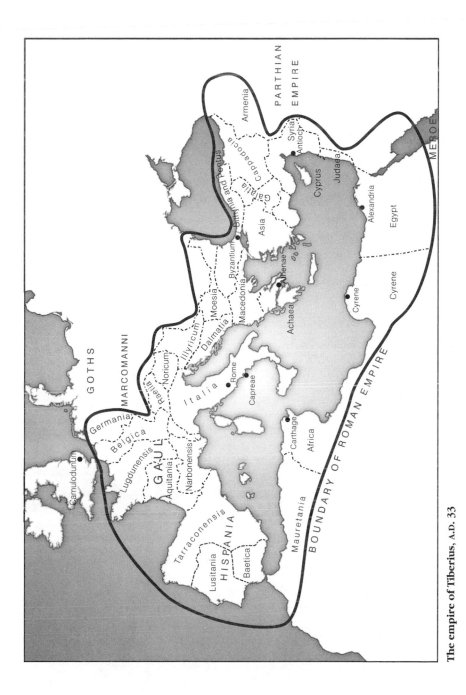

The empire of Tiberius, A.D. 33

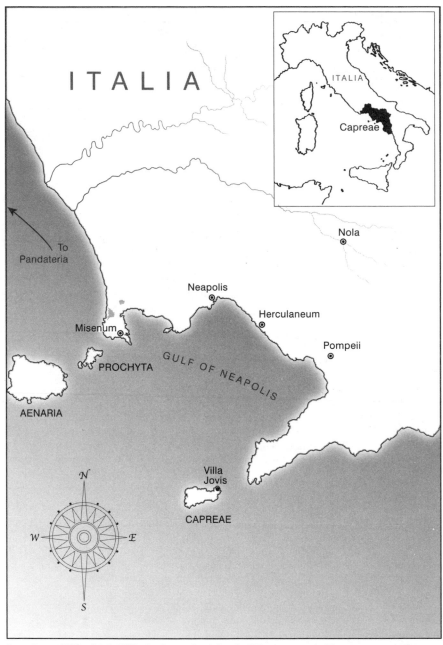

Location of Tiberius's Villa Jovis on the island of Capreae, A.D. 33

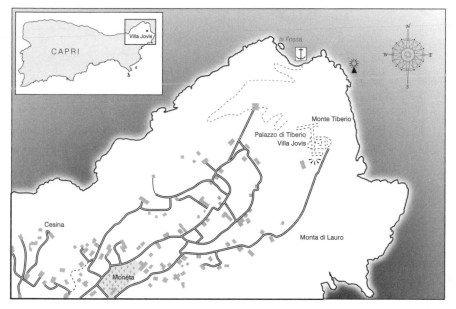

Site of the Villa Jovis on modern Capri

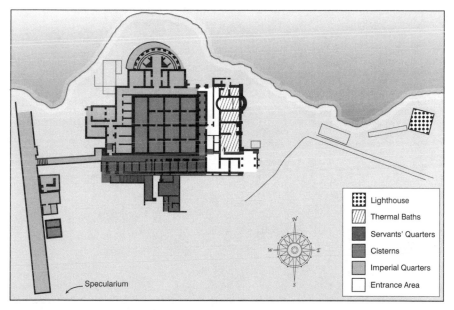

Layout of the Villa Jovis

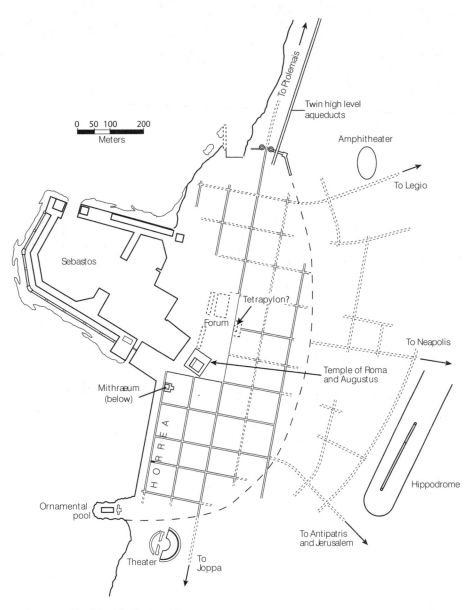

Caesarea Maritima in Roman times

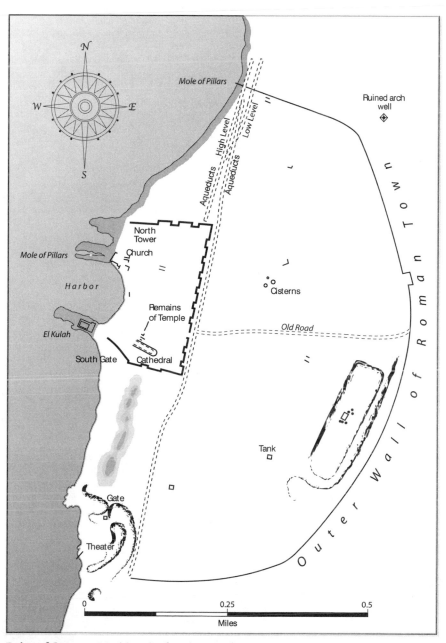

Ruins of Caesarea Maritima in the nineteenth century

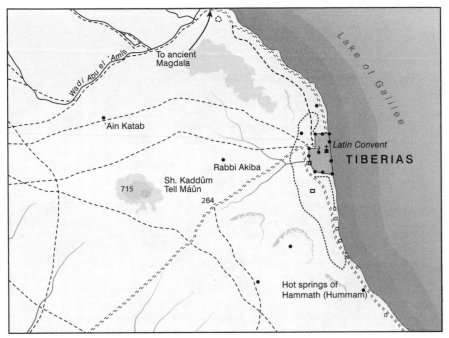

Tiberias in the nineteenth century

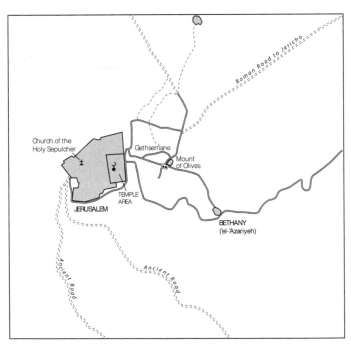

Jerusalem and Bethany in the nineteenth century

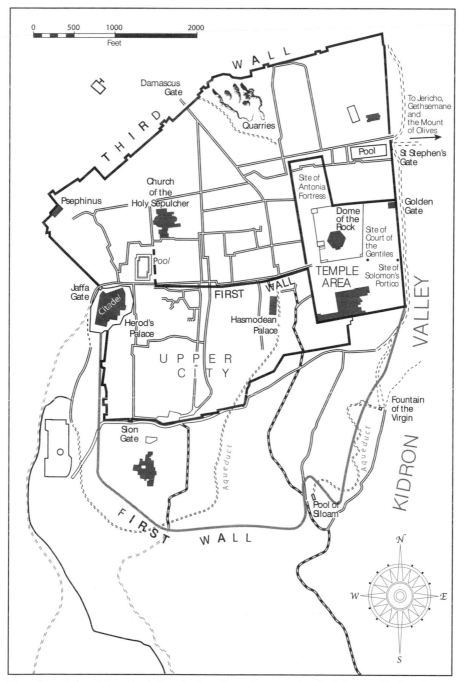

Map of Jerusalem taken from the nineteenth-century map by the Palestine Exploration Fund

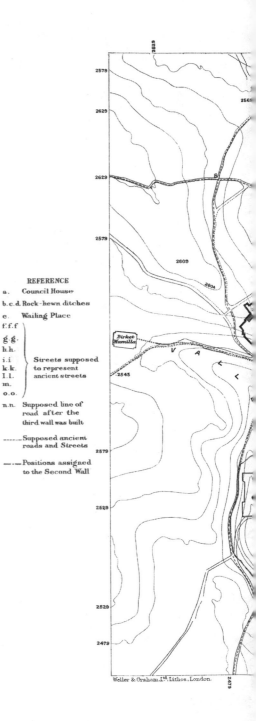

REFERENCE

a.   Council House

b.c.d. Rock-hewn ditches

e.   Wailing Place

f.f.f

g.g.

h.h.

i.i

k.k.   Streets supposed
           to represent
l.l.   ancient streets

m.

o.o.

n.n.   Supposed line of
       road after the
       third wall was built

------ Supposed ancient
       roads and Streets

--·-- Positions assigned
      to the Second Wall

Weller & Graham, Lᵗᵈ. Lithos., London.

Jerusalem in the nineteenth century, before subsequent urbanization obscured features of the landscape that would have been recognizable in A.D. 33. Bethany lies southeast of the Mount of Olives, just off the map to the right. The Roman road to Jericho runs northeast from St. Stephen's Gate. *(Palestine Exploration Fund)*

JERUSALEM

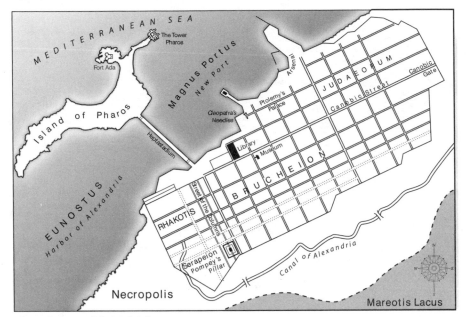

Plan of Alexandria in the first century A.D.

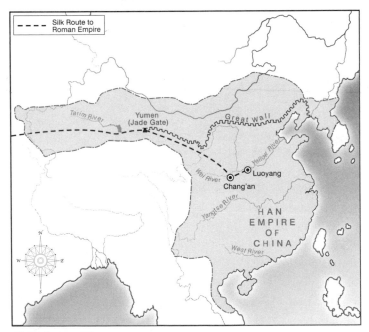

China in A.D. 33

PREFACE

A.D. 33 WAS A REMARKABLE YEAR BY ALL ACCOUNTS, dominated, so far as the hindsight of world history is concerned, by two people, a Roman and a Jew. The emperor in this year is in the final chapter of his principate, trying to end the mischief caused by his deputy, Sejanus, while at the same time keeping a tight rein on the administration of the empire, in all its diversity. There existed no script for his endeavor. The other man, Jesus, was put to death by one of Tiberius's minor governors, Pontius Pilate. Belief in his resurrection from the dead three days later invigorated his demoralized followers, leading within a few weeks to the birth of the Christian movement, which was ultimately to take over the mighty empire without force and to change the world irrevocably. While momentous events unfolded in the lives of the two kings, Tiberius and Jesus, one temporal and one spiritual, millions of people carried on their daily routines, rising at dawn and going to their rest in the evening.

I have tried to portray some of the people—both humble and powerful—who were of historical importance during this year, and to give a glimpse of the world as it existed at that time. As for all historical periods, much of what has come down to us has survived by accident, and much that is important for understanding the era has been lost. The ancient documents that have survived have done so because of the labors of many unknown individuals who copied and preserved them. In particular, surviving writings that record or touch on the events of A.D. 33 I have tried to use with respect and to understand through the minds of the time, so far as their beliefs and perceptions can be reconstructed.

In writing this book I have attempted to step back into a far-off world. It is a world that is not only distant in time, but also in the very way that people saw the skies, buildings and landscapes around them. It had an utterly different consciousness from ours, one that had a greater integration, to all appearances, than we have of the spiritual and the natural. I have tried to enter into it sympathetically, listening to its voices and observing its events. My aim has been to open up that world for readers of today.

My task has been finished with a profound sense that there is far more to say about this remarkable and yet elusive year, a year that has captured my imagination and attention for a considerable period. I offer my book in the hope that it will at least be an introduction to a year that provides a master key to so much that has happened since, a year that still has a remarkable influence in the early twenty-first century on culture, politics, literature and the very way that we see the world. We owe to it those who lived then, and who touch our lives now, to take account of the world as they saw it.

Colin Duriez

PROLOGUE

TWO KINGS, TWO KINGDOMS

DECEMBER A.D. 32: CAPREAE

An elderly but upright figure walks weightily along the wide balcony, looking to his left as usual at the high Monte Solaro, catching the early sun across the dip in the island. Then Tiberius's eyes take in the dark blue sea far below as he moves on. In a couple of minutes he reaches the end of the balcony. Here the emperor can see the whole of the Gulf of Neapolis, from the islands of Aenaria and Prochyta close by the imperial base of Misenum, along the villa-dotted bay and Vesuvius's high pyramid, and right around to the point of Campania, separated from Capreae by a narrow channel. His eyes sweep back to the northernmost point of vision, the cool horizon mist beyond the distant islands. There, somewhere solitary in the deep ocean, is the tiny island of Pandateria. It gives him satisfaction to know that Agrippina, granddaughter of the former Augustus himself, is tormented there by her exile—queen of the only territory he allows her. Maybe she is looking this way at the moment, in hatred of him. He smiles at the thought. If she is, it would only be through one eye, thanks to the beating he caused her.

Even this early, of course, Tiberius is not alone; there are the inevitable background slaves, keeping a distance, awaiting any order he might utter. The emperor is a man of few words; missing them may incur his dangerous anger. There are other fears, too. Those who are young—whether female or boys—are in terror of stories of his obscene, scrabbling hands, and of what may follow in private, away from eyes that may judge. Yesterday, a slave had carelessly spilled wine over the emperor's toga. It looked like blood— there was panic for a second in the superstitious Tiberius's face. After torture—"exquisite torture" is how the emperor likes to put it—he had the trembling slave thrown over the precipice upon which the villa stands. The slaves knew he enjoyed watching how far his victims could fall in a clean drop before scraping the cliff face and bouncing off. Such an interruption in the fall usually silenced the screams. If it didn't, he was delighted.

Tiberius liked to have as much of the first hour as he could here on the roofed promenade, even though the air was still sharp this winter morning. Away from the thrall of Rome he could enjoy the idea of it. The city, with its order and its humane law, extended throughout the world. This broad sea before him was the road to all his kingdoms. It was his—only one almost like a god could have so much. In this stillness before the day he would think around the provinces, from Hispania and Gaul in the west to Judea and Syria in the east, from wooded Germania in the north—so familiar to him as a soldier—to the hot lands of Africa in the south. He could usually see the daily naval ship from the mainland passing below, its oars flashing or sail swelling and its wake widening, as it made its way to Capreae's modest harbor. Today was no exception. The vessel was moving swiftly in the breeze. There might be a dispatch from his friend Avilius Flaccus, enthusiastic in his new governorship of Egypt. In his last dispatch he had mentioned speculation about a possible reappearance of the phoenix, the fabled bird of the sun which stood for undying life. Tiberius is not yet expecting an answer from Pontius Pilate, in Caesarea Maritima. His order to remove the offensive votive shields from Jerusalem would barely have reached him, given the winter travel conditions—a long, hard journey overland for the courier. What offense that man had already caused to the stubborn Jews, before this! It is just as well that he is kept informed of his governor's occasional misjudgments.

His thoughts are interrupted by a greeting from Thrasyllus, his personal astrologer. Tiberius, a keen amateur himself, is always anxious to hear his prognostications. Thrasyllus clutches a parchment in his hands. The two sit down on a bench while Thrasyllus unfurls the document. It is inscribed with intricate patterns relating to movements in the heavens. "There was a good omen, last night," Thrasyllus begins. "I was walking as usual down to the Specularium. On the path in front of me I saw a snake. The serpent followed the path before me a while, as if leading me, before disappearing. The omen confirms what I saw in the skies last night. My chart shows a good year ahead for the world. Soon you will appoint an heir, and he will be a serpent to Rome."

"Excellent!" Tiberius says. "I think the shadow of Sejanus will be gone before long—after I make more of those who were his friends take their journey across the Styx. I dreamed of him last night, and your words have eased the disquiet this gave me."

"What was your dream?" asks Thrasyllus on cue.

"I dreamed of having all the kingdoms of the earth, beyond the empire to Britannia, Parthia, Bactria and further east. But a dark figure who looked like Sejanus mockingly said he had given them to me. Sejanus—if it was he—took me to the cliff-drop beside the villa and said that I was a god. If I threw myself off the angeli would carry me down unharmed. He then took up a large stone from the ground and began to eat it like a starving man."

"The weight of Sejanus is indeed heavy. But he is gone, and deceives as usual. He starves for your soul. Laugh at him in torment in hell. Better times are ahead."[1]

◆ ◆ ◆

The unpleasant Tiberius just pictured may partly be created by the second-century histories of Tacitus and Suetonius. Dio Cassius similarly creates a negative picture of the emperor's life in Capreae, perhaps influenced by those earlier historians. It may be that they did not realize the extent to which Tiberius kept his private and public life in separate compartments. A contemporary, Philo of Alexandria, portrays Tiberius in a much more favorable light, perhaps in contrast to Gaius Caligula's wickedness when he succeeded Tiberius as emperor. Philo may, however, have had limited access to official documents. Certainly Tiberius, following the example of Augustus, tended to restrain injustices in the provinces, typically enjoining one of his governors (a previous prefect of Egypt, Aemilius Rectus): "I want my sheep shorn, not flayed." He may have liked to see himself as a Shepherd Prince. As part of this shepherding he protected the Jewish populations in the empire, both in Palestine and in the Diaspora. It is unlikely that he was aware of the strong anti-Jewish tendencies of his deputy Sejanus, who in effect administered Rome for many years until Tiberius realized his treachery and swiftly acted to remove him in A.D. 31.

Tiberius had forsaken Rome and had lived in Capreae since A.D. 27. Astrologers had predicted that he would not set foot in Rome again, so he never did, in case it would mean his death. He was prone to voluntary exile. Before he was prince of the empire, in the days of Augustus, he had gone to Rhodes for many years. There he had met Thrasyllus, who had taught him his Chaldean brand of astrology. Tiberius was no mean amateur—according to Roman historians he would predict the brief reign of Galba in A.D. 69, the "year of four emperors."

His magnificent Villa Jovis in Capreae, named after the main Roman deity, Jupiter, was in effect a palace, with its court. Along with thousands of slaves, Tiberius surrounded himself with Greek scholars (a custom he had long followed) as well as his personal astrologer (who was a restraining influence on his excesses). One such scholar was Seleucis the grammarian.[2] It was Tiberius's practice at supper to raise questions, based on what he had been reading during the day. Seleucis had the bright idea of inquiring of his attendants which authors he was currently reading. This allowed him to come prepared for Tiberius's questions. When the strongly built Tiberius discovered this, he was furious, laying into Seleucis and throwing him out of his household. As well as reading widely, the emperor had an absorbing interest in rhetoric and philosophy.

It is plausible that his excesses increased as he became elderly and his sexual powers decreased. Despite his indulgent, predatory sexual life (if the accounts have a core of truth, which is likely) he tried to be plain living and kept a grip on the worldwide affairs of the empire through his provincial governors, whom he encouraged to stay long term, and to whom he allowed initiative and discretion in their administration. He particularly followed the work of the imperial appointees—those governing frontier provinces like Judea and Syria. They would be either *legati* or lesser *procuratores,* depending on the perceived importance of the province. Both kinds had extensive discretionary powers in enforcing Roman rule and law. The *legati,* however, had a much more formidable military backing. By ill-judgment Judea had been assigned a prefect rather than a high-ranking ambassador. Pontius Pilate was appointed back in A.D. 26, almost certainly chosen by Sejanus, Tiberius's former deputy, on the emperor's behalf. Any former friend of Sejanus feared the emperor now. The ruthless slaughter of his associates by Tiberius continued, though perhaps not on the scale reported by his historians.[3]

DECEMBER 18, A.D. 32 (KISLEV 25)

The charismatic rabbi from Galilee is again in Jerusalem. Though the inhabitants, beginning their joyful Feast of Hanukkah, do not know it, this is to be the valedictory of his public teaching. On this winter's day he has made his way to Jerusalem, two miles from the small village of Bethany, over the hills to the west, where he habitually stays while visiting the holy city.

He has already entertained a crowd with his vivid, figurative teaching. As usual he teaches, like others, under the broad colonnade that skirts the lower court of the temple, known as the Court of the Gentiles. Its broad pillars provide shelter from cold winds in the winter and shade from the sun the rest of the year. Though Jesus of Nazareth lacks the educated Judean accent of the official religious teachers, he speaks with authority. As usual, the common people hear him gladly. Today there has been a hard edge to his words, for, as he expected, in the crowd are a number of the religious professionals—chief priests, scribes and others of Jerusalem's wealthy elite. He has spoken of being the good shepherd, and of being the protective gate for his sheep, for whom he cares. He has talked about gathering his flock and laying down his life for them. This bit of his teaching is easy for the crowd—they know the sheep are the Jews, God's chosen people, defined by the life and procedures of the temple in Judea. The result of his words, inevitably, is a division among his hearers. Some say he is insane, demon-possessed.

Afterward, Jesus walks in the long colonnade of Solomon's Portico, which runs along the edge of the huge artificial plateau of the temple area. He can see in the center of the court, raised above balustrades, the colossal temple proper, the sanctuary which only Jews can enter. Stone tablets warn Gentiles not to go in. Walking to Jerusalem early that morning, in the first hour, he had seen the rising sun's rays burn back from the gold plate of the high temple. It looked like a mountain covered with snow—the blaze of fire was so intense he saw its after-image as he turned away his gaze.

The temple, with its vast lower courtyard and high colonnades, is an immense structure, taking up one-sixth of the area of the city. The colonnade of Solomon extends along the eastern side of the temple complex.

Jesus does not enjoy the peace of his walk very long, or his professional appreciation of the cedarwork of its ceiling high above. Some of the religious leaders wall him about and confront him impatiently, stirred up by his teaching about being the one true shepherd of the Jews. There had been many in Israel before him with messianic claims.

"How long are you going to goad us? You hide your words in parables and figures of speech. Out with it, man! Are you the Messiah who has been promised through the ages? Come on, spit it out!"

Jesus answers in a deliberate and measured tone, "I've already told you many times, but you don't believe. What I've done in my father's name bears witness to who I am." (He is referring to his much-talked-about teaching, healings and other supernatural signs.) "The only reason you don't believe is because you are not part of my flock." As he says "my flock," his gesture takes in some men and women listening nearby who are known to be his disciples. Among them are individuals who are certainly not fit company for pious Jews.

He continues to speak penetratingly over the rising murmurs of dissent on the part of his interrogators: "As I said to you, my sheep hear my voice, and I know them, and they follow me, and I give to them life that is everlasting, and they shall never perish, neither shall anyone pluck them out of my hand. My father, who gave them to me, is greater than all, and no one is able to take them out of my father's hand."

Then there is a pause before the punchline, as Jesus looks directly at his critics, knowingly condemning himself to destruction: "And I and my father are one."[4]

◆ ◆ ◆

We are told in John's Gospel that, at this point, his accusers picked up stones (which they may have brought with them). They were incensed by his blasphemy—his claim to be one with God, Maker of heaven and earth. Jesus was known by contemporary historians such as Tacitus and Josephus as the "Christ," or as claiming to be the Christ (Greek, *Christos,* Messiah). A messianic claim by itself would not be blasphemy. Jewish belief at this time was diverse. Some groups looked for a messiah who would deliver the nation by force as an insurrectionist leader. Others placed their hope in a holy man or priest who would come apocalyptically at the end times. None of these concepts of messiah implied a divine claim.

By now, either the group had moved outside the temple area through one of the great entrances where rocks could be found in the Kidron Valley, or perhaps they armed themselves with building material (parts of the temple area were still under construction nearly fifty years after its foundation was laid by Herod the Great).

History would be very different, unrecognizable in fact, if the small mob had stoned him there and then. They might have pushed him over the edge of the steep Kidron Valley, then finished off the job with rocks, smashing his head and body before soldiers had time to arrive from Fortress Antonia. His distraught followers would have dragged away his body, buried him and venerated his tomb for a while as one of many failed messiahs and potential saviors, more memorable perhaps than Theudas,[5] Judas the Galilean, and his sons James and Simon,[6] but not much more. Jesus, however, continued to reason with his interrogators in rabbinic fashion, from a point within the scriptural Torah where people entrusted as divine agents were called "sons of God," which was clearly not blasphemous. This exposition made them remain a group instead of a mob. They may also have feared the vast number of people round about, increased because of the feast, who favored Jesus. They changed their minds about stoning, and instead tried to arrest him. We are told simply that he evaded capture and left Jerusalem, escaping beyond the River Jordan.

It was no accident that Jesus chose the Feast of Dedication for his valedictory public teaching. The winter feast was heavy with symbolism. Its purpose was to celebrate the rededication of the temple after its desecration under Syro-Grecian domination. The festival—called the "Feast of Lights" by Josephus—was established by Judas Maccabaeus in 164 B.C.[7] The feast began on Kislev (December) 25 and lasted eight days. On each day the "Hallel" was sung, and people joyfully carried palms and other branches. The temple was magnificently illuminated, and so were all private houses. The head of the household might light one lamp for all family members or a lamp for each. The particularly devout might increase the number each day, so if a household had ten lights on the first day, there would be eighty on the last day of the festival.[8]

Jesus by his presence at the feast was signaling that this year the temple was undergoing a rededication even more radical than that of 164 B.C. It was not simply remembering that great event. In this case, according to the New Testament accounts, Jesus himself was the new temple. This claim was based on his identity—he was, he said, one with God (his Father). In the Christian view, he replaced the existing temple as the place where all are to come for forgiveness of sin and to meet God.[9] He was simultaneously the final sacrifice and the "place" of worship. With the destruction of the temple in A.D. 70, the Christian and rabbinic versions of Judaism were to gradually diverge—for Christians, Jesus replaced the temple worship and sacraments; for the rabbinic Jews, the synagogue and the Torah filled the aching void.[10]

Significantly, Jesus announced this claim in the Court of the Gentiles, not in the higher sanctuary of the temple proper, where non-Jews were forbidden access. As always with Jesus' actions, a living iconography was enacted.

The apostles later understood him as signifying the inauguration of the kingdom of heaven, of which he had so often spoken, that transcended all nations, states and civilizations. In his claim it transcended even the temple of
the nation of the chosen people, which was only a copy of the original. His
claim was that he is the Original.[11]

◆ ◆ ◆

Rome and Jerusalem at this time were both cities that were symbols as well
as places. Under Augustus and Tiberius, the Roman empire had established
a civilizing "Pax Romana," and Jerusalem's very name could mean "foundation of peace." These two cities hereafter symbolically would dominate the
history of Western and world civilization. Rome represented the rule of civilized law—an idea that transcended the works of bad men like Caligula and
Nero. Jerusalem, and its temple in particular, defined the monotheism, allegiance to the Torah and moral clarity of ancient Jewish faith. Rooted in this
ancient faith, the new allegiance to Jesus would forever in its essence have
the character of that faith, however ignorant of this inheritance some of its
followers might become. By a strange irony the idea of a "new Jerusalem,"
associated with following Christ, would win over the mighty empire without
force in less than three hundred years. The result would be mutual enrich-
ment and a creative tension, what George Steiner calls "the dual currents
which determine Western consciousness, that of classical antiquity and that
of scriptural-Christian inheritance."[12]

1

PAPYRI AND PUZZLES

IF YOU WANDERED INTO A PRIVATE ROMAN LIBRARY IN A.D. 33—of which there were many, as it was the height of fashion to have one—you might be surprised to find that it was quite small, even though, likely enough, well furnished and decorated. If you stretched out your arms you might be able to touch both sides of the room. Yet a room this size could house up to 1,700 scrolls—each the equivalent of a small book. The rolls would typically be in cases around the walls, all numbered, with a rectangular case in the middle of the room.

Such manuscript rolls—for, of course, literature at this time was hand-written—comprised sheets made out of papyrus (the source of the English word *paper*), stitched together end on. Unrolled they could be up to as much as about 20 to 40 yards in length. Many of the ancient sources used in writing this book would have had their lengths, or the lengths of their divisions, determined by the physical length of the scrolls used.

As well as many private libraries, there were also large libraries such as the magnificent one at Alexandria, in Egypt, which may have housed as many as 500,000 rolls, or that in Pergamum with about 200,000 rolls. A whole industry surrounded the making of written works. An author might dictate to a group of scribes. A copy might be loaned or hired out to use for further copying by a single scribe or a group, with one person dictating. Even in modern publishing, where the best publishers have stringent methods for checking and double-checking proofs before a text goes to the printers, errors can creep in. In the copying system of first-century publishing, words could be misheard or handwriting misread. Once introduced, errors could be passed on if the faulty copy were used as the basis for further copies, rather like the telephone game or Chinese whispers. It is not surprising that scholars trying to determine meanings of ancient texts, whether Gospels or works by Latin or Greek authors, often find it difficult to gauge the true meaning of some details.

Later in the first century came the remarkable development of the codex, which is far more like our concept of a book. Pages were stitched together and written on, on both sides. It is possible that the technology of the codex was driven by the need of Christian churches throughout the empire to group together their writings. Certainly, by the mid-second century, and perhaps earlier, the four Gospel accounts were collected together—the accounts that became known as the Gospels of Matthew, Mark, Luke and John. One of the earliest fragments of a Gospel from a codex has been dated around A.D. 130, from the Gospel of John. Remarkably, some forty-two papyrus fragments of the Gospels have so far been discovered from codices. T. C. Skeat pointed out the significance of this: "This is an astonishing statistic, if we reflect that among non-Christian papyri the roll form predominated for centuries, and it was not until about A.D. 300 that the codex achieved parity of representation with the scroll, and another two or three centuries passed before the roll disappeared altogether as a vehicle for literature."[1]

Graham Stanton, an eminent British New Testament scholar, agrees with T. C. Skeat's belief that Christians adopted the codex because it could contain all four Gospels. (The individual Gospels only fit on to a scroll.) This has profound implications for the complex issue of canon (how the early Church decided which texts were authoritative as holy Scripture).

The Gospel accounts, of course, must be an important source for the task of discovering events in A.D. 33. Scholars for several centuries have debated the nature of these accounts. Are they history (in which case, how do we weigh up elements that appear to be historically unlikely, such as miracle-working)? Are they biography (and if so, why are they so different from a modern perception of the genre of biography)? Are they religious texts (and therefore may have a totally different purpose from that of the historian)? Also essential are the Roman histories of Tacitus, Suetonius and Dio Cassius, all of whom write of events of the year A.D. 33 or preceding and subsequent events that are relevant to that year. Tacitus is the most helpful, as his *Annals,* by its nature, recounts events year by year. Then too there are the Jewish histories of Josephus. Other literature of the period casts incidental light on the lives, thinking and beliefs of people throughout the empire. Outside of the Roman and Jewish world, carefully preserved documentation of the era is to be found in China, whose civilization had already flourished for many centuries. In exploring these ancient texts, my overwhelming feeling has been delight in what has survived for us to read, and today is so easy to access through cheap paperbacks and the Internet, but also sorrow at what has been lost to us. My admiration for textual scholars, historians, translators and archaeologists concerned with this period is immense.

In using the four Gospel accounts I have made the same assumption as with employing the three accounts of the emperor Tiberius to be found in the Roman historians Tacitus, Suetonius and Dio Cassius. From these can be built up a picture of events that is reasonably consistent, supplemented by any other available source (e.g., archaeological finds). I have focused on this broad picture rather than on very detailed differences in the accounts, which are really the realm of the textual scholar. This is because my purpose is to try to give a consistent portrait of the events of A.D. 33, in which various strands, particularly Roman and Jewish, interrelate. It is possible to weigh the individual purposes of each Gospel, just as it is to weigh the antipathy of the three Roman historians to the Julio-Claudian period of Tiberius, without dismissing their historicity. The closeness of the accounts to the actual events is of course an important issue. We assume that the Roman historians drew (with varying closeness) on older documents. Many scholars similarly assume that the Gospel writers drew on older sources, or were eyewitnesses or drew upon eyewitness accounts. Some scholars, however, believe that the Gospel accounts are too distant from the events, in the sense that Christian beliefs radically developed and modified the stories of Jesus for them to be accepted at historical face value. They have to be deconstructed to reveal the original Jesus, prior to Christian spin, a Jesus who turns out to be one of several holy teachers whose charisma attracted followings or an eschatological prophet or a wandering philosopher. A problem with these views is that such a figure would hardly set the world alight in the way that Jesus did—the overriding causal element in the rapid expansion of the Christian movement in its first generation was its conviction that Jesus had returned from death and that this authenticated his claim to be the Messiah. The considerable number of scholars who do not put a radically late view on composition suggest a maximum range between the mid-60s (with Mark's Gospel) and the 90s (John's Gospel). Dating of writings of this period is notoriously difficult. The fact that a fragment from John's Gospel exists from a codex dated early second century (Rylands Papyrus 457, dated around A.D. 130) indicates publication well before the date of that codex.

The fact that there are four Gospel accounts has led to intense debate over many generations as to their interrelationship. Though all are indepen-

dently authored, with differing purposes, three of them in particular have
striking similarities, suggesting that at least two may have used at least one
of the others as a partial source. A persuasive theory has posited that a core
of lost oral or even written material, mainly comprising segments of Jesus'
teaching, was a source the three Gospels (Matthew, Mark, and Luke) had in
common. The content of this core is also the subject of extensive debate.
Some scholars argue that similarities between the three can be explained
without this core material, called by scholars "Q" (that is, if Luke made use
of both Mark's and Matthew's accounts).[2] The majority view is that Mark's
Gospel was written first and that Luke and Matthew made use of Mark and
another source (the material called Q) as well as material unique to each
(such as accounts of Joseph and Jesus' birth in Matthew). The Fourth Gospel
was, in the view of scholars, written independently of the other three and
most likely was written last.

As well as literary and source criticism of the Gospels, there has been a
great deal of scholarly debate over the dates of their composition. Judg-
ments about this are inevitably swayed by one's views of how close the
Gospels bring us to the actual events of Jesus' life and his teaching. If the
view is that much of the material is anachronistic, being in fact the expression of later developments in Christian thought, then later dates are posited, as writers who were eyewitnesses or who drew on eyewitness accounts were unlikely to modify the material in this way. Inevitably,
therefore, larger questions are involved. One very fruitful line of inquiry is
to consider the Gospel accounts in the context of the diversity of Jewish
beliefs in the period before A.D. 70, when the fall of Jerusalem and the destruction of the temple had such an impact on both Jewish and Christian
communities, and when so much was lost to us (see chap. 6). Such inquiry
can take into account the Jewish nature of the New Testament writings, in,
for example, the letter to the Hebrews or the late-written book of Revelation. There is strong evidence that the church in its first generation was predominantly Jewish. If one considers the Gospels as literary narratives, their
affinities are with the Jewish Scriptures rather than with Hellenistic literature. An example of racy narrative by a Latin author is Petronius's *Satyricon*. Although, like the Gospel writers, Petronius includes characters from
common life, he has no interest in a distinctive historical context: what he
writes is intentionally fiction that is close to the genres of its time, particularly of comedy and satire. The *Satyricon* was probably written around the

same time as the Gospel of Mark, and so makes a significant comparison.

It is true, however, that the Gospel writers had some knowledge of contemporary Greco-Roman history writing, which affected the structuring of their material rather than its distinctive narrative character. Building on the work of some earlier scholars, Richard A. Burridge has offered a convincing case for genre similarities between the Gospels and contemporary Greco-Roman biography. In his *What Are the Gospels? A Comparison with Graeco-Roman Biography,* after a detailed examination of the structure of representative biographies by Xenophon, Satyrus, Nepos, Philo, Tacitus, Plutarch and others, he concludes that the Gospels belong to the genre of Greco-Roman biography. Generic features in common with the Gospels include length (between ten thousand and twenty thousand words, fitting a typical scroll of about 10 yards long), absence of a strict chronological sequence in the narrative, and inclusion of selected stories, anecdotes, sayings, and discourses in the middle sections. In content there are also similarities between such contemporary biography and the Gospels. Burridge explains:

> They begin with a brief mention of the hero's ancestry, family or city, followed by his birth and an occasional anecdote about his upbringing; usually we move rapidly on to his public debut later in life. Accounts of generals, politicians, or statesmen are much more chronologically ordered when recounting their great deeds and virtues, while lives of philosophers, writers, or thinkers tend to be more anecdotal, arranged around collections of material to display their ideas and teachings. While the author may claim to provide information about his subject, often his underlying aims may include apologetic (to defend the subject's memory against others' attacks), polemic (to attack his rivals) or didactic (to teach his followers about him). Similarly, the gospels concentrate on Jesus' teaching and great deeds to explain the faith of the early Christians. As for the climax, the evangelists devote between 15 and 20 per cent of the gospels to the last week of Jesus' life, his death and the resurrection; similar amounts are given over to their subjects' death in biographies by Plutarch, Tacitus, Nepos and Philostratus, since in this crisis the hero reveals his true character, gives his definitive teaching or does his greatest deed.[3]

In his *The New Testament and the People of God,* N. T. Wright extends Richard Burridge's conclusions to consider a unique blending of genres in each of the four Gospels. He accepts the genre similarities between Greco-Roman biography and the Gospels. The blending of genres is distinctive in each of the Gospels, but similarities outweigh differences. He builds a strong case for each Gospel being a Jewish story intended for a wider Gentile readership. Thus each brilliantly blends a Jewish genre with Hellenistic biography, making their accounts accessible to both Jewish and Gentile readerships. The Jewish genre in itself is superbly accomplished, being an integral whole that includes strongly distinctive elements such as apocalyptic, fulfillment of ancient prophecy and sense of the ending of a millennia-old story, as Jesus fulfils the Old Testament. The emphasis on particular elements, of course, varies from Gospel to Gospel.[4] On top of their accomplishments in employing the Jewish story, the Gospel writers also brilliantly succeeded in using the Hellenistic genre of biography, in such a way that it would be recognizable by a Greco-Roman readership.

Dr. Wright points out this unique blending of genres, for example, in Luke:

> How do these genres—the Jewish story reaching its climax, and the Hellenistic bios, the life-story of a human individual within the Greco-Roman world—fit together? . . . Luke believed that, prior to Jesus, Israel's story had yet to reach its climax. . . . But at the same time Luke clearly grasped the equally important Jewish belief that when Israel was redeemed the whole world would be blessed. . . . The good news of the established kingdom would have to impinge on the Gentile world. Since, therefore, he believed that this good news had taken the form of the life, and particularly the death and resurrection, of one human being, and since this was a Jewish message for the Gentile world, Luke blended together two apparently incompatible genres with consummate skill. He told the story of Jesus as a Jewish story, indeed as the Jewish story, much as Josephus told the story of the fall of Jerusalem as the climax of Israel's long and tragic history. But he told it in such a way as to say to his non-Jewish Greco-Roman audience: here, in the life of this one man, is the Jewish message of salvation that you pagans need.[5]

As well as their uniqueness in blending genres, the Gospels are also remarkable from a literary point of view in having a "low-class" setting, even though, of course, their biographical subject is a great man, mockingly dubbed "The King of the Jews" by Pontius Pilate. In this Jewish heritage they anticipate the rise of the realistic novel very many centuries later, and also the related genesis of documentary journalism in Daniel Defoe's account of the plague year and the recording of ordinary life in diarists such as Samuel Pepys.

Tacitus's *Annals,* though part of the work has been lost, nevertheless gives an essential account of the year A.D. 33 as part of a portrayal of the emperor Tiberius. It also recounts preceding events that bear on the year, particularly the rise and fall of Sejanus, Tiberius's deputy. It may have been written around A.D. 115-117. Suetonius's *Lives of the Caesars* includes a much more anecdotal and colorful account of Tiberius than is found in Tacitus's measured and concise history. His *Lives* were written later in the second century. The third substantial account we have of Tiberius and events relating to A.D. 33 is found in Dio Cassius's *Roman History,* written in Greek around the end of the second century.

The remaining major history that documents the period is Flavius Josephus's *History of the Jews* (covering Jewish history from ancient times to A.D. 66—the beginning of the Jewish wars—which he leaves to another book). As he was born in A.D. 37, four years after the death of Jesus and the birth of the church, Josephus is the closest to the period after the authors of the Gospels. His work provides many insights into the Jewish world of that time and its key players.

THE EAST

TIBERIUS AND
THE EASTERN EMPIRE

ROME'S EASTERN EMPIRE—taking in areas such as Greece, Asia Minor, Syria, Palestine and Egypt—was essentially the advanced civilization bequeathed by Greece through its former empire, and it was still deeply influenced by Hellenism. This empire had been established by Alexander the Great (356-323 B.C.) and, after his death, was dominated by the Seleucids and Ptolemies. Expanding Roman Republican rule gained the extremities of Syria and Egypt in the first century B.C. The common language of this vast area was, tellingly, Koine or common Greek. It stood in dramatic contrast to the western empire, in which the processes of Romanization were generally more radical for the indigenous cultures.

The influence of Greek civilization was relatively unobtrusive, and the imposition of Roman rule followed the same pattern, enabling cultural diversity to continue. An example of this accommodation was that Jewish people were allowed to continue their monotheism, exempt from worshiping the Roman pantheon of gods. They were also not required to submit to the cult of the emperor. Even though Augustus had been deified, Jews were not expected to participate in his worship. A similar benign attitude operated in the western regions such as Gaul, Germania and later Britannia. Though not a national entity, Celtic cultural identity was distinctive and affected every area of life. Resistance to the alien Roman culture was at first strong, though the Celts were eventually pacified. Those outside the Roman economy, like the Germanic tribes of the northeast, were considered barbarians.

This is not to say that in the east there were no parts that resisted Romanization; Judea had only partly been Hellenized. Syria, Macedonia, Greece and Egypt had all been part of a dying Hellenistic empire before being defeated by Rome. These lands became provinces of Rome, under the control of governors appointed by the Senate or directly by the emperor. Roman legions were stationed across the eastern empire ready to bring to bear appropriate force when necessary.

To get an insight into the complexity and diversity of the eastern empire in A.D. 33, we can visit several important locations and individuals in those places who played significant roles in the unfolding events of that year. The most significant figure, historically, Jesus of Galilee, we shall leave to other chapters.

TIBERIUS AT CAPREAE, ITALY

Tiberius's choice of the tiny island of Capreae as his main base after A.D. 27, when he was 67 years old, perhaps reflected a changed perception of Rome. Its city civilization had become, with the emperors, an ideal to be realized across the world—or at least in the vast domains of the empire east and west. Julius Caesar had pointed the way for the future emperors as he conquered Gaul and tried to invade Britannia. It also suited the reclusive emperor personally to live at Capreae. Like the first emperor, Augustus, Tiberius had been invested with powers that were novel and untried, such as that of being active sovereign over an immense and diverse region of the world. Powers that had been tailored for Augustus, as first citizen rather than self-consciously emperor, were exercised by a very different man. Later Roman historians were to see a corrupt dynasty beginning with Tiberius, and perpetrated by Caligula, Claudius and Nero. Tiberius's territories extended beyond the farthest horizons south and north, west and east of the city. Although he relied on his provincial governors and allowed them great discretionary powers, he took a detailed interest in the provinces, particularly where the governors were his direct responsibility. Hence his intervention in Pilate's characteristic misjudgment in sending inscribed shields into Jerusalem, probably at the Feast of Tabernacles in autumn A.D. 32.

Suetonius describes Tiberius as "being greatly delighted with the island, because it was accessible only by a narrow beach, being on all sides surrounded with rugged cliffs, of a stupendous height, and by a deep sea."[1] Capri is merely four miles long, two miles wide, and only three miles from the Point of Campania, from which it continues geologically. The air is pure and the vegetation nearly tropical. The highest point is Monte Solaro (1,932 ft). When Tiberius moved to the island the population was scanty. Suetonius repeats some gossip about Tiberius:

A few days after he reached Capreae and was by himself, a fisherman appeared unexpectedly and offered him a huge mullet; whereupon in his alarm that the man had clambered up to him from the back of the island over rough and pathless rocks, he had the poor fellow's face scrubbed with the fish. And because in the midst of his torture the man thanked his stars that he had not given the emperor an enormous crab that he had caught, Tiberius had his face torn with the crab also.[2]

Tiberius benefited from roads, aqueducts and villas that Augustus had built on Capreae during his reign. During the ten years Tiberius was there, he built villas at dominant points, most likely dedicated to various Roman gods. The most important was Villa Jovis, honoring Jupiter, which was effectively his palace, near the lighthouse (pharos). Here there was a sheer cliff (970 ft) over which Tiberius reputedly had victims of his displeasure thrown.

Villa Jovis, crowning the high point at the eastern edge of the island, covered an area of over 200,000 square feet. At its center four large cisterns were cut out of the rock to provide the water supply. The north-facing villa had a high vestibule, its roof supported by four marble columns. Nearby were the rooms of the guard corps, and the inevitable thermae or baths— made up of a dressing room, a frigidarium (a cold room), a tepidarium (a warm room), a calidarium (a hot room), and rooms for the heating and distribution of the water. To the east of the thermae were the state rooms. The imperial apartments were in the west wing, past the servants' quarters, looking across the island. From here a corridor and steps led down to the 300-foot-long imperial promenade. This was set into the rim of the north-facing cliff, 60 feet below the level of the palace. Steps along the west flank of the villa, going inland, led down to vaulted store rooms and to the kitchens, isolated from the rest of the villa.

From the highest point it was possible to see the island, the sea, the Point of Campania and the mainland's two gulfs—the Gulf of Neapolis (Naples) to the north, toward Misenum, and the Gulf of Salerno to the south. Vesuvius lay brooding eastward in the distance.

Tiberius (Tiberius Caesar Augustus) had been born seventy-four years before on November 16, 42 B.C. He was the son of Tiberius Claudius Nero (d. 33 B.C.), a high priest, magistrate and former fleet captain for Julius Caesar, and the young and beautiful Livia Drusilla (c. 58 B.C.-A.D. 29)—who may have only been thirteen when Tiberius was born. Augustus forced Tiberius's father to divorce the desirable Livia, and she became the emperor's third wife in 39 B.C. Eventually Tiberius and his brother Drusus came to live in the imperial household.

Tiberius's first wife was Vipsania. Their only son, Drusus (13 B.C.-A.D. 23), was later probably murdered in secret by Tiberius's trusted deputy, Sejanus, commander of Rome's prestigious praetorian guard. Tiberius's second wife, Julia, was daughter of Augustus. When Agrippa, Julia's first husband, died, Augustus compelled Tiberius to divorce Vipsania, whom he loved, and marry Julia. Julia was well known to Tiberius, as he had grown up with her in the imperial household. He was under no illusions about her character.

Tiberius, cold to Julia, requested fighting commands away from Rome. On one occasion, when he happened to be back in the capital, he came across Vipsania. On Augustus's orders, she had married a senator. Tiberius was so grief-stricken that he trailed her, sobbing, through the streets. Hearing of this, Augustus forbade Tiberius to see her again. Five years after marrying Julia, when the extent of her infidelities was becoming clear, Tiberius asked for leave of absence and retired to Rhodes, even though he had been appointed to a five-year term as the equivalent of chief tribune of the people. There he became increasingly reclusive, perverse and self-preoccupied. Meanwhile, Augustus was forced by revelations of his daughter's behavior to exile Julia to the tiny island of Pandateria. Tiberius eventually returned to Rome in A.D. 2. After this he was adopted as Augustus's son. In A.D. 4 he was sent to command the imperial armies, based outside Italy. There he excelled as a military commander.

Tiberius, described by Suetonius as strong and above average height, eventually became emperor. Tiberius had been Augustus's fourth choice, preceded by Agrippa (late husband of Julia, Augustus's daughter) and their sons, both of whom died while Augustus was still alive. On September 17, A.D. 14, at the age of fifty-six, he succeeded to the principate.

Initially Tiberius's reign appeared to be exemplary, modeled on the ideals set up by Augustus. The simmering violence of his character emerged from time to time to serve to protect his power. A possible rival, Postumus, was murdered, most probably on Tiberius's orders. The Roman Senate was subdued by the concentration of the praetorian guard near Rome. The guard was controlled by Sejanus, who effectively became Tiberius's deputy. He quickly took advantage of the emperor's trust. Tiberius's laws and policies resulted in a cautious and stable administration that fostered the Roman peace. Sometimes this was upheld by vicious repression, as when he exiled the entire Jewish population from Rome. After the death of his son Drusus in A.D. 23 he entrusted the administration of his affairs more and more to Sejanus, the man, unknown to him, perhaps most culpable in his son's murder. It seems that Sejanus seduced Drusus's wife, Livilla, and enlisted her help in removing Drusus, potential heir to the emperor. Sejanus cleverly hid this and other treachery for many years.[3]

In his last years Tiberius became even more of a recluse and, it seems, a tyrant. It is likely that he subjected the major personages of Rome—most of whom inevitably had had some kind of contact with the deposed Sejanus—to a reign of terror.[4] Tiberius's unfavorable portraits by the second-century historians Tacitus, Suetonius and Dio Cassius are probably colored by this late period, in which he lived, drank constantly, and evidently followed his every whim in Capreae. Significantly, Seneca, a young contemporary, wrote much more positively of Tiberius. Writing after the death of Caligula and Claudius, he conceded that the earlier part of Tiberius's principate had been as good as that of Augustus. Tiberius at that stage was a model emperor, he argued, and thereby superior to Caligula and Claudius. Another contemporary, Philo of Alexandria, was also positive toward Tiberius, though he was considering him in contrast to Caligula's vicious incitement of Jewish anger.[5]

Despite his reputation for boorish cruelty, Tiberius undoubtedly had an absorbing interest in rhetoric and philosophy.[6] On Capreae he had a retinue of literary men, historians and poets—Greek professionals.[7] In the year that concerns us, he had in his company at Villa Jovis a young man as his protégé—one Gaius, nicknamed "Caligula." Caligula was the son of Germanicus Caesar and Agrippina, and nephew of Tiberius (Tiberius had adopted Germanicus). He gained the nickname Caligula ("little boots") from the boots and miniature military uniform he wore as a child in Germania, where he was a favorite of the troops. Gaius Caligula in effect had been confined to Capreae for his own safety since being summoned there in the autumn of A.D. 31. During A.D. 33 Tiberius increasingly marked out Caligula as his successor, and it may have been in this year that he said, "I am nursing a viper in Rome's bosom."

PILATE AT CAESAREA MARITIMA, PALESTINE

Pontius Pilate was Roman Prefect of Judea from A.D. 26 to 37. We learn about him from the New Testament Gospel narratives and from Tacitus, Josephus, and Philo. A fragment from a codex that included the Gospel of John dates back to around A.D. 130[8] and comes from the passage describing the trial of Jesus before Pilate. In 1961 a large piece of damaged masonry inscribed with Pilate's name was found in excavations of Caesarea Maritima. The surviving text includes the words: "[Thi]s Tiberieum [Pon]tius Pilatus, Prefect of Judea, [mad]e." The building that had Pilate's dedicatory inscription on it, the Tiberieum, was clearly constructed to honor Tiberius.[9]

Caesarea Maritima was Pilate's base as governor of Judea (which, as a Roman territory, included Samaria as well as Judea proper). His wife accompanied him to the post, but unfortunately we lack her name. His troops were stationed there, ready to act to police the population or take military action in the case of insurgency. Some years later one of the officers of a cohort of Caesarea, by the name of Cornelius, would become a follower of Jesus. (We do not know if he was stationed here at this time.) Many of the troops adhered to the popular cult of Mithras, and some, like Cornelius, were attracted to Judaism. He had, like many others (possibly including Pilate's wife), been attracted to Judaism in some form—Judaism was varied at this period, much more so than after the devastating destruction of Jerusalem and the temple in A.D. 70. Teachings of rabbis, worship and prayer at the synagogue or temple, celebrations of festivals, and the quest for purity may have attracted them. Unusually, Mithraism had regular religious meetings. Normally only the Jewish synagogue had regular meetings at this period. Most Roman worship was a matter of attending religious temples for sacrifices, without an established time of meeting, even on holy days. The apostle Paul would be imprisoned in Caesarea Maritima for two years by a later Roman procurator, Felix.

Caesarea Maritima was one of many magnificent architectural achievements of Herod the Great, a client king of Rome and father of Herod Antipas. The coastline of Palestine lacked natural harbors for long stretches. According to Josephus, the coast of Palestine was "not fit for havens, on account of the impetuous south winds that beat upon them, which rolling the sands that come from the sea against the shores."[10] Herod's brilliance lay in constructing a harbor, with deep walls and a lighthouse. He also constructed a temple to Roma and the deified Augustus, and other buildings of white stone, including a palace, a theater, and an amphitheater. There was a large forum, in Roman style, north of the temple. There was also a boundary wall, and a double aqueduct that carried water from springs at the foot of Mount Carmel. The temple, which dominated the city, was built on a high podium facing west toward the harbor. Broad steps led from the harbor to the temple. The construction of the harbor was a great feat of engineering, and it was beautiful, as Josephus explains:

> This he effected by letting down vast stones of above fifty feet in length, not less than eighteen in breadth, and nine in depth, into twenty fathom deep; and as some were lesser, so were others bigger than those dimensions. This mole which he built by the sea-side was two hundred feet wide, the half of which was opposed to the current of the waves. . . . There were also a great number of arches where the mariners dwelt. There was also before them a quay, which ran round the entire haven, and was a most agreeable walk to such as had a mind to that exercise; but the entrance or mouth of the port was made on the north quarter, on which side was the stillest of the winds of all in this place: and the basis of the whole circuit on the left hand, as you enter the port, supported a round turret, which was made very strong, in order to resist the greatest waves; while on the right hand, as you enter, stood two vast stones, and those each of them larger than the turret, which were over against them; these stood upright, and were joined together. Now there were edifices all along the circular haven, made of the politest stone, with a certain elevation, whereon was erected a temple, that was seen a great way off by those that were sailing for that haven, and had in it two statues, the one of Rome, the other of Caesar.[11]

When the Roman administration originally came to Judea it had appropriated Caesarea Maritima as its headquarters, and it was here that Pilate spent most of his year. Under the Roman administration Herod Antipas, son of Herod the Great, had reduced powers (he had the inherited title of "Herod" rather than "King"), and smaller territories—merely Galilee and Perea. He was tetrarch, that is, a subordinate ruler (literally, ruler of a fourth of a territory). During A.D. 33 Pilate would leave Caesarea several times a year for the assizes in the districts of Samaria, Idumea and Jerusalem. This meant that in early spring he would to ascend to Jerusalem with troops for the major Jewish Feast of Passover. The soldiers would keep a watchful eye from Fortress Antonia, overlooking the temple courts, and from above the colonnades. The Passover period presented hazards for the Roman peace, particularly as the population of Jerusalem swelled enormously with pilgrims, including many from Galilee, noted for its tendency toward insurrection. It has been calculated that the population of the densely inhabited city was between 60,000 and (more likely) 120,000, swelling to at least double that figure on principal feasts, with sometimes maybe as many as one million pilgrims. Some visitors were hosted by local people, some in emergency accommodations, while

very many camped around the city.[12] The previous Passover, in the spring of
A.D. 32, had proved a particularly difficult time for Pilate. It was the occasion
reported to Jesus: "There were some present at that very time who told him
about the Galileans whose blood Pilate had mingled with their sacrifices.
And he answered them, 'Do you think that these Galileans were worse sin-
ners than all the other Galileans, because they suffered in this way?' " (Luke
13:1-2). The massacre of the Galileans at Passover time A.D. 32 would have
particularly offended Herod Antipas, who, as tetrarch, was responsible for
the region of Galilee. We do not know the details of this incident in Jerusalem—Josephus doesn't include this in his selection of Pilate's misjudgments
and indiscretions against the native population, which would eventually get
him sent to Tiberius to answer for his actions.

Pilate had not started well when he arrived as Judea's prefect in A.D. 26.
Josephus records that he brought military standards into Jerusalem that had
an image of Tiberius on them, which deeply offended the faith of its inhabitants. Rather like Islam today, first-century Jewish faith prohibited the use of
images as idolatrous (Exodus 20:4-5). A prolonged protest afterward at Caesarea Maritima forced Pilate to relinquish and remove the standards. For another incident Josephus gives two accounts, the first in his *Antiquities of the
Jews* and the other in *The Jewish Wars*.[13] This was when a riot by militants followed the disclosure that Pilate had used sacred temple funds (the "Corban")
to finance an aqueduct to the city. It is quite possible that Pilate used the holy
money with the concurrence of the chief priests and other city elders. In both
accounts Pilate's men mingle with the crowd in disguise, ready for trouble. In
one account they are carrying cudgels and in the other daggers—most probably both were in use, resulting in many injuries and deaths.[14]

But an even more serious event had happened later in A.D. 32, at the autumn Feast of Tabernacles. This time it was not just Antipas whom Pilate offended but also the ruling aristocracy in Jerusalem, on whom he depended
to maintain the civil peace. It was so serious that it ultimately led to the direct intervention of Tiberius himself. The Jewish philosopher Philo, writing
in Alexandria, records the incident several years later, after Pilate's term as
prefect had been curtailed:

> Pilate was one of the emperor's lieutenants, having been appointed governor
> of Judaea. He . . . dedicated some gilt shields in the palace of Herod, in the
> holy city; which had no form nor any other forbidden thing represented on
> them except some necessary inscription, which mentioned these two facts, the

name of the person who had placed them there, and the person in whose honor they were so placed there. But when the multitude heard what had been done, and when the circumstance became notorious, then the people, putting forward the four sons of the king [the late Herod the Great], . . . and his other descendants, and those magistrates who were among them at the time, entreated him to alter and to rectify the innovation which he had committed in respect of the shields; and not to make any alteration in their national customs, which had hitherto been preserved without any interruption, without being in the least degree changed by any king or emperor. But when he steadfastly refused this petition (for he was a man of a very inflexible disposition, and very merciless as well as very obstinate), they cried out: "Do not cause a sedition; do not make war upon us; do not destroy the peace which exists. The honor of the emperor is not identical with dishonor to the ancient laws; let it not be to you a pretence for heaping insult on our nation. Tiberius is not desirous that any of our laws or customs shall be destroyed. And if you yourself say that he is, show us either some command from him, or some letter, or something of the kind, that we, who have been sent to you as ambassadors, may cease to trouble you, and may address our supplications to your master." But this last sentence exasperated him in the greatest possible degree, as he feared lest they might in reality go on an embassy to the emperor, and might impeach him with respect to other particulars of his government, in respect of his corruption, and his acts of insolence, and his rapine, and his habit of insulting people, and his cruelty, and his continual murders of people untried and uncondemned, and his never ending, and gratuitous, and most grievous inhumanity. Therefore, being exceedingly angry, and being at all times a man of most ferocious passions, he was in great perplexity, neither venturing to take down what he had once set up, nor wishing to do anything which could be acceptable to his subjects, and at the same time being sufficiently acquainted with the firmness of Tiberius on these points. And those who were in power in our nation, seeing this, and perceiving that he was inclined to change his mind as to what he had done, but that he was not willing to be thought to do so, wrote a most supplicatory letter to Tiberius. And he, when he had read it, what did he say of Pilate, and what threats did he utter against him! . . . Immediately . . . he wrote a letter, reproaching and reviling him in the most bitter manner for his act of unprecedented audacity and wickedness, and commanding him immediately to take down the shields and to convey them away from the metropolis of Judaea to Caesarea . . . in order that they might be set up in the temple of Augustus.[15]

The main features of the incident are clear: Pilate, perhaps to show his loyalty to Tiberius, set up inscribed shields in Herod's palace in Jerusalem. He had learned not to put images on them. They bore an inscription of the name of the dedicator and the person dedicated, which carried religious associations. High-ranking Jews, whose delegation was headed by the sons of Herod, including Antipas, pleaded with him to remove them, but he was adamant. They wrote to Tiberius, who angrily instructed Pilate to move them to the temple of Augustus in Caesarea. This was in keeping with his policy of toleration of Jewish faith, which included the concession of exemption from emperor worship.

The incident most probably happened at the feast around the end of September and beginning of October. Allowing for the deliberations of the chief priests of Jerusalem and other dignitaries, and given the lengthy time for winter communications with Tiberius on Capreae (around two months each way), it was probably not until early spring A.D. 33 that Pilate received the summons from Tiberius and implemented it. By then resentment on the part of Antipas, and the Jewish authorities in Jerusalem, had been simmering for a lengthy period.[16]

Could it have been that Pilate's crass behavior toward the inhabitants of his province was simply anti-Semitism? After all, it is most likely he had been employed originally by Sejanus, acting as Tiberius's deputy, and Sejanus was overtly anti-Semitic. The historian Barbara Levick thinks not. She explains Pilate's behavior not as anti-Semitism inspired by Sejanus but simply

> stupid officiousness and, especially when the fall of the Prefect [Sejanus] brought on a period of fear and uncertainty, a desire to demonstrate loyalty to the Princeps at all costs. It is in accord with this suggestion that the inscription found at Caesarea shows, not only that the official title of the governor in Tiberius' time was Praefectus, but that Pilate had constructed a building known as the Tiberieum.[17]

ANTIPAS "THE FOX" AT TIBERIAS, GALILEE

Antipas was appointed by Rome to rule over the territories of Galilee and Perea in the Palestine area. Like his father, King Herod the Great (or Elder), Antipas (20 B.C.-A.D. 39) was an inveterate builder.[18] His first major project was the rebuilding of Sepphoris (modern-day Zippori) in Galilee, which had been razed by the Romans, and its inhabitants made slaves after an uprising. The uprising happened after the death of Herod the Great. A revolutionary leader, Judas, provided his followers with weapons from the royal palace there, and it became the center of the insurrection.

Antipas probably began restoring Sepphoris soon after returning from Rome, where the trials concerning Herod the Great's will had taken place soon after his death, and may have completed the new city by A.D. 8 to 10. The work was so magnificent that the city became "the ornament of Galilee," the largest city in the region. From archaeological evidence it seems that the work included a theater and a sophisticated waterworks. As Nazareth was only four miles south-southwest of Sepphoris, it is likely that Joseph, step-father of Jesus, obtained work there as a carpenter/builder, and it is possible that, as the oldest in the family, Jesus assisted him in the late stages of the city's construction. This would have been but part of the youthful Jesus' exposure to Hellenism, for the city was built on Greek lines. Its rebuilding was more than physical—through it, ideologically, Antipas attempted to replace the fervent nationalism of Judas's days with a Romanized culture. Indeed, in the later war of A.D. 66-70, Sepphoris was pro-Roman. It was, however, a wholly Jewish city, albeit Hellenized, with an important Sanhedrin or Jewish Council located there. This pro-Roman attitude was likely enough shaped by the bitter memory of its former devastation by the Roman forces.

The next major building project was probably Livias (or Julias, modern-day Teller-Rameh, in Jordan), named in honor of Livia, wife of Augustus (and mother of Tiberius), who was held in high esteem in the Roman world. Livias was a fortified city built on the site of an existing town. "Julias" may have been the official name, but not the employed name, after Livia was adopted in A.D. 14 into the gens Julia, an important family connected with the imperial Julio-Claudian dynasty. The city may have been officially founded in A.D. 13 (though it is likely it was completed before then)— January 17, A.D. 13, marked the fiftieth wedding anniversary of Livia and Augustus. That year also marked Livia's seventieth birthday. Livias was probably located about six miles north of the shores of the Dead Sea and several miles east of the River Jordan opposite Jericho.

Antipas's next project was arguably his most important, for Tiberias became his capital, and it was the first city in Jewish history that employed the municipal framework of a Greek polis. It was built from scratch on the western shore of the Sea of Galilee, where the hills did not press so tightly to the waterline, and provided for Antipas a convenient midway location for accessing Perea and Galilee. It was also on the major north-south trade route that in one direction led to Syria and in the other to Egypt. Nearby to the south were the warm springs of Ammathus (Hammath), favored by Antipas. The city was named in honor of the current emperor, out of political expedience. It may have been founded between A.D. 18 and 23, with 23 a strong possibility. That was the year of Tiberius's sixty-fifth birthday, and the tenth anniversary of his succession to the throne.

There is evidence that Antipas built at Tiberias a large synagogue, a stadium and a beautiful, golden-roofed palace. So he sought to please his Jewish subjects and his Roman superiors, and he certainly looked after himself. He had some difficulty in populating Tiberias as, in the course of the construction, he disturbed a cemetery, which for devout Jews made the place unclean. He compelled local people to move in from the countryside, brought in some immigrants and liberated slaves in return for living in Tiberias. Though the result was a mixed citizenship, it was largely Galilean. This did not stop Antipas from implementing a course of Hellenization. An important aspect of this was establishing the semi-autonomous government and constitution of the city. Its council was so large that it must have included virtually all the important citizens. The city was also allowed to date its records from its founding and to issue coins. It did not, however, control the surrounding region, as a true Greek-style city-state, but remained under Antipas's rule, administered by royal officials living in the city. This suited Antipas's personal desire for power, and was more acceptable to Rome, particularly in the period in which Sejanus virtually ruled. We know the name of one of Antipas's staff—Chuza was his steward—and his wife, Joanna, was a disciple of Jesus, helping him and his close followers financially out of her own means. From Joanna (and possibly also from Manaen, a friend and foster brother of Antipas, who knew Jesus) news about Herod and his household may have been received by Jesus and his disciples.

Antipas was a complex character, and it is of great interest that Jesus referred to him as "that fox" when warned, possibly in Herod's territory of Galilee, that Antipas desired to capture him. This was after the death of John the Baptist at Antipas's hands.

> At that very hour some Pharisees came and said to [Jesus], "Get away from here, for Herod wants to kill you." And he said to them, "Go and tell that fox, 'Behold, I cast out demons and perform cures today and tomorrow, and the third day I finish my course. Nevertheless, I must go on my way today and tomorrow and the day following, for it cannot be that a prophet should perish away from Jerusalem.' " (Luke 13:31-33)

Calling Antipas a "fox" mostly likely refers to his lack of real power, and his employment of cunning and deceit to achieve his purposes. The fox was often contrasted with the lion, and Jesus may have seen himself like this. (In the late book of the New Testament, Revelation, he is called "the Lion of the tribe of Judah" [Revelation 5:5].) Jesus is being ironic: Antipas has no real power over him (as, he will later claim, Pilate has no effective power over him). Jesus also seems to be ironic in referring to his fate if he returns to Jerusalem—for Antipas had killed the prophet John the Baptist in Machaerus, not Jerusalem, the location almost being a matter of bad taste. Jesus may be alluding to the fact that Jerusalem was the real center of Jewish faith and practice, more strictly orthodox, and therefore more likely not to recognize prophets from God, who characteristically ruffled the status quo!

Antipas's foxlike character may be seen in his capture and execution of John the Baptist, the prophet in the desert in Perea. John was a relation of Jesus', possibly a second cousin. John's death probably took place in A.D. 31 or 32, some time after his arrest, and is mainly recounted in two accounts that superficially seem to be contrary to each other, the New Testament Gospels and Josephus's *Antiquities.*[19] In Josephus the motive for arresting and killing John is that Antipas feared that, because of his sway over the people, the Baptist might incite a sedition, which would be disastrous for his relations with Rome. John was imprisoned at Machaerus, Antipas's fortress by the Dead Sea, and executed. In the Gospels John is imprisoned for denouncing Antipas's illegal marriage to his half-brother's wife, Herodias. Josephus's account focuses on the political, and the Gospels on the moral. In fact, the two motives are indissolubly linked. This is because John's preaching against Antipas's marriage could easily have had political consequences, in terms of fomenting unrest. Josephus in the same section in fact brings out political consequences of the marriage, which later led to war with the Arabian King Aretas, the father of Antipas's first and abandoned wife. It is likely that Antipas held John for a considerable time in prison, vacillating about what to do with him, weighing the consequences of killing him, in foxlike manner. He is quite likely to have found that John was not the political threat he feared (as he was to find with Jesus soon after). Herodias lacked this indecisiveness and pushed Antipas into a decision, employing alcohol and his passions to rule his brain, as her daughter, Salome, danced for him. Later, when he heard reports of Jesus' teachings and the wonders he performed, Antipas feared that John had been resurrected. It may be that John and Jesus had a superficial physical resemblance because of their kinship. Of John, Josephus said:

> John, that was called the Baptist . . . was a good man, and commanded the Jews to exercise virtue, both as to righteousness toward one another, and piety toward God, and so to come to baptism; for that the washing [with water] would be acceptable to him, if they made use of it, not in order to the putting away [or the remission] of some sins [only], but for the purification of the body; supposing still that the soul was thoroughly purified beforehand by righteousness. Now when [many] others came in crowds about him, for they were very greatly moved [or pleased] by hearing his words, Herod, who feared lest the great influence John had over the people might put it into his power and inclination to raise a rebellion, (for they seemed ready to do any thing he should advise,) thought it best, by putting him to death, to prevent any mischief he might cause, and not bring himself into difficulties, by sparing a man who might make him repent of it when it would be too late. Accordingly he was sent a prisoner, out of Herod's suspicious temper, to Machærus . . . and was there put to death.[20]

The Gospel of Matthew says:

> For Herod had seized John and bound him and put him in prison for the sake of Herodias, his brother Philip's wife, because John had been saying to him, "It is not lawful for you to have her." And though he wanted to put him to death, he feared the people, because they held him to be a prophet. But when Herod's birthday came, the daughter of Herodias danced before the company and pleased Herod, so that he promised with an oath to give her whatever she might ask. Prompted by her mother, she said, "Give me the head of John the Baptist here on a platter." And the king was sorry, but because of his oaths and his guests he commanded it to be given. He sent and had John beheaded in the prison, and his head was brought on a platter and given to the girl, and she brought it to her mother. And his disciples came and took the body and buried it, and they went and told Jesus. (Matthew 14:3-12)

Herod Antipas had inherited part of the kingdom of his father, Herod the Great, after Augustus had adjusted his will. He worked hard to restore the territories of Galilee and Perea, and to secure his standing with Rome. Many of the dignitaries there, including Tiberius, he knew from the years he had spent in Rome for his education (from 8/7 B.C. to 5/4 B.C.). His closeness to the emperor's family would later lead to him being employed successfully in mediating between Rome and Parthia. In A.D. 33 he was to have a dramatic involvement in the trial of Jesus before Pilate, when Jesus was charged with the capital offense of being an unauthorized leader of the Jews.

CAIAPHAS AT JERUSALEM

Jerusalem in A.D. 33 was surrounded by wooded hills, with a break to the southeast, toward the desert. It rose among the hills, presenting a splendid sight. Most of its buildings were the golden color of the local stone, but there were many of marble and cedar covering, looking white and rich brown amid the gold. Although it was built between 2,000 and 2,500 feet above sea level, it lay in a basin, and between two valleys—the Hinnom and the Kidron—which joined southeast of the city. Jerusalem was divided down its middle by a lesser valley, widening southward—"the valley of the Cheese-makers," Josephus called it. A viaduct ran across this middle valley, connect-ing the west side of the city with the temple area to the east. The valleys to each side and south of the city were deep, giving to the city the appearance of a natural fortress. To the north, slopes rose above Jerusalem. A man being crucified on these upper slopes, lifted up on his cross, could see over the city. From the Mount of Olives, across the Kidron to the east, there were dra-matic views—beyond the steep valley to the golden city, east to the green plains of the Jordan valley and Jericho, to the south to glimpses of the hill-country of Judea, and to the west to the haze beyond the mountains of Bether, indicating the distant Mediterranean—the Great Sea.

Jerusalem was dominated by the temple courts, taking up a sixth of the urban area, with the Fortress of Antonia towering above them on its north-west corner. Across the viaduct to the west of the temple, near the city wall, lay Herod's palace, usually occupied by Pilate, the Roman prefect, when he was in Jerusalem. Antipas would habitually stay in the older Hasmonean pal-ace, in the center of the city, near the temple area. The house of the high priest, Caiaphas, probably lay on the south slope, in the upper city, where the larger houses of the wealthy were located.

Because the city was built on hills, most of the streets went up and down, with connecting alleyways. Space was at a premium in the densely packed city, so the roads were narrow and unsuitable for wheeled transport. Don-keys, horses and camels were driven along them, sharing the thoroughfares with pedestrians and wealthy people in litters. The streets gained their names from the various city gates to which they led or from the plentiful bazaars. They had names like Water Street, Fish Street and East Street. There was a Baker Street, Butcher Street and Strangers' Street.[21] In Jerusalem, it was claimed by rabbis in later years, no house could be rented for a stay. Rather the houses in a sense belonged to all—pilgrims visiting for the great festivals were welcome to use them.

As Caiaphas's house was built on the slope of a hill, a lower story was built under the principal apartments, with a porch in front. We get a hint of its character from a description of events in spring A.D. 33 in a similar house that may indeed have been part of the same complex of housing—events that take place in the courtyard of Annas, his father-in-law, the former high priest and probably the most powerful man in Jerusalem. This is when Peter is secretly trying to find out what is happening to the arrested Jesus. He stands "below in the courtyard" while Jesus is questioned by Annas in the rooms above (Mark 14:66, probably Peter's own words). He is near a brazier warming himself in the chill night air. He is suspected, rightly of course, of being a disciple by some of the high priest's servants. In the same incident we learn that John, who got Peter access to Caiaphas's courtyard, is known to the high priest, or at least to his attendants (John 18:15). Some scholars believe that he had connections with the wealthy and powerful in Jerusalem, most probably through his family's trade in fish.

Joseph Caiaphas had been high priest for about fifteen years. Caiaphas seems to have worked in close cooperation with Annas, because Annas, a kind of high priest emeritus, continued to exert formidable power. The high priesthood had a long tradition of political involvement that continued even after its powers were greatly reduced by Herod the Great. According to Josephus, Caiaphas was appointed by the Roman procurator Valerius Gratus, the predecessor of Pontius Pilate, around A.D. 18.[22] The fact that the high priest was a political appointee reveals the extent of Romanization, even among the notoriously recalcitrant Jewish subjects.

In November 1990 twelve ossuaries, or bone chests, were discovered, including two bearing the name of "Joseph, son of Caiaphas," who was possibly the same high priest. They were found in Jerusalem's Peace Forest, about a mile south of the Old City, in an ancient burial cave. Six of these ossuaries were undisturbed—the others had been rifled by grave robbers. One contained the skeletons of children, a teenager, a young adult female and a man in his 60s. It bore inscriptions which may be the names *Yehoseph bar Qapha'* and *Yehoseph bar Qayapha'*—probably variants of one name. Some scholars believe that this is the Joseph Caiaphas mentioned by Josephus and the New Testament accounts.[23]

The "house of Annas," to which Caiaphas belonged, is later condemned and cursed in the Talmud, along with "the corrupt leaders of the priesthood," whose presence defiled the sanctuary.[24] Caiaphas, his father-in-law and others of the Jerusalem hierarchy were wealthy and unscrupulous, and evidently concerned at all costs to maintain the Roman status quo that supported them. It seems that they were heartily disliked by a group of devout Jews called the Pharisees, who were generally anti-Roman, more resistant to Hellenistic influences and strict observers of both scriptural and ritualistic law. This piety did not stop Pharisees from sometimes collaborating with the pro-Roman leadership out of expediency. Our knowledge of the Pharisees and other groups within Judaism before the catastrophic destruction of Jerusalem and the temple is very limited (see chap. 6).

PHILO AT ALEXANDRIA, EGYPT

Alexandria was the largest city in the empire after Rome, with a population of perhaps half a million or more people. This included a large Jewish community—the largest outside Palestine—which played a full part in city life. It took its name from Alexander, who founded it in 331 B.C. The Nile Delta was close by to its east, and from its large harbors grain was shipped to Rome. It was one of the world's foremost cultural centers, with its great library and intellectual life. Here a basic steam turbine was invented by Hero, and later Claudius Ptolemaeus, geographer and astronomer, mapped the known world and developed theories of the cosmos.

Pliny the Elder was a great contemporary naturalist, with an insatiable curiosity not only about natural phenomena but also about the geography of the world. (Characteristically, he died investigating the eruption of Vesuvius in A.D. 79.) In a survey of northern Africa he writes of Alexandria:

> With the greatest justice, however, we may lavish our praises upon Alexandria, built by Alexander the Great on the shores of the Egyptian Sea, upon the soil of Africa, at twelve miles' distance from the Canopic Mouth and near Lake Mareotis. . . . The plan of this city was designed by the architect Dinochares. . . . Building the city upon a wide space of ground fifteen miles in circumference, he formed it in the circular shape of a Macedonian chlamys [cloak, mantle], uneven at the edge, giving it an angular projection on the right and left; while at the same time he devoted one-fifth part of the site to the royal palace.[25]

The great harbor area was protected from the open sea and the constant winds from the north by a narrow strip of rock running parallel to the coast, about a mile off shore. The center of this strip of island was connected to the mainland by a causeway. This separated two deep sea harbors. From the western harbor a canal led to Lake Mareotis. That freshwater lake provided an inland harbor for the city. It was also a gateway to the Nile and therefore to the Red Sea via a network of canals.

The four-hundred-foot-high lighthouse, famous as one of the seven wonders of the ancient world, was on the eastern end of the protective island strip. This is the earliest lighthouse, so far as is known, and became called Pharos, after the name of the narrow island. It had three stories, one square, one octagonal and the highest cylindrical, crowned by a statue to Zeus Soter. Light from a fire inside the lighthouse was reflected through a mirror mechanism, which made it visible for a huge distance—perhaps more than thirty miles, as suggested by Josephus.[26]

The city was separated into ethnic regions. In the southwest of the city was the poorest district, the Egyptian, which was situated in the area of the original village and called by its name, Rhakotis. A Ptolemaic king had rebuilt the temple of Serapis, an invented hybrid of Egyptian and Greek deities, in this Egyptian quarter. Under Roman occupation this temple became one of the great centers of pagan worship. The Brucheion, the Greek quarter, included an immense royal palace, which, according to the first-century geographer Strabo, may have taken up as much as a quarter of the city's area.[27] As well as the palace there were many official buildings, such as the Soma (Alexander's mausoleum) and the museum, including the great library. The Jewish population was located in the northeast.

The population was thoroughly Hellenized, and Greek, not Latin, was the official administrative language. The general policy at this time was of mutual tolerance. However, the multiethnic mix brought tensions that would soon explode. Jewish citizens generally tried to balance being pro-Greek with maintaining a confessional separation according to their religious and scriptural heritage.

It was probably among the Jewish community in Alexandria that Mary, Joseph and the infant Jesus took refuge near the end of the previous century to escape the brutality of Herod the Great.[28] The Jewish community had undergone a long exposure to Greek influence, and, significantly, between the third and first century B.C. the Hebrew Scriptures had been translated into Greek. The translation, known as the Septuagint (after the number of the translators, which according to legend was seventy or seventy-two), was a remarkable accomplishment. Not least it has allowed scholars subsequently over many centuries to expand their knowledge of both ancient Hebrew and ancient Greek. Josephus writes that Rome had granted equal citizenship to the Jewish population of Alexandria: "Julius Caesar made a pillar of brass for the Jews at Alexandria, and declared publicly that they were citizens of Alexandria."[29] Even in the time of Augustus, fewer Jewish people lived in Judea than in the rest of the Roman empire.[30] The stabilizing influence of first the Hellenistic states and then the empire had facilitated the Diaspora. Some Jewish people had settled in Mesopotamia and Arabia and even parts of western India.

In the first century Alexandria was arguably the leading center for scholarship in the world. Early in the third century B.C. a museum had been founded. The museum included the magnificent library that became renowned in the ancient world. The community associated with the museum included both poets and scholars. Zenodotus of Ephesus (c. 325-260 B.C.) was its first librarian. He edited the first critical edition of Homer and also made editions of Pindar and Anacreon, and perhaps other lyric poets. Others are said to have prepared editions of the tragic and comic poets. Then the eminent poet Callimachus (c. 305-c. 240 B.C.) compiled the Pinakes (or "Tablets"), an immense catalog of the chief holdings that included explanatory biographical and bibliographical information. Some later librarians added lexicons and treatises about literature. One wrote commentaries on Homer, Pindar, and on the genres of tragedy and comedy. To give some idea of the scope of its collections, the library in the first century included around 500,000 works, including Aristotle, Plato, Socrates, Aeschylus, Sophocles and Euripides. It is possible that Aristotle's own library was purchased for the collection. It encompassed works of geometry, mathematics and applied science as well as philosophy and poetry. Part of the collection was evidently destroyed by a large fire caused in 47 B.C. by Julius Caesar, whose army supported Cleopatra in a civil war. The great library, however, survived to continue its work for over four hundred years.

Egyptian civilization was millennia old by the time of Roman expansion in the aftermath of the Greek empire and the rule of the Ptolemies. Cleopatra VII was the last of the Ptolemaic queens. After the suicides of Mark Antony and Cleopatra, Egypt became part of the Roman empire in 30 B.C. By annexing Egypt the Romans effectively depoliticized it. Political changes thereafter

were initiated in Rome, not Alexandria. Rather than a state, Egypt became
an important Roman province. As a province Egypt achieved a stability it
had lacked under the Ptolemies. This also meant, however, that its resources
were exploited by Rome.

Augustus established Egypt as a significant territory. His system of administration was still in existence in A.D. 33 and remained so for several centuries. Tiberius was held to be Pharaoh. Egypt was of huge importance to
Rome—one-third of the city of Rome's annual grain supply came from the
fertile Nile Valley. Therefore the chief procurator was directly appointed by
the emperor and was recruited from the high-ranking equestrian class. He
was held directly accountable to Tiberius.

The senior administration was based at Alexandria. At a local level the
province was run by a Hellenized elite that had become powerful under the
Ptolemies. Three Roman legions were stationed in Egypt to provide security.
With the Sahara to the south, Egypt lacked troublesome barbarians overrun-
ning the borders of empire, unlike in the northern provinces, though there
were many bandits.

In A.D. 33 Egypt, like the empire itself, was experiencing a large measure
of stability—the Pax Romana. The burden of efficient Roman tax collection,
administered locally, forced some to flee and some to turn to banditry. But
there was no significant social unrest at this time, though soon after there
was a systematic mistreatment of the Jewish population in Alexandria.[31] As
elsewhere in the Roman empire, the overlords were essentially tolerant of
religious diversity. In Alexandria the indigenous Egyptians worshiped what
the Romans regarded as pagan deities, such as Osiris, the most widely revered of the Egyptian gods. In another, and large, quarter Jews attended synagogues and traveled to Jerusalem for festivals, such as Passover, drawn by
the temple cult.

The economy had expanded over the Ptolemaic period—thanks in part
to more efficient irrigation tools (such as the ox-driven water-wheel and the
Archimedean screw)—reaching its high point by the period of Roman occupation. This is why the population of Alexandria may have been as high as
half a million in A.D. 33, about half that of the world's largest city, Rome.
Egypt also benefited from the international trade routes made possible by
the stability of the empire—south into Meroe and central Africa, north across
the Mediterranean, east into western Asia, and even to India and China.[32]

South of Egypt lay the independent kingdom of Meroe, in the area where the White Nile and Blue Nile converge. It was in a good geographical position for trade. There was access to the Red Sea by an overland route. It was linked into the trade of the Roman empire, with its exports of ivory, leopard skins, ostrich feathers, ebony and gold. In the years of Tiberius's reign, Meroe had reached its peak of power and wealth. Relations with the Roman administration in Egypt were peaceful and trade links were strong. Although Meroe had a close association with Egypt, it also diversified in many respects. While Egyptian gods were worshiped, Meroe added its own deities, most notably the lion god, Apedemek. He was usually portrayed as a lion's head on the body of a snake or of a man. As its own culture developed, its own language, eventually with an alphabetical-style script, replaced Egyptian. In time, its culture and agriculture were to develop away from the Egyptians into a more African style.[33]

Meroe was dominated, politically, by its queen mothers, who had the title of Candace. We know that a steward from its court traveled to Jerusalem by chariot on one occasion, possibly in A.D. 34 or soon after (Acts 8:26-28).

Avilius Flaccus, a friend of Tiberius, was appointed as prestigious governor of Egypt in A.D. 32 or 33, after the death of the freedman Hiberius. His full name, Aulus Avilius Flaccus, was found on an inscription from Tentyra in Egypt. It was also discovered on a fragment of papyrus concerning a decree of Flaccus (though some scholars read "Lucius" rather than "Aulus"). The first years of his governorship were exemplary, but he later began to be hostile toward the Jewish population, and his brutal persecution had far-reaching ramifications. Philo, a dignitary of Alexandria, wrote that at first he fulfilled his office peacefully and uprightly, surpassing all his predecessors. It is through the writings of Philo that most of our knowledge of Flaccus comes—these provide insights into his life and character.

Flaccus was an important figure in Roman politics. He had grown up with the sons of Augustus's daughter, and later became a friend of Tiberius. He was heavily involved in the downfall of Agrippina the Elder, Augustus's granddaughter, resulting in her banishment to the island of Pandateria, east of Italy. His denunciation of her may have resulted from his devotion to Tiberius. He also supported the ill-fated Gemellus as heir to Tiberius.

But an even more significant figure associated with Alexandria was Philo, a Jewish intellectual whose writings have been carefully preserved through the ages. He was one of several Jewish leaders who are important in this year, along with Antipas, Jesus, Peter and other disciples close to Jesus, and the young Saul (Paul), though he would not take an active part in events that appear on the stage of what history has preserved until several years later, when he went to Rome.

Philo, who lived from around 20 B.C. to about A.D. 50 and was therefore in his fifties in our year, was successful and established in the thriving Jewish community in Alexandria. He was employed as a customs agent, collecting what was due on all goods imported from the east via the busy trade routes. Many if not the majority of his large corpus of books were probably written by then, ranging from allegorical interpretations of the five books of Moses to themes such as drunkenness or dreams. They thus give contemporary insights into the leading-edge thinking of the period. He demonstrates an evident diversity in Jewish thinking. Philo combined Plato and the Old Testament Scriptures in a way that anticipated the scholars of the Middle Ages.[34] He seems to have preceded St. Augustine in believing that God created time—an idea that has far-reaching philosophical and scientific consequences.[35] Much of his work was interpreting Scriptures such as the books of Moses in the light of Plato's philosophy.

Philo was undoubtedly one of the important Jewish writers of the first century. He wrote in Greek and most of his writings survive in this, but a few have come down to us only in their Armenian translation. He lived his early life in Alexandria, but visited Rome later as part of an official delegation to Gaius Caligula protesting at the unjust treatment of Jews, particularly by the Roman governor Flaccus. On another occasion, probably much earlier in his life, he visited the great temple in Jerusalem "for the purpose of offering up prayers and sacrifices therein."[36]

Philo came from a prominent and wealthy family, therefore he had the best education available anywhere at the time. He himself became a leader in the Jewish community at Alexandria. He had all the resources of the Alexandrian library available to him for his scholarly writings, and he was surrounded by scholars. In one place he gave us a rare insight into his life and work. It was a familiar picture of the conflict between sustained philosophical thought and the demands of public responsibility. "There was once a time when, devoting my leisure to philosophy and to the contemplation of the world and the things in it, I reaped the fruit of excellent, and desirable, and blessed intellectual feelings. . . . I appeared to be raised on high and borne aloft by a certain inspiration of the soul." He was, however, dragged down by envy "into the vast sea of the cares of public politics, in which I was and still am tossed about without being able to keep myself swimming at the top."[37]

Philo had a distinguished brother, Alexander, whose two sons were later, like their father, active in Roman affairs. Alexander served the Roman administration in Egypt and used some of his wealth to enhance the gates of the Jerusalem temple with gold and silver.

Philo made use in his thought and writings of the concept of the Logos, or Word, connecting Platonic metaphysics with the distinctive scriptural notion of Wisdom.[38] One of his works, perhaps written before A.D. 33, presciently employs the Logos or Word as a mediator between God and humanity, and thus gives vivid insight into the thought forms of his day. Such thinking was to become important in rabbinic Judaism after the catastrophic destruction of Jerusalem and the temple in A.D. 70. The idea of a divine messenger and savior was part of his Zeitgeist:

> And the Father who created the universe has given to his archangelic and most ancient Word [Logos] a pre-eminent gift, to stand on the confines of both, and separated that which had been created from the Creator. And this same Word is continually a suppliant to the immortal God on behalf of the mortal race, which is exposed to affliction and misery; and is also the ambassador, sent by the Ruler of all, to the subject race. And the Word rejoices in the gift, and, exulting in it, announces it and boasts of it, saying, "And I stood in the midst, between the Lord and you;" [Numbers 16: 48] neither being uncreated as God, nor yet created as you, but being in the midst between these two extremities, like a hostage, as it were, to both parties: a hostage to the Creator, as a pledge and security that the whole race would never fly off and revolt entirely, choosing disorder rather than order; and to the creature, to lead it to entertain a confident hope that the merciful God would not overlook his own work. For I will proclaim peaceful intelligence to the creation from him who has determined to destroy wars, namely God, who is ever the guardian of peace.[39]

Later, in writing the Gospel of John, its author would remarkably transform Philo's already adapted term, the *Logos,* to apply to Jesus Christ:

> In the beginning was the Word [Logos], and the Word was with God, and the Word was God. He was in the beginning with God. All things were made through him, and without him was not any thing made that was made. In him was life, and the life was the light of men. . . . And the Word became flesh and dwelt among us, and we have seen his glory, glory as of the only Son from the Father, full of grace and truth. (John 1:1-4, 14)[40]

The Word here was mediator between God and his creatures, ambassador, and distinct from God as in Philo, but also tangibly part of creation and of the human race (strongly contra Platonism), and, at the same time, one in identity with God. According to the author of John's Gospel, God himself had entered human history at a definite time and place as a particular human being. It was rather like a master storyteller entering his own story.

Many scholars see the author of the Gospel of John as "Christianizing" (i.e., fictionalizing or "spinning") the events of Jesus' life, transforming them out of their original Jewish context, as a result of cultural distance. These scholars usually place the Gospel late in the first century (Geza Vermes is unusual as placing it as late as A.D. 100-110).[41] Many other scholars have a much earlier date for the Gospel. (John A. T. Robinson is unusual in dating it as early as A.D. 50-65.)[42] Such scholars often regard the Gospel as not being heavily invented or Christianized but as reflecting the diversity of the Jewish context before A.D. 70. This view fits better with the Jewish nature of the Gospel, and its setting largely in Jerusalem and its vicinity (more than two-thirds of the book)—the defining center of Judaism.

NEAR JERUSALEM

THE ROAD OF COURAGE

JESUS OF NAZARETH, EARLY SPRING A.D. 33

A YOUNG WOMAN MAKES HER WAY NIMBLY through the gnarled and twisted trunks of a large olive grove. The ascent is steep and she is soon panting and hot, burdened with the bundle she carries. The small, cream flowers of the olive blossom are beginning to appear on the branches she stoops under, tucked into the gray-green leaves. Above her she can now see the path descending from the direction of the Jericho-to-Jerusalem road. She clambers on to the path and finds a large rock to sit on while she waits. It is warm from the early spring sunshine. Her shoulders sag, and she begins to weep silently amid the occasional hum of early bees.

Her thoughts are interrupted by distant voices. Into view over the brow of the slope come a number of men, grouped in threes or fours. Looking intently, she soon makes out Jesus, with John to one side and Thomas to the other. Thomas appears to be disagreeing with something that Jesus has said, and is gesticulating wildly. Then they spot her and salute.

Martha pulls herself up and walks toward the disciples. Now that she can see Jesus' face, it is clear that his expression is somber, even though he gives a quick nod of greeting. She knows that he has always liked to see her, Mary and Lazarus, and has always stayed with them, or encamped nearby, when visiting Jerusalem at feast times and on other occasions. She says, "Master, if you had been here, my brother would not have died." Jesus says nothing, but puts his hand on the shoulder of the sobbing woman. He gestures for them all to sit down beside the path and takes a drink from the skin of cool water that Martha has brought, passing it to the others.

Martha continues, "But I know that whatever you ask of God, he will give you."

He says, looking directly at her, "Your brother shall rise from the dead."

Martha says to him, as if nobody else is there, "I know that he shall rise at the resurrection on the world's last day."

"Martha, I am the resurrection and the life," he says. "The one who trusts in me, even though he were dead, yet shall he live. Whoever lives and trusts in me, shall never die. Do you believe this?"

She turns her face again to him, "Yes, Master, I believe that you are the Messiah, the son of God, the one who is to come into the world."

At this, Martha gets to her feet, turns and drops away from the path into the olive grove, quickly making her way back to Bethany to tell her sister, Mary, that their Master has come at last.

Jesus watches her quick movements through the trees until she is lost from sight, then drops his gaze.

The group of disciples and their rabbi continue to rest, recovering from the unrelenting steep ascent from Jericho, until the other sister appears at the turn of the path below. A group of mourners following her comes into view, wailing. Mary walks up to Jesus, falls at his feet, and says, "If only you had been here, my Lord, my brother would not have died."[1]

◆ ◆ ◆

The above vignette is based on the account in the Gospel of John of the raising of Lazarus—an account that does not appear in the other, synoptic, Gospels. Some scholars see it as a later Christian and Hellenistic addition to a core of older narrative (even though the resurrection of the body is a Jewish concept). Others see it as an early narrative formulated in the diverse context of the Jewish world before the destruction of the temple, even if penned shortly after A.D. 70, and as complementing the other Gospel accounts.

In the course of events, there would have been no peace to talk to Martha had she met Jesus at the house rather than outside the village. This is but one of a number of closely observed details (or invented details, in the opinion of some) in the Gospel account. The narrative goes on to tell what happens when Jesus entered the village and the house of Mary and Martha. The prevailing worldview of that century was a spiritual one, in which most Jews believed in the possibility of miracles, even that of being raised from the dead, though some, particularly the group called Sadducees, rejected this idea. (We explore the contemporary Jewish worldview in chap. 6.) Even those who believed in the possibility of raising the dead hardly expected it to happen more than a secularist would in the twenty-first century (though they would, of course, be more ready to accept its reality if it did). Indeed,

people then were more likely to have experienced the hurt and disorienta-
tion of bereavement from early in life, with a much higher mortality rate
among the young. They knew first hand the irrevocable loss of a family
member or friend. Although Martha found it plausible to believe in the resurrection of the dead at the end of the world, she appears not to have entertained the idea of her brother's resurrection here and now, even though
she was clearly convinced that Jesus could have healed him if he had arrived
before Lazarus's decline into death. Jesus' arrival, however, seemed to her
to be a sign of hope. She may have reflected that he had risked stoning to
come so near to Jerusalem—it was only a matter of weeks since he had
nearly been set upon by his enemies at the Feast of Dedication.

In John's account, Jesus was deeply distressed by Mary's weeping, and
the wailing of the mourners for his friend Lazarus.[2] John indicates that, like
himself, Lazarus was an especially close friend of Jesus. The kind of distress
that Jesus experienced could not be contained. Perhaps the shortest sentence in all Scripture records, "Jesus wept."

John tells us that Jesus asked to be led to the tomb and the mourners followed. Bodies were either buried in the ground or (what seems to have
been the preference) in caves. In the limestone and sandstone hills around
Jerusalem, natural caves were plentiful, and artificial ones for tombs were
easily cut out of the soft rock. The custom was for a large stone to be rolled
across the cave entrance to keep out wild animals that might feed on the
fresh body—hyenas and jackals were common. Bodies were anointed and
wrapped in linen, including a separate cloth for the face. When the flesh had
fully decayed, the bones would be placed in a small ossuary. Jesus asked
for the stone to be rolled away. The practical Martha protested: "Master, he
stinks to high heaven—he has been dead four days." John writes that Jesus
shouted, "Lazarus, come out," and the buried man emerged with difficulty
from the tomb, his hands and feet still bound with linen strips, and his face
wrapped with a cloth (John 11:40—12:2).

In John's carefully structured narrative this event is a catalyst. It precipi-
tates opposition against Jesus, further uniting the rival groups of the orthodox Pharisees and the majority of the city and temple leaders, who were
dominated by the Sadducees. The latter seem to have been particularly pro-
Roman and more radically Hellenized, and mediated and influenced Roman
rule in their volatile city. John tells us that many believed in Jesus as the
promised Messiah after seeing Lazarus emerge, but some reported the event

to the Jerusalem leaders as a further threat to their power and authority. The event was discussed by the Sanhedrin, the central ruling council, and a plan was initiated to do away with Jesus. Jesus had some supporters in the Sanhedrin, two of them named elsewhere in the Gospel as Nicodemus and Joseph of Arimathea, but not enough to counteract the prevailing consensus. John, who it seems from the Gospel had contacts among the household of the high priest's influential father-in-law, Annas, records the remarkable discussion in which Caiaphas is seen as making a prophecy, the significance of which was greater than he realized:

> So the chief priests and the Pharisees gathered the Council and said, "What are we to do? For this man performs many signs. If we let him go on like this, everyone will believe in him, and the Romans will come and take away both our place and our nation." But one of them, Caiaphas, who was high priest that year, said to them, "You know nothing at all. Nor do you understand that it is better for you that one man should die for the people, not that the whole nation should perish." He did not say this of his own accord, but being high priest that year he prophesied that Jesus would die for the nation, and not for the nation only, but also to gather into one the children of God who are scattered abroad. So from that day on they made plans to put him to death. (John 11: 47-53)

It was part of the function of the high priest in this period to be a prophet. Not only is this passage remarkable for the interpretation of Joseph Caiaphas's words as prophecy, but also for the light it sheds on the motives for seeking Jesus' death, which are strikingly plausible. The ruling elite, together with other religious authorities, were evidently afraid that the teaching and wonders performed by Jesus, most especially the event concerning Lazarus, would bring about a popular insurrection against the Romans, which was likely to result in both the loss of their hard-won power and their national identity. Later history reveals that this fear of insurrection, on the face of it, was not ill founded or exaggerated: after the Jewish insurrections of A.D. 66 and the following years, the city of Jerusalem was razed and the magnificent temple destroyed. The survivors were forced out of the city. In the second century, after another revolt, the city was forcibly secularized by the Romans and renamed Aelia Capitolina. Ironically, however, their fears were ill founded in that Jesus in his teaching and even his miracle working made it clear, according to the Gospel accounts, that his kingdom was not one of earthly power, necessarily temporal and political, but to do with the eternity within real men, women and children. The apostle Paul would, in his letters to fledgling churches, grasp the significance of this Jesus kingdom and establish it as foundational Christian teaching: it was an invisible power of love for God and one's neighbor that would bring down the barriers between male and female, slave and free, rich and the poor, powerful and the helpless, Jew and Gentile (Galatians 3:26-29). This kingdom teaching was far more radical than an insurrection, but would not present a political threat to Rome, according to its ideals of law and peace (rather than according to the spirit of later abuses, especially by Nero).

As well as being an important element in the rising opposition to Jesus on the part of the authorities, the events in Bethany draw attention to Jesus' female followers. Mary and Martha of Bethany probably became disciples during earlier visits by Jesus to the area. Many, however, seem to have become his followers during his lengthy ministry to the north, in Galilee. These include Mary Magdalene (that is, Mary from Magdala, a small town or region on the west shore of Lake Galilee), Susanna, Mary the mother of James and Joseph, or Joses, (members of the Twelve, the close disciples), Salome the mother of another James, and John (also of the Twelve), and Joanna, wife of Chuza, Antipas's steward. Salome by this time might have been resident in Jerusalem, as part of the family fish business, and some scholars consider Mary Magdalene and Mary of Bethany to be identical. The importance of these women is clear, as they are named—unlike the majority of the larger group of disciples.

Between the incident at the Feast of Dedication in December A.D. 32 and the raising of Lazarus in early spring A.D. 33, Jesus had removed himself and his close disciples into the territory of Perea, eastward beyond the River Jordan. This was because of the danger he was in from the city authorities. To get to Perea meant a sharp descent to below sea level in the great Rift Valley in which the River Jordan meandered its way into the Dead (or Salt) Sea. After their descent into its flat-bottomed basin, the group passed New Jericho and Herod's huge winter palace, and crossed the Jordan at one of the many fords. Jesus' destination, which he had revealed to his friends in Bethany, was the place where John had formerly performed baptisms—at the Jordan a few miles north of the Dead Sea, about a day's journey from Jerusalem or, according to some scholars, further north up the Jordan, several days' journey, at Batenea, in the territory of Antipas's brother Philip. Many people came to him there, perhaps some who had formerly gone to hear John the Baptist—for they mentioned that John had worked no sign and that all that John had said of this man Jesus was true. As well as a protective move, it was also symbolic: Jesus was identifying with the ministry and message of his relative John the Baptist, who had been an important feature of Jewish life and belief at that time, to the extent of being featured in Josephus. Jesus clearly perceived a continuity between his message and John's.

The danger to Jesus' life was even more real after Lazarus's restoration, and this time he retired to Ephraim, north of Jerusalem in the central mountains. The town was accessed by a circuitous route north of Jerusalem, through part of Samaria. In another direction from Ephraim the way led down to Jericho. It is described in the Gospel of John as "the region near the wilderness." Here Jesus stayed, along with his disciples, awaiting the forthcoming Passover feast in Jerusalem and preparing himself for what lay ahead. When they finally returned to Jerusalem, they made their way via Jericho, joining the throng of pilgrims from Galilee. Many of these pilgrims would have known Jesus from his itinerant ministry of several years in Galilee. The number may have included Galilean disciples like Mary Magdalene and Susanna, on their way to observe the Passover.

ROME

4

TIBERIUS AND
THE SHADOW OF SEJANUS

A MAN WHO DIED LATE IN A.D. 31 continued to exert an enormous impact on the events of the year A.D. 33 in Rome and elsewhere. This was Sejanus, Tiberius's deputy and even co-consul with Tiberius not long before his death on October 18, A.D. 31. Being consul with Tiberius was a position so honored that, in the circumstances, it suggested that Sejanus might one day be emperor. Many of the great and the good curried favor with him and wished to be considered his friends. In the months after his death and into A.D. 33 and the year beyond, any close connection with Sejanus was a liability and often a cause for terror. Later Roman historians depict the immediate years following Sejanus's death as a period of terror, although some modern historians consider this an exaggeration in view of the likely number of executions that were carried out by Tiberius on those closely associated with the disgraced leader. Tacitus in his *Annals of Imperial Rome* attributes the sway of Sejanus over Tiberius as due to "heaven's anger against Rome." He saw in the events the working out of the judgment of the gods on a corrupt imperial regime. In this view, Sejanus was Tiberius's evil daemon, who, if he had succeeded in his designs on the empire, would have brought even greater moral ruin on Rome than transpired through Tiberius and his successors Caligula, Claudius and Nero—emperors in the Julio-Claudian dynasty, which was broken at the death of Nero by civil wars in A.D. 68-69.

Aelius Sejanus was born at Vulsinii, in Etruria (modern Tuscany) in 20 B.C. He was the son of the commander of the elite praetorian troops at the close of the reign of Augustus, in A.D. 14. The praetorian guard was a special force of bodyguards protecting the emperor. This pedigree was to give him access to the center of Roman power. That very year Sejanus was promoted to share in the command of the praetorian guard of his father, Seius Strabo.

When his father was moved to the prestigious post of governor of Egypt, Sejanus took on the sole command of these troops. He carefully gained such influence over Tiberius that the reclusive emperor made him his confidant.

Dio Cassius records that Sejanus consolidated the power of the praetorian guard and thus his own military power:

> He strengthened his authority in many ways, especially by bringing together into a single camp the various cohorts which had been separate and distinct from one another like those of the night-watch. In this way the entire force could receive its orders promptly, and would inspire everybody with fear because all were together in one camp. This was the man whom Tiberius, because of the similarity of their characters, attached to himself, elevating him to the rank of praetor, an honor that had never yet been accorded to one of like station; and he made him his adviser and assistant in all matters.[1]

Sejanus was intoxicated with his growing influence. Not content with his access to the emperor, it seems likely that Sejanus was planning to become emperor himself, or at least to have ultimate control of power. With his lifetime immersion in the military, he knew the strategic importance of finding favor with the troops. He worked hard at gaining the popularity of the soldiers and made sure that the right people were given posts of honor or rewarded in other ways.

A bigger obstacle lay with the existing heirs to the imperial seat and those in the emperor's family who worked against his designs. As part of a well-ordered and daring strategy he seduced Livilla, the attractive wife of Drusus, who was Tiberius's son. This seems to have been one of many seductions.

By promising Livilla marriage and involvement in the imperial power, Sejanus in A.D. 23 succeeded in poisoning Drusus with her agreement and help.[2] This same year he divorced his wife, Apicata, perhaps to sooth Livilla's jealousy or to convince her of his intentions toward her. Everything seemed to be going Sejanus's way. With Drusus out of the picture an important impediment to supreme power was removed. He also felt that he had an influential woman like Livilla in his hand because of his charm. Then a freak of nature occurred that increased Sejanus's standing in the eyes of Tiberius, convincing him of his friendship and trustworthiness. Tacitus recounts the event:

> They were dining in a country house called "The Cave," between the gulf of Amuclae and the hills of Fundi, in a natural grotto. The rocks at its entrance suddenly fell in and crushed some of the attendants; thereupon panic seized

the whole company and there was a general flight of the guests. Sejanus hung over the emperor, and with knee, face, and hand encountered the falling stones; and was found in this attitude by the soldiers who came to their rescue. After this he was greater than ever, and though his counsels were ruinous, he was listened to with confidence, as a man who had no care for himself.[3]

Sejanus encouraged the reclusive Tiberius, who needed little persuasion, to retire from the troublesome environment of Rome in A.D. 26, settling on the island of Capreae the following year. Sejanus could now follow his plans with much less hindrance. He insinuated himself into the position of gatekeeper for the emperor, so that correspondence and other business passed through his hands, as a trusted deputy. When Livia, the mother of Tiberius and widow of Augustus, died in A.D. 29, a powerful restraining influence was removed. Indeed, the strong-minded Livia apparently was one of the reasons Tiberius had been glad to be out of Rome. Soon afterward, Sejanus achieved the banishment of the distinguished Agrippina, granddaughter of Augustus (see chap. 12), and her sons Nero and Drusus, potential heirs to the emperor. She had been at the forefront of opposition to him. Sejanus exploited the jealousy Tiberius had long harbored against the unfortunate Agrippina.

One of the best accounts of the growth of Sejanus's power is to be found in Tacitus's *Annals of Imperial Rome*. Sadly, the last part of the fifth book and the beginning of the sixth, which covered the marriage of Sejanus and his disgrace, a period of nearly three years, are lost. Tacitus does, however, refer to the events elsewhere in the *Annals,* and there are accounts in Suetonius and Dio Cassius. To increase his power Sejanus had asked Tiberius if he could marry Livilla, Drusus's widow, but Tiberius had turned down the request on the grounds that Sejanus was not sufficiently high born. However, Tiberius left open the possibility that she might one day be allowed to marry him. It was not until A.D. 31 that he agreed to the marriage.

Despite his isolation in Capreae, Tiberius began to suspect the ambitions of Sejanus, ambitions that put his own life in danger. When faced with evidence of the appalling reality of Sejanus's involvement in the death of his son, Drusus, and other machinations, Tiberius decided that he must be eliminated. It had to be done in a way that bypassed the powerful praetorian guard that Sejanus commanded. Important evidence for Sejanus's treachery, in the form of his part in Drusus's death, was supplied by Antonia, Tiberius's sister-in-law.

Dio Cassius records portents of Sejanus's fall around the time of his pe-

riod as consul early in A.D. 31, which in his arrogance he ignored. The listing
of these portents is characteristic of the beliefs in auguries of the time:

> Now on a New Year's day, when all were assembling at Sejanus' house, the
> couch that stood in the reception room utterly collapsed under the weight of
> the throng seated upon it; and, as he was leaving the house, a weasel darted
> through the midst of the crowd. After he had sacrificed on the Capitol and was
> now descending to the Forum, the servants who were acting as his body-guard
> turned aside along the road leading to the prison, being unable by reason of
> the crowd to keep up with him, and while they were descending the steps
> down which condemned criminals were cast, they slipped and fell. Later, as
> he was taking the auspices, not one bird of good omen appeared, but many
> crows flew round him and cawed, then all flew off together to the jail and
> perched there.
>
> Neither Sejanus nor anyone else took these omens to heart. For, in view of
> the way matters stood, not even if some god had plainly foretold that so great
> a change would take place in a short time, would anyone have believed it. So
> they swore by his Fortune interminably and called him Tiberius' colleague, co-
> vertly referring to the supreme power rather than to the consulship.[4]

Making Sejanus joint consul with himself might have been part of the emperor's scheme to be rid of his treacherous deputy. It hid his suspicions and
gave Sejanus a false picture of his prospects. Tiberius's eventual agreement
to the marriage with Livilla was possibly part of this same disarming strategy.

Sometime early in September Tiberius summoned Gaius Caligula to Capreae for safety; it was clear to the emperor now that he was in danger, as
a possible heir, from Sejanus. On October 18 Tiberius sent a favorite and
trusted officer, Sertorius Macro, to Rome with a commission to take the command of the praetorian cohorts. Macro ensured that Sejanus did not have his
usual guard and led him to believe he carried a letter of substantial promo-
tion from the emperor intended for the Senate. Sejanus sat in the Senate
while Tiberius's deliberately rambling letter was read. It slowly became apparent that the letter condemned Sejanus as a traitor. As the condemnations
began to emerge from the dense prose, senators moved away from Sejanus,
not wanting any association with him in his downfall. When the letter concluded, the stunned Sejanus was arrested. Sejanus appeared dazed by the
turn of events, according to Dio Cassius:

> Regulus summoned him to go forward, but he paid no heed, not out of con-
> tempt—for he had already been humbled—but because he was unaccustomed

to having orders addressed to him. But when the consul, raising his voice and also pointing at him, called the second and third time, "Sejanus, come here," he merely asked him, "Me? You are calling me?" At last, however, he stood up.[5]

One of the great English playwrights, Ben Jonson, wrote a play called *Sejanus: His Fall,* which is now little known. When it was first performed in 1603, Shakespeare was in the cast. Jonson recreates the dramatic letter from Tiberius in the last act, with senators shifting away from places near Sejanus as Tiberius's import gradually becomes clear. As they do so, Jonson has the distinguished senator Lucius Arruntius remark, "Gods! How the leaves drop off, this little wind!" The consul Regulus conducted him to prison, with the people outside vilifying the prisoner as he passed them. The Senate passed a death sentence, and he was immediately strangled. His body was dragged about the streets, mutilated and finally thrown into the Tiber. Seneca added the gruesome detail that "there scarcely remained a fragment of it for the executioner to drag to the river."[6]

Because of the severity of his treason, even his youngest children were not spared, despite their ages. His eldest son, named Strabo after Sejanus's father, was executed in less than a week. The culling of the other children followed later. His younger son, Capito Aelianus, who had been adopted, probably knew what was coming, but the youngest, Iunilla, said as they were carried off that she was sorry for being naughty, and if they whipped her she would not be bad again. Tacitus describes the events, the horror of which has shocked people through the centuries since.

> It was next decided to punish the remaining children of Sejanus, though the fury of the populace was subsiding, and people generally had been appeased by the previous executions. Accordingly they were carried off to prison, the boy, aware of his impending doom, and the little girl, who was so unconscious that she continually asked what was her offense, and whither she was being dragged, saying that she would do so no more, and a childish chastisement was enough for her correction. Historians of the time tell us that, as there was no precedent for the capital punishment of a virgin, she was violated by the executioner, with the rope on her neck. Then they were strangled and their bodies, mere children as they were, were flung down the Gemoniae.[7]

Their mother, Apicata, appalled at the sight of their bodies lying on the Gemonian Steps, ready to be dragged by hooks into the Tiber, killed herself. According to Dio Cassius, she first composed a damning statement about Livilla's involvement in the death of Tiberius's son, Drusus, and sent the document to Capreae. Out of regard for her mother, Antonia, Tiberius did not execute Livilla, but passed the daughter over to her. Antonia locked up Livilla until she starved to death.[8]

The praetorian guard, so recently under Sejanus's iron control, assisted in a widespread slaughter of his friends and associates. After the initial excitement died down, what the later Roman historians saw as a "reign of terror" continued for three years, into A.D. 34.

Tiberius's strategy for ridding Rome of Sejanus and removing a palpably real threat to his position as emperor was full of risks. Tiberius himself had paraded the strength of the praetorian guard to the Senate to emphasize his power over them, not realizing then that the military power was in fact in Sejanus's hands. He had accordingly made plans to escape from Capreae if his plan failed, and anxiously looked out from Villa Jovis for a beacon signal from the hill above Misenum, across the Gulf of Neapolis, a signal to be transmitted fire by fire from the capital. He had a fleet standing by and intended to flee, probably to Syria but perhaps to Alexandria, if the signal came that his plan had failed.

The Roman historian C. Velleius Paterculus perished around the time of Sejanus. He had the misfortune to publish his *History of Rome,* promoting Sejanus, in A.D. 30. His work closes with a prayer that was decidedly not answered by his gods:

> Let me end my volume with a prayer. O Jupiter Capitolinus, and Mars Gradivus, author and stay of the Roman name, Vesta, guardian of the eternal fire, and all other divinities who have exalted this great empire of Rome to the highest point yet reached on earth! On you I call, and to you I pray in the name of this people: guard, preserve, protect the present state of things, the peace which we enjoy, the present emperor, and when he has filled his post of duty—and may it be the longest granted to mortals—grant him successors until the latest time, but successors whose shoulders may be as capable of sustaining bravely the empire of the world as we have found his to be: foster the pious plans of all good citizens and crush the impious designs of the wicked.[9]

Sejanus would be soon executed, and within seven years Tiberius would be gone, succeeded by the infamous Gaius Caligula, then Claudius, to be followed by Nero, whose ignominious death brought to an end the dynasty of Augustus and Tiberius and opened a brief period of civil war.

During A.D. 33 the consequences of Sejanus's fall continued to play out. One may have been that Tiberius, recovered from his period of depression the year before, exploited the climate of terror for his own ends. Tacitus has an intriguing reference to one Sextus Marius, richest man in Spain, executed for his wealth, according to the *Annals*.[10] He was thrown from the Tarpeian Rock in Rome (the traditional place from which traitors were hurled). The charge under which Sextus Marius was executed was that of incest. After his death, Tacitus notes, Tiberius personally appropriated his lucrative gold and copper mines. Dio Cassius also refers to the incident: "When this Marius, now, had sent away his daughter, a strikingly beautiful girl, to a place of refuge, in order to prevent her from being outraged by Tiberius, he was charged with having criminal relations with her himself, and because of this he perished together with his daughter."[11]

This year also marked the death of Gaius Asinus Gallus, who was hated by Tiberius because he married Vipsania, his former wife, and because of his freedom in expressing his opinions in the Senate. The emperor had resolved to get rid of him before the downfall of Sejanus. In A.D. 30 he invited Gallus as a guest to his table at Capreae. While the hospitality was going on, the Senate, as Tiberius had arranged, sentenced him to death. The emperor spared his life, but only so that Gallus could be made to suffer. Tiberius kept him imprisoned for three years, and on the minimum of food so that his hunger was never satisfied but he had enough to sustain life. Some time in the autumn of A.D. 33 he died in his dungeon of starvation, but whether it was self-chosen is unknown. According to Tacitus, Tiberius killed him. Certainly the emperor seemed to explore the possibilities of torment afforded by starvation, and it is almost a theme of the year—in it first Gallus, then Drusus, then his mother Agrippina, and then Nerva died from starvation.

As the year progressed many people continued to be killed for their connection, real or imaginary, with Sejanus. On one day up to twenty of Sejanus's imprisoned followers, including boys and women, were executed, their bodies exposed on the Gemonian Steps. Suetonius makes much of the "reign of terror," as later does Dio Cassius. Dio Cassius writes, in his *Roman History*:

> His relatives, his associates, and all the rest who had paid court to him and had proposed the granting of honors to him were brought to trial. The majority of them were convicted for the acts that had previously made them the objects of envy; and their fellow-citizens condemned them for the measures which they themselves had previously voted. Many men who had been tried on various charges and acquitted were again accused and now convicted, on the

ground that they had been saved before as a favor to the man now fallen. Accordingly, if no other complaint could be brought against a person, the very fact that he had been a friend of Sejanus sufficed to bring punishment upon him. . . .

It happened not only that those who had accused others were brought to trial and those who had testified against others now found others testifying against them, but also that those who had condemned others were convicted in their turn. So it was that neither Tiberius spared anyone, but employed all the citizens without exception against one another, nor, for that matter, could anybody rely upon the loyalty of any friend; but the guilty and the innocent, the timorous and the fearless, stood on the same footing when face to face with the inquiry into the charges involving the acts of Sejanus. . . .

All who incurred any such charge, senators as well as knights, and women as well as men, were crowded together in the prison, and upon being condemned either paid the penalty there or were hurled down from the Capitol by the tribunes or even by the consuls, after which the bodies of all of them were cast into the Forum and later thrown into the river.[12]

Whether or not Suetonius and Tacitus before him exaggerated the extent of Tiberius's retributions over Sejanus, a very poignant testimony to the moral confusion of the period is found near the end of the year A.D. 33. This comes from a prominent member of Tiberius's household on Capreae and friend of the emperor. Nerva simply lost the will to live in the face of what was happening in Rome.

Tacitus tells us that Marcus Cocceius Nerva, a brilliant lawyer who had once been a consul in Rome, was among those who accompanied Tiberius when he originally moved from the capital in A.D. 26 and then to Capreae the following year. He was one of a group of learned men with whom Tiberius liked to be surrounded. Most of them were Greeks, but Nerva was one of several Romans of "liberal culture." Members of the group, versed in astrology, told Tiberius that the movement of the heavenly bodies when he departed Rome forbade the possibility of his return. Thereafter, the nearest Tiberius would go to Rome was the vicinity of the city walls, as when Livilla and Drusilla, the daughters of Germanicus and Agrippina, were married in A.D. 33.

Nerva died in November or December of A.D. 33 as a result of a slow suicide by starvation. Day after day Tiberius had sat beside him, pleading with him to eat. Although Nerva said nothing of the reason for his action to Tiberius, it was in response to calamities at Rome, according to Tacitus.[13] Suetonius believed that he did this because he could no longer endure being with Tiberius and his court in Capreae.

There was a financial crisis due to a currency shortage that year. This threatened to ruin very many of the landed classes, a sector Tiberius had always favored. Nerva was particularly unhappy, in response to blatant abuses, that "Tiberius had reaffirmed the laws on contracts enacted by Caesar" that had been ignored. These, in Nerva's view, "were sure to result in great loss of confidence and financial confusion." Julius Caesar had established these laws to control loans and land ownership.[14] Tiberius had allowed eighteen months in which all private finance was to be brought into accord with the law. As a result there was a shortage of hard currency because all debts were called in simultaneously and the land and property of many was put at risk. In response to Nerva's unhappiness, Dio Cassius tells us, "Tiberius modified his decision regarding loans and gave one hundred million sesterces to the public treasury, with the provision that this money should be lent out by the senators without interest to such as asked for it."[15] By establishing the interest-free loan fund Tiberius averted the crisis.

Tiberius also took steps to obviate injustices that were occurring over the punishments of those associated with Sejanus. Dio Cassius records that "he . . . commanded that the most notorious of those who were bringing accusations against others should be put to death in a single day. And when a man who had been a centurion desired to lodge information against someone, he forbade anyone who had served in the army to do this, although he allowed the knights and senators to do so."[16]

These steps were of no avail. Nerva continued to refuse food and eventually died. The death of such a great and eminent friend was a powerful loss to Tiberius. Their friendship went back a long way, and Tiberius had given him the superintendence of the aqueducts of Rome. A measure of his importance is that he was the grandfather of the emperor Nerva (A.D. 96-98).[17]

As well as managing this financial crisis Tiberius also had to deal with a shortage of bread in Rome this year. He did so by importing as much grain as he could from the nearer provinces. Egypt was a particularly important supplier. He reminded the citizens of Rome that it was more than Augustus had ever supplied. When there were disturbances by some who wanted lower prices for the bread as well, Tiberius ordered them crushed by the Senate and the city magistrates.

All in all, it was a difficult year for Tiberius, still affected by the treachery of Sejanus. The year A.D. 33 was the tenth anniversary of the death of his son Drusus. The fact that he now knew the death was not natural, but brought about by Sejanus, added to the pain, and the desire to obliterate Sejanus's malevolent influence. He continued to seek solace in the movement of the heavenly planets as influences on the events of earth. Historians record a remarkable outcome of his astrology.

In the spring or summer of A.D. 33 Galba became a consul in Rome. According to Tacitus, Tiberius prophesied Galba's brief rule after the death of Nero in A.D. 68.

> I must not pass over a prognostication of Tiberius respecting Servius Galba, then consul. Having sent for him and sounded him on various topics, he at last addressed him in Greek to this effect: "You too, Galba, will some day have a taste of empire." He thus hinted at a brief span of power late in life, on the strength of his acquaintance with the art of astrologers, leisure for acquiring which he had had at Rhodes, with Thrasyllus for instructor.[18]

Galba had become a senator before the usual age, and was 36 when he became consul in A.D. 33. Tiberius realized his potential as a leader. He was from an ancient family and hugely wealthy, and within six years Galba would receive command of the Upper German army.

Tiberius was much preoccupied with the question of leadership. He needed to establish an heir. His eyes were upon Gaius Caesar, nicknamed "Caligula," the son of the late Germanicus and Agrippina, exiled on the island of Pandateria. Caligula became twenty-one this year, on August 31. At his coming of age Tiberius allowed him to hold a quaestorship, giving him access to the Senate. He also married him to Julia Claudia, an arranged marriage that linked him to the powerful Julio-Claudian dynasty. Caligula, along with Tiberius's grandson Gemellus, was clearly flagged as Tiberius's possible successor by then. Gemellus was the son of Drusus, but some later said that he was fathered during Sejanus's adultery with Livilla. The favoring of Caligula presents one of the paradoxes in Tiberius's character, for he was the son of the hated Agrippina, and brother of Drusus, who died this year at Tiberius's hand. Perhaps Tiberius, who may have glimpsed a darkness in Caligula that corresponded with his own, enjoyed the thought of nursing a viper in the bosom of Rome. Perhaps it was an elaborate way of torturing the young man, fanning a mental conflict that eventually unbalanced him.

JERUSALEM

DARKNESS AT NOON

(MARCH 28-APRIL 3)

SATURDAY EVENING, MARCH 28, TO SUNDAY, MARCH 29 (NISAN 9)

Mary can't take her eyes off Lazarus. She can see that Martha, her sister, is similarly overwhelmed. They can't view him simply as a brother any more. One day he lies rotting in the family tomb, the next he is out and about, eating and drinking as if he's never seen a meal before. Martha keeps bringing him extra helpings and giving him the best wine. Meals in Jewish households are painstakingly prepared, and in this Bethany home meals are varied. Greek and Roman influences shape the cuisine, though of course there is no unclean food, as prescribed in the Torah. Red meat tends to be eaten only on festival days, but there is an abundant supply of fish from the nearby markets of Jerusalem. Many vegetables are eaten raw (such as small cucumbers), while lentils and greens are boiled in oil or water. A kind of porridge is made out of corn, and a variety of cakes is created out of crushed and malted grain. For sweetening, honey, dates, raisins and figs are used. There is a plenitude of fruits. Olive oil is an essential feature of meals, as is wine, which might be flavored with myrrh or other spices.

Then one day Mary remembers a story she's heard about a dubious woman who had anointed the Master's feet and wiped them with her hair. Jesus hadn't rebuked her or recoiled from her touch.

The family is rich—like many in Bethany, so close to the holy city—and Mary has many possessions. Martha tends to live more simply. Mary knows her sister gives a great deal out of her means to support Jesus and the disciples. In particular, Mary has some spikenard, a rare perfumed oil, which she has been saving for special occasions, perhaps even for her wedding one day. Perfumes are used to give fragrance to clothes or for cosmetics. Some are used for burials. As days become weeks since Jesus raised her brother, her thoughts return to the precious nard again and again. It came from far away, across distant seas to the east. It cost her about a normal man's wages for a year.

Now word has come that Jesus is returning for the Passover Feast. Simon the Leper has invited him, together with his disciples, to a feast in his house. Lazarus, something of a celebrity, is also to be a guest—he is the talk not only of Bethany but of the villages round about, and even of Jerusalem. Martha typically has offered to help serve at the feast. Mary loves Martha, and her readiness to serve. She knows too that it will give Martha the opportunity to see Jesus. But Martha's greatest joy is to have the chance to serve him.

It is now some hours after sunset has closed the sabbath. It is Nisan 9 (the equivalent of the evening of Saturday, March 28). The guests recline on pallets around the laden table, Greek style. They have eaten their full and the wine and conversation is fast flowing.

It is at this point that Mary comes into the room, carrying the alabaster flask that contains her ten ounces of nard, a substantial amount. At first the guests don't notice her—servers have been coming and going all evening. But then, as she opens the flask, her movements start to tug at their attention, especially as Jesus has stopped talking and is looking intently at Mary. She begins anointing Jesus' head with the liquid, amber-colored nard, so that his locks are dampened. Its fragrance suddenly fills the room. She continues by putting the spikenard on to his wrists and hands, after which she kneels at his feet and applies the perfume liberally to them. She does something then that jolts the guests even more than the anointing—she loosens her hair so that her long braids roll down her back and over her shoulders. Usually this act in such a public setting comes across as erotic. She reaches back, gathering her hair with her hands. With her hair she carefully wipes Jesus' feet.

The silence is quickly broken by indignant male voices of the guests. One disciple after another upbraids her. Judas speaks for them all (but with a darker motive unknown to them) when he says, "What a waste! This ointment should have been sold and the money given to the poor. A fortune has been poured away." The others add their agreement, calling the squandering of the precious nard a scandal.

Jesus has been silent through all this, observing Mary's increasing distress.

He turns on the disciples and other guests and tells them to let the woman alone. He says that Mary has done a beautiful thing to him. He declares that the poor are always with them, but those present will not always have him. In pouring this ointment on his body, he says, she has helped to prepare him for burial. Wherever this gospel, or good news, is proclaimed throughout the wide world, he says, what she has done will be retold to remember her.

◆ ◆ ◆

This account of Mary's anointing of Jesus is recorded in three of the Gospel narratives, which is a measure of how important the incident was considered to be. The spikenard came from India, via the new sea routes. There it was called Jatamansi.[1]

Mary's anointing was particularly important to Jesus because, whether intentionally or unconsciously, the act acknowledged Jesus' role of suffering as the Messiah. This went against what we know of contemporary expectations of such a figure, particularly for those geared to political success. Grasping the role of suffering was likely to have been a paradigm shift.[2]

Jesus used the occasion to give one of several warnings of his impending fate. He saw his time as having come, and he no longer withdrew from danger, as previously. His attitude was implicit in coming up to the Passover Feast when his blood was sought. He would soon poke the wasps' nest even more. Even as the feast in Bethany happened, people in high places were planning his death as a matter of utmost expediency. Judas was to be caught up in these plots, and indeed would precipitate them. In reaction to what he saw as Mary's waste of a fortune, he mentally took a further step in making possible Jesus' demise. On one level his motive was simple greed: he saw that he could make some easy money by providing intelligence to the city and temple authorities about Jesus' movements. Perhaps on another level he wished to force the hand of his erstwhile master into insurrection, but no hints of such a more noble motive are given. John's account of the anointing alleges that Judas regularly dipped into the common purse that was entrusted to him, a habit that weakened him morally. With this and his subsequent betrayal of the innocent Jesus, he must count as one of history's most unpleasant characters. Yet the Gospel narratives do not demonize him. The faults of other disciples, such as Peter the future church leader, are aired with his. Theirs is no hagiography.

Judas is a complex figure: he is portrayed both as an agent of Satan and as a central agent of providence—without his approach to the authorities, Jesus' arrest, trial and execution would not have happened at this particular time. Such complexity is typical of the Gospel narratives, which are rooted in Jewish scriptural narratives, requiring an interpretative response, because of their multilayered reference to reality.

Jerusalem and the area around it was, at this time, awash with pilgrims preparing themselves for the forthcoming Passover. The number of inhabitants had swelled to perhaps as many as one million. The popular preacher and healer had been missed. Many of those who had made their way to Jerusalem from Galilee had expected to find him there. Some were saying as they mingled in the crowded temple courts, "What do you think? That he will not come to the feast?" Then word started to spread that he was in Bethany, visiting Mary, Martha and Lazarus. Both the chief priests and the pious Pharisees had given orders that anybody who knew his whereabouts was to let them know, so that they could detain him. Instead, many of those who knew made their way across the top of the Mount of Olives, or skirted its flanks, to the little village of Bethany. A large crowd ended up congregated around the house of Mary, Martha and Lazarus, either that night or the next day—perhaps both. Not only did they want to see Jesus but also the much-talked-about Lazarus, the man back from the dead. The authorities could do nothing in full view of such a crowd, but the interest in Lazarus made them start planning to put him to death also. A dead Lazarus would be preferable to a live one, who simply by being alive was stirring the popular following of Jesus. An uprising was in the air. It was only a year since the bloody suppression by Pilate at the feast of a group of Galileans—people who could be notoriously anti-Roman. It may be that the Galileans, because many had been exposed to Jesus' ministry there, were much more favorable to him than the local residents of Jerusalem.

◆ ◆ ◆

At this point in the narrative Lazarus is walking about larger than life, and Jesus is poised to suffer an injustice of horrific proportions. This is a good place at which to consider the scope of a historical account of these events. Is it only Jesus as a human being who is of interest, the man who undoubtedly died under Pontius Pilate's governorship? Was he only an outstanding charismatic teacher, a holy man, as we will explore in chapter six, or should we also take seriously his evident claims to be divine as well as human, and to replace the temple cult, which also means taking seriously the consequent outrage felt at these claims by the majority of those who were in charge of the temple and Jerusalem? As Michael Grant points out, blasphemy and treason were indivisible in the Jewish context of the time—"any challenge to the Jewish religious authority inevitably seemed to imply political opposition to the Romans."[3] Even to restrict the account to human agency is not as simple as it sounds. A historian who is a materialist will have to reduce human actions to natural causes. For a materialist, a historical cause would be identical with a natural cause. The interest of history, however, is in its dealing with historical causes as transcending natural causation, in its dealing with culture as well as nature, in its concern with the subtleties and motives of human beings, which can be interpreted but never easily explained. For the theistic historian (such as the writers of the scriptural narratives), human agency and its mysteries point to an even higher causation—the hand of God in history. A polytheistic historian (like Tacitus or Suetonius) would have a similar orientation. Tacitus finds it natural to include the arrival in Egypt of the fabled phoenix in his account of the Caesars. The working out of historical causes is parallel to the complex relationship between human freedom and the intricate causalities that shape it—those of nature, society, thought and belief. To try to understand the world of A.D. 33 it is necessary to step inside a Zeitgeist in which events are shaped not only by free human agency as well as natural causes but also by causes that are supernatural, spiritual, angelic and divine. We need to understand the events surrounding Jesus and his claims against the background of the beliefs of the time. Jesus lived, breathed and taught in a Jewish milieu.

SUNDAY, MARCH 29 (NISAN 9)

Jesus started out on foot for Jerusalem. There was a choice of three ways, it seems, from Bethany over the Mount of Olives to Jerusalem. One, a path, passed between the northern and central summits of the mountain. Another ascended to the highest point of the mountain and then down toward Jerusalem. The third, which was the main track, skirted the southern shoulder of the mountain, between it and the "Hill of Evil Counsel." Because of the crowds, Jesus most probably took the third and easiest route. Soon after leaving Bethany, they approached the fig gardens of Bethphage, the "House of Figs." This was a small suburb or hamlet, the exact site of which is now unknown. It probably lay a little to the south of Bethany and in sight of it.

To this village, or another near it, Jesus dispatched two of his disciples. These may have been Peter and John. Jesus instructed them that when they got to the village, they should find an ass tied and a foal with her.[4] These they were to loose and bring to him. If anybody objected, they were to say that "the Lord had need of them" ("the Lord" implied Jesus for any of his followers). The disciples put their garments over the foal in festive fashion and hoisted Jesus upon it. The event acted out an allusion to the coming messianic king of an ancient scriptural prophecy well known to the crowd (Zechariah 9:9-10). Instead of a war horse, Jesus deliberately rode a symbol of peace. The procession, which would have been largely made up of pilgrims from Galilee, where Jesus was well known, set forth along the steep side of the Kidron Valley and down the slope toward Jerusalem, finally ascending to the temple gate. The green slopes of the valley would have been thickly populated by tents and booths of the many pilgrims, the mood rather like a rock or folk-music festival today. All the while the crowd flung garments and branches before Jesus on the young donkey—a first-century red carpet. They were boisterous and shouted words from their Scripture: "Hosanna! [literally, "Save now!"] Blessed is he who comes in the name of the Lord! Blessed is the coming kingdom of our father David! Hosanna in the highest!" (Mark 11:9-10). Some Pharisees in the throng irritably demanded that Jesus rebuke the people for shouting this. Jesus replied: "I tell you, if these were silent, the very stones would cry out" (Luke 19:40). The Pharisees said to one another that they could do nothing—"the world has gone after him" (John 12:19). Jesus' entry into Jerusalem, hailed in this way by the crowd of pilgrims, could not be ignored by the Jewish authorities, and thus the confrontation deepened.

When Jesus drew near to the city across the valley from him, heading for the Susa Gate, it is noted that he wept over it. Luke records words that, with other statements of Jesus throughout this final week, were taken as prophetic of the destruction of Jerusalem thirty-seven years later. He spoke of their enemies setting up a barricade around the city, hemming them in with a siege in which they and their children perish. Not one stone would be left upon another because of Jerusalem's ignorance of his messianic visitation (Luke 19:41-44).

◆ ◆ ◆

Because of the vividness with which Luke's words recall the Roman siege of Jerusalem, many scholars argue that they were written after A.D. 70. There are, however, difficulties with the assumption (and it is always an assumption) that because Jesus' words were taken as referring to the fall of Jerusalem in A.D. 70 and because, in this view, true prophecies cannot happen, this (and similar accounts) must have been written after the event. In fact, it is possible that the three similar (Synoptic) Gospels—Matthew, Mark and Luke—were written earlier, or at least Matthew and Mark were, their writing precipitated by the savage repression of Christians by Nero in the 60s. During this time, one apostle after another, each a repository of knowledge about Christ's life, seemed to be falling to the executioner within a brief period—the pillars of the young church, Paul and Peter, certainly died then. The apostle James, brother of John and cousin of Jesus, had earlier died in Jerusalem under the persecution of Herod Agrippa I in A.D. 44 (Acts 12:2).

Furthermore, Luke's words are not as explicit about the A.D. 70 siege as they might at first appear. They refer to what was a standard Roman military strategy. As Nazareth was so close to Sepphoris, Jesus was no doubt familiar with its destruction by Roman forces after a revolt not long after the death of Herod the Great, and that event would therefore provide ready imagery of a siege for his prophecy.[6] Those who wish to account for Christ's uncanny words need a more convincing explanation. By the time of the fall of Jerusalem, it seems that most Christians had left, as if they had been warned.[7] This is even more remarkable given the fact that until the city's fall and the destruction of the temple, Christianity seems to have been perceived either as an offshoot or a variant of Judaism.[8] It was only after A.D. 70 that, in the words of F. F. Bruce, "the divergence of the paths of Jewish Christianity and orthodox Judaism was decisive."[9]

According to a later Roman authority, Sulpicius Severus, apparently basing his account on Tacitus, Titus, the leader of the siege of Jerusalem, was eager to destroy the temple. This was "in order that the Jewish and Christian religions might more completely be abolished; for although these religions were mutually hostile, they had nevertheless sprung from the same founders; the Christians were an offshoot of the Jews, and if the root were taken away the stock would easily perish."[10] The Romans were eager to eliminate the resistance of Jews to Roman rule. Not only was there widespread revolt in Judea from 66 to 70 but also unrest in other parts of the Diaspora, such as Alexandria. Rome seems to have realized that the existence of Jerusalem, and the temple cult in particular, was central to Jewish identity. In Rome, furthermore, the large Christian group was blamed by

Nero for the Great Fire, which started on July 19, A.D. 64, and destroyed two-thirds of the city; as far as the Romans were concerned, Christianity was a Jewish sect.

Furthermore, Jesus was not alone in prophesying the destruction of Jerusalem, and thus the temple, nor alone in the language and imagery he used. According to Craig A. Evans there is significant evidence in Jewish literature of similar predictions of destruction by a variety of persons and literary traditions.[11]

◆ ◆ ◆

When the procession neared the city walls, the inhabitants were stirred with excitement and some distrust. "Who is this?" they shouted. Some in the crowd accompanying Jesus responded, "This is Jesus, the prophet from Nazareth!" perhaps with some regional pride. It may be that here there is a distinction between the concerns of the local inhabitants and those of the visiting pilgrims from Galilee. The latter had been more exposed to Jesus' teaching and perhaps more ready to espouse it.

Once in the city, Jesus went into the temple. Many blind and lame people came to him for healing, and small children clambered after him, yelling, "Hosanna to the Son of David!" This reference to the Son of David linked Jesus to an expected messiah, descended from King David, the famous king of antiquity.[12] It was either on this day or the following that Jesus attacked the traders in the temple courts. In any event preparations for Passover were well under way and F. W. Farrar describes the scene before Jesus:

> The tessellated floors and pillared colonnades of the Court of the Gentiles had been again usurped by droves of oxen and sheep, and dove-sellers, and usurers, and its whole precincts were dirty with driven cattle, and echoed to the hum of bargaining voices and the clink of gold. In that desecrated place He would not teach.[13]

Jesus was clearly deeply grieved at what he saw. At the beginning of his ministry, around A.D. 30, he had driven out the traders to cleanse the temple.[14] He would do it again. This time, in the context of the opposition to him of the temple and city leaders, it would be a provocative confrontation. According to Michael Grant, the act of cleansing the temple was a breach of public order imposed by the Roman political administration. At the same time it attacked the Jewish priestly authority that controlled temple affairs.[15]

Jesus would simultaneously be antagonizing the Romans and the Jewish authorities. He would be striking at the very core of his people's identity in challenging the temple cult. Jesus saw the temple primarily as a place of prayer and worship rather than elaborate sacrifice with its attendant merchandising. Jesus remained in the temple area for some time and then returned with his disciples to Bethany.

MONDAY, MARCH 30 (NISAN 10)

Early the next day Jesus set off again for Jerusalem from Bethany with his disciples. He was hungry. (Perhaps he had bivouacked with his disciples on the slopes of the Mount of Olives and had had no breakfast.) Seeing in the distance a fig tree in leaf, he went to look for fruit on it. When he got to the tree, he found nothing but leaves: the season for figs had not yet arrived, though an earlier type of fig might have been expected. His disciples heard him say to the tree, "May no one ever eat fruit from you again." This is not a vindictive act against a poor little tree, but a symbolic act, which links the tree with the end of the temple in Jerusalem. The tree seemed healthy and vital, but without fruit it had lost its purpose. Jesus may have been inspired to act out this parable by the words of the ancient scriptural prophet, Micah, whose image of a fig tree without fruit symbolized the moral and religious failure of Israel (Micah 7:1).

When he arrived at the temple, he was again confronted with the bustle of buying and selling in the lead-up to the feast. Incensed at the commercialization, he drove out the merchants. It was a deliberate sequel to his earlier triumphant entry into Jerusalem, an assertion of his countercultural authority. He kicked over the stalls of the moneychangers and those selling sacrificial doves at inflated prices. The anger in his face and the approval of the pilgrim crowds, especially the Galileans, meant that there was no resistance. This was the anger of a prophet. He said to the traders, "Is it not written, 'My house shall be a house of prayer for all the nations'? But you have made it a den of robbers." Clearly, for him the temple should be defined as a center of prayer and worship rather than the location of an elaborate system of sacrifices related to the ritual purification of human life. His anger is not simply against the traders but their customers—all who bought and sold. In hindsight it became clear that he was signaling the end of the sacrificial system, as well as its misuses. It was an enacted parable, in the style of the Old Testament prophets and the recent declamations of John the Baptist,

who enjoined a purity of body and spirit by repentance, not ritual. In order
to provide sacrificial animals for pilgrims who had come from a distance, of
course, it was necessary to have some kind of market. The authorities, however, had allowed the marketing to dominate the huge outer court of the
Gentiles, and this indicated their spiritual lack of substance. It was not a permanent reform on Jesus' part; almost certainly the stalls were soon back, and
life went on as usual. Presumably Jesus ignored the trading later in the
week. Inevitably, however, as they were intended to do, his actions incensed and challenged the temple and city leaders. His popularity with the
people, however, prevented the authorities from openly harming him. Nevertheless, they continued plotting to do away with him. His fate was fixed.
The act of cleansing the temple reinforced the stress of his farewell message
that week that the institution of the temple was to be destroyed. It was this
message that was the reason for his subsequent arrest and trial.

With the temple court cleared, Jesus taught among its colonnades, as he
was to do throughout much of this week. The crowds were astonished and
hung upon his words. Because of this, we are told in the Gospel accounts
that "the chief priests and the scribes and the principal men of the people,"
those who had authority in the city and temple, were thwarted in their plans
to detain Jesus and have him destroyed. They had a limited window of opportunity: Pontius Pilate, the Roman prefect, was on his annual visit to the
city for the assize. If Jesus was to be punished by the Roman authority, this
was the most expedient time. At the end of that day, after meeting with a
group of Greek proselytes who wished to see him—presumably visiting
Jerusalem because of their attraction to Judaism—he returned to Bethany.

During these events there was a remarkable indication of Jesus' internal
struggle as he faced inevitable destruction. He knew the time had come to
be sacrificed. It is one of several poignant soliloquies that recur through the
week: "Now is my soul troubled. And what shall I say? 'Father, save me from
this hour'? But for this purpose I have come to this hour." These occasional
insights into Jesus' inner state deepen the power of the Gospel narratives,
which have gripped people over the subsequent centuries.

TUESDAY, MARCH 31 (NISAN 11)

Jesus returned to Jerusalem and the temple early next morning. This was his
custom. The Gospel narratives state: "early in the morning all the people
came to him in the temple to hear him." On the way Peter noticed the fig

tree they had passed the previous day. According to the account of Mark's Gospel, which may have been based on Peter's reminiscences years afterward, he recalled saying, "Rabbi, look! The fig tree that you cursed has withered" (Mark 11:21). At the temple Jesus faced a series of dialogues with the official leaders of the nation. This would climax in his forceful denunciation of those in their company who saw themselves as the gatekeepers of the nation's moral and religious conscience. The scene was set for a mutual rejection. In the Gospel narratives those opposed to Jesus are called by a variety of names—chief priests, scribes, elders of the people, Pharisees, Herodians and Sadducees. It is clear that groups usually in conflict with each other over important ideological and religious issues were increasingly united against Jesus, this teacher from Galilee. In sharp contrast the ordinary people (probably represented by the Galilean pilgrims) hung on his words, accepting him as a prophet from God. Jesus was bypassing the religious authorities. Here the leaders, not the people, of Israel were opposing Jesus and challenging his authority.

Jesus always had a ready and witty answer to questions intended to ensnare him. Often the opposing groups almost seem a foil for his comments. He continued to speak in parables (for instance, the parable of the vineyard, which alluded to his rejection and murder, and previous rejection of the prophets of God). Jesus was so often able to turn their questions against them that it had become a popular spectacle to see the efforts of his detractors thwarted. In the end they gave up asking further questions that might incriminate him and sought darker methods to trap him.

Jesus then withdrew from teaching in Jerusalem. As he came out of the temple, one of his disciples said to him, "Look, Teacher, what wonderful stones and what wonderful buildings!" The disciples knew Jesus' love of buildings, instilled by the many years he had spent working with stone and wood. Jesus responded to him, "Do you see these great buildings? There will not be left here one stone upon another that will not be thrown down." Later, on the slopes of the Mount of Olives with Peter, James, John and Andrew, Jesus further spoke both of the destruction of the temple and of apocalyptic events at the end of the world. He drew on familiar imagery from the Old Testament, which he saw as pointing to his parousia (or return), when his kingdom would be physically established on earth. The destruction of the temple evidently paralleled the destruction of his body, which would soon be efficiently accomplished by professional Roman soldiers (who would within a generation with similar ruthlessness dismember the city and temple). The insights of hindsight, or the spin of future developments in Christianity (depending on the varied scholarly standpoints), inevitably overlie the interpretation of his words, as they are written down. However, it is clear that there is a contrast between the destruction of the temple, which would take place within a generation, and the "end times," the date of which Jesus does not claim to know. At this period, there was a strong strand of intense interest in eschatology, or end times, which the narrators reflect. Here is a flavor of Jesus' stirring discourse:

> When you see the abomination of desolation [Gentile pollution of the sacred temple ritual] spoken of by the prophet Daniel, standing in the holy place (let the reader understand), then let those who are in Judea flee to the mountains. Let the one who is on the housetop not go down to take what is in his house, and let the one who is in the field not turn back to take his cloak. And alas for women who are pregnant and for those who are nursing infants in those days! Pray that your flight may not be in winter or on a Sabbath. For then there will be great tribulation, such as has not been from the beginning of the world until now, no, and never will be. And if those days had not been cut short, no human being would be saved. (Matthew 24:15-22)

WEDNESDAY, APRIL 1 (NISAN 12)

As usual Jesus and his disciples slept at Bethany, probably on the hillside. It seems that they did not leave early this day. The teaching in the temple courts was now over. We are told that Jesus pointed out to the disciples that it was two days to the Passover. He warned them of his imminent death, explicitly saying, "The Son of Man will be delivered up to be crucified." The title the "Son of Man" was pivotal in his messianic teaching and is variously explained by scholars. The explanations range from a claim to divinity (which I think the most likely from the context) to an identification of himself as simply a teacher from God. At this very time the religious and civic leaders opposed to him were planning to arrest and execute Jesus without causing a riot during the festival. They feared an uproar among the people. They sought a way to arrest him by stealth and kill him, gathering in the house of Caiaphas the high priest to plot. A way opened up from a surprising quarter. That evening, in the darkness, perhaps while the others slept, Judas found his way to the chief priests in order to betray his master. When they heard Judas's intention, they were delighted and agreed to pay him.

They conferred with him about how the deed might be accomplished. Clearly Jesus would need to be taken well away from the eyes of the crowds. They couldn't afford a repeat of the previous Passover, when Pilate had a number of Galileans killed by his soldiers during a riot. The Gospel accounts are at pains to point out that Jesus was not a pretender to the throne of David in a military sense or another kind of leader of revolt against Rome. The last thing the temple and city leaders wanted was to have Jesus perceived as such by the volatile Galilean pilgrims, while at the same time they wished to present Jesus as a threat to the Roman peace. Judas returned to his colleagues, looking for an opportunity to betray Jesus to his enemies.

THURSDAY, APRIL 2 (NISAN 13-14)

Nisan 13-14 was the day of the preparation of the Passover, the first day of the Feast of Unleavened Bread. (The day of preparation, according to Jewish reckoning, did not start until sunset.) During the Middle Ages it used to be called Green Thursday. There have been several explanations for this, but one conjecture is a belief that Jesus prayed on a green meadow in Gethsemane. It is remarkable that we have so much detail for a particular day nearly two thousand years ago—which is also true of the next day. We do not have one single account but four Gospel narratives, adding dimensions of depth to each other—or vexing contradictions, according to which scholarly perspective one takes. (Rather similarly, we have three accounts of Tiberius's last years, with Tacitus, Suetonius and Dio Cassius.) It is possible to give only a brief account of it; there is a vast and stormy literature about the events of this day, including complex discussion by theologians of numerous countries. Jesus, for instance, gives a long "farewell discourse" to his disciples that is in itself a remarkable document, central to the belief and practice of Christians. Some scholars see this discourse as largely a later Christian addition. They see these "anachronisms" as being very different from Jesus' original teaching. Geza Vermes attempts a fascinating Jewish reading of the passion of Christ (focusing on the last day), in which he compares the four Gospel narratives, finding many contradictions rather than eyewitness variants, but trying to establish a core of "fact." (The attempt is rather similar to the attempts of a liberal German theologian, Rudolf Bultmann [1884-1976], to "demythologize" the accounts.) Vermes generally relies heavily on a much later rabbinic literature for his interpretation. Other scholars treat the Gospel accounts as credible historical documents, though written to promote Christian faith, whose differences nevertheless have to be weighed but which can be accounted for in principle. Some scholars are midway between these positions, such as E. P. Sanders.[26]

That morning a discussion took place between Jesus and his disciples about the Passover meal, the necessity of obtaining a lamb, and a place to observe the feast.[17] As Jesus had now withdrawn from public teaching at the festival and was spending the day in seclusion in Bethany rather than making his way to the temple courts, the disciples may have assumed that he would eat the Passover meal at the village. For such purposes rabbinical authority had decided that Bethany was within the limits of Jerusalem. It turned out that his plans were otherwise. They would eat a pre-Passover meal that evening in Jerusalem. They later realized, according to the Gospel accounts, that he intended to be sacrificed as the Lamb of God in the holy city, a sacrifice proclaimed years before by John the Baptist. That Thursday evening meal, it would transpire, was intended to supersede the Jewish festival by one of a deeper significance that would fulfill it. His followers later saw this as the institution of "the Lord's Supper."[18]

He sent Peter and John to Jerusalem with a mysterious instruction. He told them that on entering the city gate (we are not told in the accounts which gate, but it was perhaps in the south of the city, still in the prosperous quarter) they would meet a man carrying a pitcher of water. While many women would be taking water from one of the fountains for use that evening, a man doing so would be odd and thus distinctive. Following him, they would reach a large house. They were to say to the master of the house, "The Teacher says, 'Where is my guest room, where I may eat the Passover with my disciples?' " They would be taken to a large upper room furnished and ready for use. There they were to make it ready for them all.

The Upper Room, located probably near the southern wall, would play an important part in events for the next few months, and perhaps longer. It would be used by the disciples after Jesus' death and after his resurrection. In the history of the Christian church, it must rank as its most important building. The Upper Room could have belonged to the parents of John Mark, probably a mere teenager at this time and a follower of Jesus. He possibly later wrote one of the Gospels, perhaps based on the direct recollections of Peter. Scholars have varying views on the authorship of the Gospel of Mark, perhaps the earliest of the accounts, but John Mark is a plausible candidate. The Gospel is most likely to have been composed between A.D.

60 and 70, though some place it after the fall of Jerusalem.

If the householder was the father of John Mark, his name is not given, perhaps because, when the events were being recounted, Christians in Jerusalem were facing persecution. He was almost certainly a wealthy follower of Jesus and is likely to have been the person who had in the past put a private walled garden on the Mount of Olives outside Jerusalem at Jesus' disposal, called Gethsemane. John Mark was later that day in the garden with the disciples, perhaps with the purpose of staying there overnight. Two Gospel narratives, those of John and Luke, tell us that Jesus "often met there [in Gethsemane] with his disciples" (John 18:2; Luke 22:39). Now Jesus was asking for the use of the large upper room as well.[30] Significantly (John) Mark, perhaps writing his Gospel in the mid-60s A.D., gives neither the name of the householder nor his own name, which does suggest that it might have caused danger to do so. It was a furnished room, already provided with the necessary tables and couches or mats for a large party of people. Peter and John bought the provisions in the busy markets and prepared the meal for that evening.

It was getting toward the evening, perhaps when the deepening dusk disguised their movements across the crowded hills and into the city, when Jesus and his disciples made their way from Bethany. They were soon assembled in that "large upper room." When they arrived, the meal was ready. Each dining couch or mat, whichever was there that evening, was laid with cushions for the guests. The arrangements bore little resemblance to Leonardo da Vinci's *The Last Supper*. The room may have had white walls, and been simply furnished. (Within a few weeks it was able to accommodate a large number of people.) If customs of the time were followed that evening, couches or mats, each large enough to hold three persons, were placed around three sides of a table. Presumably there were two of these tables, four of the disciples being forced to be apart from the main group. These tables were of brightly pigmented wood, each little higher than stools. The seat of honor was the central couch or mat. This was, naturally, occupied by Jesus. There seems to have been an undignified scuffle for places beside him and for the main table. Each guest reclined at full length, leaning on his left elbow, leaving his right hand free. At the right hand of Jesus was the "beloved disciple," most probably his close friend John.[20] In the other coveted place to his left probably was Judas, the son of Simon Iscariot.

Jesus watched his men as they struggled for their places at the meal. In the accounts, instead of reproving them he enacted a demonstration of self-sacrificial love. As people entered the room, they would leave their sandals at the door. The disciples would have done this as they entered. But another custom had been neglected. Their dusty feet had not been washed. To do this was the work of slaves or attendants. No one had offered to perform this service. Jesus stood up and removed his outer garment, wrapping a towel around himself instead. He then proceeded to wash the feet of his disciples, wiping them dry with the towel. When he got to Peter this led to an exchange, as the disciple was sharply averse to Jesus washing his feet, but Jesus insisted on it—two strong characters for a while locked will to will. We are told that when he had finished washing the feet of all the Twelve, Jesus concluded his acted parable: "If I, . . . your Lord and Teacher, have washed your feet, you also ought to wash one another's feet. For I have given you an example, that you also should do just as I have done to you" (John 13:14-15). The titles "Lord" and "Teacher" were evidently common names for Jesus used by the disciples. "Lord," in the Christian context of the Gospel accounts, refers to his status of messianic authority over his followers as master, but with a deepening meaning of the authority of God himself. "Teacher" is simply a translation of "rabbi." Geza Vermes argues that terms such as these have been anachronistically changed out of their original context and made Christian, a point further discussed in chapter six.

As Jesus leaned there on his left elbow, John lay at his right, with his head quite close to Jesus' chest. Next to John, and at the top of the next mat or couch, was likely to have been his brother James. From the few details we have, it is likely that left of Jesus lay the person about to betray him. Peter might have placed himself at the top of the next mat or couch, at the left of Judas.

The Gospel narratives say that a little later Jesus became troubled. His mood seems to have affected all in the room—this was no joyful Passover (or probably pre-Passover) meal. He said, emphatically, "One of you will betray me." The disciples looked at each other, wondering whom he meant. As John was close to Jesus, Peter gestured to him to ask Jesus who he was speaking of. John said to Jesus, "Lord, who is it?" Jesus' response was, "It is the person I give this piece of bread to, when I have dipped it." After he had dipped it in the sauce of the lamb meal on the table, scooping up some meat or rice, he passed it to his left, to Judas. Jesus told Judas to do quickly what he was going to do. He was making it absolutely clear to Judas that he was ready to be apprehended by the authorities. No one at the tables, say the accounts, knew why he said these words to Judas. Some of them thought that, because Judas had the moneybag, Jesus meant, "Buy what we need for the feast," or that he should give something to the poor. Judas immediately went out into the night and took the short journey to the house of Caiaphas, the high priest.

The Gospel narratives record that when Judas had gone out, Jesus said, adding to the gloomy atmosphere, "Little children, yet a little while I am with you. Where I am going you cannot come." Peter said, "Lord, where are you going?" Jesus answered him cryptically, "Where I am going you cannot follow me now, but you will follow afterward." (This was later taken as a reference to Peter's crucifixion under Nero.) Peter said to him, "Lord, why can I not follow you now? I will lay down my life for you." Jesus answered, "Will you lay down your life for me? Make no mistake at all about what I'm saying—the rooster will not crow till you have denied me three times." Jesus was pointing out that denial would follow betrayal. He was, it seems, confronting the action in advance, though Peter continued to affirm his loyalty. He with the other disciples drew attention to the fact that they had two swords for defense. "That will suffice," said Jesus, ironically, it seems.

Much else happened in the Upper Room that evening, including Jesus' words over the bread and wine, representing his blood that would be shed in sacrifice, and his body that would be broken. The occasion represented a radical historical moment: Jesus was evidently indicating the end of the sacrificial system of the temple itself. Some scholars see this indication as a later Christian addition—particularly the account given in the Gospel of John, which was written later than the other three Synoptic Gospels. One scholar, E. P. Sanders, regards Jesus' death as perhaps being a surprise to him, and that he died disappointed, thinking up to then that the kingdom of God was at hand.[21] Jesus' anticipation that he would die a sacrificial death, however, is consistent with a number of statements he made about his forthcoming death and with his acquiescence in Judas's betrayal of him. These many-layered interconnections are far too complex to have been created as fiction later by Christians, especially given that there was no type of fiction at this time that embodied the kind of narrative realism that the Gospel accounts have. (It was not until the seventeenth century that such fictional narrative began to develop.) This is true whether the Gospel writers were drawing on written sources that had already been radically developed in a Christian direction or whether they were inventing directly.

The narratives of the Last Supper, if they are to be believed, remarkably indicate the Jewish character of Jesus' life and ministry, rather than a "Christian gloss." According to the accounts, Jesus saw himself as fulfilling the Torah—the Jewish law. Even though he was abrogating the Passover, his sacrifice was the completion of the very reason for its existence. The Passover had been instituted at the end of the enslavement of the Jewish people in Egypt around the fourteenth or thirteenth century B.C. During the final plague to force the Pharaoh to release the Israelites, the firstborn of all the people were to die. The Jews, however, were commanded by Moses to daub the blood of unblemished lambs on the lintels of their doors so that the angel of death would pass over them. The sacrifice of the lambs brought life. As John the Baptist had prophesied, Jesus was to be the Lamb of God to take away the sins of the world and bring messianic deliverance.

The Gospel narratives tell these momentous events and those that follow in remarkably few words. According to them Jesus and his diminished band of disciples sang a hymn before departing for the walled garden of Gethsemane (where the disciples supposed they were going to sleep). Earlier, in the pre-Passover meal, they would have sung the Hallel. Now it may have been the second part they sang again—Psalms 115 to 118.

> O Israel, trust in the LORD!
> He is their help and their shield.
> You who fear the LORD, trust in the LORD!
> He is their help and their shield.

Jesus continued his long discourse to them as they quietly wended their way out of the city, across the deep Kidron Valley and up the slopes of the Mount of Olives.

Meanwhile there was much activity elsewhere, as a result of Judas's evening visit to the house of Caiaphas. There was discussion to decide the course of action, which would have included conferring with Pontius Pilate, the prefect, so that Jesus could stand trial early the next morning. The trial and execution of Jesus is one of the best-attested events of this year, and indeed of the first century, referred to not only in the Gospel narratives but (directly or indirectly) in Roman and Jewish histories—Tacitus, Suetonius, Josephus—and may be alluded to elsewhere in Roman literature. The trial and the sequence of events is both complex and controversial. What is most clear is the involvement of the Roman prefect, Pontius Pilate, in Jesus' death.

By this time Pilate in the assize may already have condemned three men to death—or he would do so early the next morning—one of whom we know was called Jesus Barabbas (Jesus son of Abbas). These were most likely political insurgents rather than mere robbers. The Jewish authorities may have consulted with Pilate at Herod's palace. (He may have been staying there and holding his assize at Antonia Fortress.) Pilate was led to believe that Jesus was a threat to the Roman peace and should be eliminated. At any event, Pilate's wife must have heard about the intention to arrest and try Jesus, causing her troubled dreams that night. Possibly she was among a number of Roman expatriates attracted to the religious beliefs of the Jews and may have heard accounts of Jesus' doings. The outcome of the conferences was that a party of temple guards, apparently backed up by some Roman soldiers, was made ready to set off for the private walled garden where Judas knew Jesus and the disciples would be heading. When it eventually did get under way, the band of guards and soldiers was accompanied by a number of the city and temple elders.

While these events were taking place within the nearby city, Jesus took aside the inner circle of the disciples—Peter, James and John—and led them deep into the garden. He needed the companionship of close friends. (James and John were cousins as well as friends.) The others remained by the entrance. The garden itself may have been large enough for an olive press and some buildings as well as an orchard—the term *Gethsemane* means "oil press."

Jesus then withdrew from the three about a stone's throw and knelt down and prayed. They heard him say, "Father, if you are willing, remove this cup from me. Nevertheless, not my will, but yours, be done." His distress became so acute that in the moonlight his sweat looked like blood pouring out. But tiredness and the effects of the meal overcame the three watchers and they dozed off. Jesus roused them several times. Clearly he needed companionship; there was no martyr mentality here, where death would be faced cheerfully for some large cause. Jesus clearly had a choice of continuing or not continuing his course. They could all escape before Judas arrived. He had only to tell them what Judas intended. At last Jesus roused them with the news that his betrayer was at hand. As the disciples became alert, they would be able to see flaming torch lights from a group of people ascending the slope below—"a great crowd with swords and clubs" (Matthew 26:47). Peter clutched his sword—a weapon Jesus was aware that he was carrying and presumably knew that he might use, which he does clumsily, trying to protect his master.

With Jesus' betrayal and arrest the disciples fled for their lives, probably in the opposite direction from the guards and soldiers, that is toward Bethany, where they might well have alerted Lazarus and the others to Jesus' arrest. Other disciples, such as Mary Magdalene and Cleopas and his wife, may have been staying at John's house in the city or with others of Jesus' followers living there and would hear later. Peter and John, however, soon recovered their wits and made their way on their own to the house of the former high priest, Annas, perhaps following the arrest party. James presumably stayed with the main body of disciples. As Jesus had predicted, the Shepherd would be struck and his sheep scattered. Although we cannot know for certain, it may now have been around midnight or even later.

FRIDAY, APRIL 3 (NISAN 14)

Now followed a complex series of events in which Jesus was interrogated by various groups before Pontius Pilate handed him over for crucifixion on an insurrectionist charge, mockingly calling him "the King of the Jews." The fact that this most serious of charges was not followed by the arrest of Jesus' main followers reveals just how complex the situation was. Among the factors shaping events were Pilate's rift with Antipas (following two incidents the previous year, Pilate's killing of the Galileans and his introduction of votive shields into Jerusalem) and the continuing shadow of Sejanus, Tiberius's fallen deputy, brought down so suddenly a year and a half earlier. These factors created a situation in which the city and temple authorities were able to exert more power over the strong-willed Pilate's actions than usual. They flexed their muscles with a vengeance. Perhaps not unrelatedly, within three or four years Pilate would be gone and perhaps be dead. With the accession of Claudius in A.D. 41 Judea would again have a popular client king, Herod Agrippa I, who had been brought up in the imperial court in Rome as a friend of Claudius, Gaius Caligula and Drusus. It would be a happy compromise, except for the followers of Jesus in the church in Jerusalem—still Jewish in character and membership—whom Agrippa persecuted.

After his arrest Jesus was first escorted to the house of the former high priest, the wealthy and powerful Annas, who was father-in-law of the current high priest. It was a large building constructed on the slope of the plush upper city, near or perhaps adjoining the home of Caiaphas. Peter and John followed behind and, because of John's contacts in Annas's household, were able to enter the lower courtyard. It is likely that while Peter remained in the courtyard, John was able to gain access to the inner building and hear ✔ Jesus' interrogation by Annas. Jesus was possibly visible but inaudible in the distance to the group in the courtyard. Peter was soon suspected of being one of Jesus' men, his Galilean accent being a giveaway.

> When they had kindled a fire in the middle of the courtyard and sat down to-gether, Peter sat down among them. Then a servant girl, seeing him as he sat in the light and looking closely at him, said, "This man also was with him." But he denied it, saying, "Woman, I do not know him." And a little later someone else saw him and said, "You also are one of them." But Peter said, "Man, I am not." And after an interval of about an hour still another insisted, saying, "Certainly this man also was with him, for he too is a Galilean." (Luke 22:55-59)

This scene in the courtyard, where Peter warms himself in the chill night air, and where he denies that he is one of Jesus' followers, was chosen by Erich Auerbach, in his groundbreaking study, *Mimesis,* to illustrate an essential difference between Greek (classical) and Hebrew narrative. Both have fundamentally shaped Western narratives and continue to do so today in electronic as well as literary media, with films, television and DVDs. Our lives are shaped by such narratives. Auerbach points out that while Greek authors like Homer had a compulsion to explain and rationalize, the scriptural authors had a background and psychological depth to their narrated ● characters and events that came from the presence of a real historical context. People and events had a background and history that was many-layered and required interpretation rather than a flat explanation. Furthermore, everyday settings and humble characters entered world history—even a figure like Peter, who had been such a failure and who was tormented by remorse at denying his Master, who also seemed a failure, but a more heroic one. Auerbach observes:

> From the humdrum existence of his daily life, Peter is called to the most tre-mendous role. Here, like everything else to do with Jesus' arrest, his appear-ance on the stage—viewed in the world-historical continuity of the Roman Empire—is nothing but a provincial incident, an insignificant local occurrence, ✔ noted by none but those directly involved. . . . The nature and the scene of the conflict . . . fall entirely outside the domain of classical antiquity. Viewed superficially, the thing is a police action and its consequences; it takes place entirely among everyday men and women of the common people; anything

of that sort could be thought of in antique terms only as farce or comedy. . . .
Peter and the other characters in the New Testament are caught in a universal
movement of the depths which at first remains almost entirely below the surface and only very gradually . . . emerges into the foreground of history. . . .
For the New Testament authors who are their contemporaries, these occur-
rences on the plane of everyday life assume the importance of world-revolu-
tionary events, as later on they will for everyone.[22]

Auerbach highlights the radical difference between the Gospel narratives
and contemporary classical genres. The narratives drew on Hebrew scriptural patterns.

Annas's preliminary questioning of Jesus appears to have been extensive.
According to the Gospel of John, which alone speaks of this preliminary
hearing with Annas, he was interrogated about his disciples and his teaching. The informal session was inconclusive because Jesus refused to answer
direct questions put by the former high priest. The first abuse of the prisoner
took place when he was struck across the face for saying to Annas, "I have
spoken openly to the world. I have always taught in synagogues and in the
temple, where all Jews come together. I have said nothing in secret. Why do
you ask me?" (John 18:20-21).

Having failed to incriminate Jesus, Annas sent him as a prisoner to Caiaphas. He presumably had first crack at questioning Jesus due to his status
as former high priest and head of a powerful family. Caiaphas, his son-in-
law, was the current high priest and head of the Sanhedrin, the ruling council. It may be that it was as he was led out that Jesus looked at Peter before
the cock crowed.

When he was led before the whole council, or Sanhedrin, which had been
hastily convened, it was after daybreak. It is very likely that this was held
within the temple precincts, which had been locked for the night, as was the
custom. Mark's account calls it a gathering of "all the chief priests and the elders and the scribes," under the presidency of the high priest, Caiaphas. The
charge was that, according to witnesses, Jesus had prophesied the destruction
of the temple and his building of a new one. This claim seemed to imply that
he was the Messiah, the ultimate catalyst in Israel's destiny. Jesus in fact had
not taught a political message—he referred to himself as the temple of God.

Caiaphas decided to make an incriminating challenge, "Are you the Christ
[*Christos*, Greek for Messiah], the Son of the Blessed [God]?" Jesus replied,
"I am," which was also the divine and sacred name, Yahweh ("I am who I

am"). In the past Jesus had usually been ambiguous over any such blasphemous identification—habitually flinging the question back on the challenger.
To be absolutely clear, Jesus used of himself the title "the Son of Man" and
quoted two passages from the Psalms and the Prophets (Psalm 110:1; Daniel
7:13-14). These composed an unmistakable claim to divinity, as is evident
from Caiaphas's reaction—he was quick to see Jesus' words as blasphemy.
The claim to be the Messiah was not itself blasphemous, nor was the title
"the Son of Man" in many contexts. To speak confidently of sharing the
throne of God and of being the fulfillment of Daniel's vision was blasphemy,
however, unless, of course, Jesus was who he claimed to be—an idea unthinkable to Caiaphas and most, but not all, of the Sanhedrin. Nicodemus,
who had once interviewed Jesus secretly at night, and Joseph of Arimathea
were covert disciples who may have begun to grasp the full import of the
Galilean's claims. There may have been others.

Securing a blasphemy charge was still not enough for Caiaphas. As he
had said not long before, "It was expedient that one man should die." The
Sanhedrin might technically have been able to stone Jesus on a such a
charge, but such a procedure most probably would not have killed off his
popular following.[23] The situation might well be worse than before his
death, bringing in the might of Rome and the end of Jewish civic rule in
Jerusalem. Jesus had to die in a more public way that would be unutterably
shameful and put to rest for ever the idea that he was the triumphant, all-
conquering Messiah, come to free Israel. At best, he would be another failed
messiah. The death of a claimant was always seen as a decisive sign of in-
authenticity. The authorities were uncomfortable not only with those who
sought to save Israel from Gentile rule by armed force but also with more
holy messiah figures who wanted radical change by religious means. This
meant charging him with what Rome would consider a capital crime, that is,
insurrection, with its punishment being lifted up on a cross, making him in
Jewish eyes an accursed figure. The abuse of Jesus continued. He was spat
on and blindfolded. He was also struck about the face many times and asked
to "prophesy" who it was that struck him.

The prisoner was after this led away to Pilate for the sentence of death
to be considered, with the evident expectation that it would be pronounced.
Though it was still early morning, time was progressing. The punishment
had to take place before sunset (a little after 6 p.m.), when the sabbath began. The allegation put to Pilate is a direct political one. It turned on Jesus'

claim to kingship. The charge was of treason against the Roman imperial authority. The accusation may have been put at Fortress Antonia, where Pilate was likely to have held his assize. Pilate, understandably, was suspicious of these charges. He presumably had had time to ponder them since the likely meeting the previous night with some of the Jewish authorities, hurriedly setting up the trial of Jesus. He had at all costs to avoid incurring the displeasure of Tiberius again. No doubt the words of the recent letter from the emperor in Capreae, ordering him to remove the offensive shields from Jerusalem, burned into his memory.

Pilate would have sat in judgment on a raised platform outside his headquarters. (The Jewish leaders would have considered a Gentile building ritually unclean.) From the four Gospel narratives the exchanges between the Jewish leaders and Pilate, and between Pilate and Jesus, can be reconstructed in vivid detail, though the sequence is not always clear. The dialogue displays Jesus' rabbinic virtuosity but, unlike his public exchanges with Pharisees and officials trying to catch him out, Pilate is more than an apparent foil for Jesus' insights and repartees. The exchange is more like his engaging encounters with Nicodemus, when he came to Jesus secretly at night, or with the Samaritan woman at the well, or with the blind man that he healed (John 3:1-15; 4:1-42; 9:1-41).

They led Jesus from the house of Caiaphas to the governor's headquarters. It was early morning. They themselves did not enter the governor's headquarters, so that they would not be defiled and could eat the Passover.

So Pilate went outside to them and said, "What accusation do you bring against this man?"

They answered him, "If this man were not doing evil, we would not have delivered him over to you."

Pilate said to them, "Take him yourselves and judge him by your own law." The Jews said to him, "It is not lawful for us to put anyone to death [for such a crime]."

They began to accuse him, saying, "We found this man misleading our nation and forbidding us to give tribute to Caesar, and saying that he himself is Christ, a king."

So Pilate entered his headquarters again and called Jesus and said to him, "Are you the King of the Jews?"

Jesus answered, "Do you say this of your own accord, or did others say it to you about me?"

Pilate answered, "Am I a Jew? Your own nation and the chief priests have delivered you over to me. What have you done?"

Jesus answered, "My kingdom is not of this world. If my kingdom were of this world, my servants would have been fighting, that I might not be delivered over to the Jews. But my kingdom is not from the world."

Then Pilate said to him, "So you are a king?"

Jesus answered, "You say that I am a king. For this purpose I was born and for this purpose I have come into the world—to bear witness to the truth. Everyone who is of the truth listens to my voice."

Pilate said to him, "What is truth?" (Matthew 27:1-14; Mark 15:1-5; Luke 23:1-5; John 18:28-38).

In the light of the many accusations against Jesus, Pilate asked him if he had any answer to make. When Jesus remained silent, to Pilate's amazement, the prefect went back outside to the chief priests and the crowds, where he said, "I find no guilt in this man." Their response was that Jesus "stirs up the people, teaching throughout all Judea, from Galilee even to this place."

It was at this point, according to Luke's account, that Pilate realized that Jesus was a Galilean. He decided to send Jesus to Herod Antipas, who had jurisdiction of Galilee and Perea. Antipas, conveniently, was close by in the Hasmonean palace. It was an important gesture of good will on Pilate's part; he was keen to heal the rift between himself and Antipas, particularly as this would be useful in mending relations with the Jewish authorities in Jerusalem, which were still volatile following the incidents the previous year of the killing of Galilean pilgrims and the introduction of the inscribed shields into Jerusalem. Here, as throughout, the prisoner Jesus is moved to and fro on a political gameboard. The irony, not lost on the Gospel narrators, is that all was going as Jesus had predicted and planned.

The New Testament accounts tell us that when Antipas saw Jesus, he was very glad. His reaction may have been reported by Chuza or his wife Joanna, disciples of Christ, who would have been staying in the palace as part of Antipas's household. The tetrarch had desired for a long period to see him. Jesus at one stage had been warned in Galilee that Antipas desired to apprehend him. Antipas had heard about him and was hoping to see some sign done by him. Although Antipas questioned Jesus at some length, he made no answer. Throughout, the "chief priests and the scribes" stood by, accusing him forthrightly. We are told in the Gospel account that, gaining only silence from Jesus, Herod reacted by joining with his guard in treating him with contempt and mocking him. They ridiculed the idea of his being the King of the Jews by dressing him in purple robes (the color of royalty). By a strange irony of history Antipas's successor, Herod Agrippa I, was treated with similar contempt when he passed through Alexandria on his way to Palestine from Rome later in the decade, in A.D. 38. The anti-Jewish crowds dressed a madman in mock royal clothes to ridicule Agrippa. Philo records the event in *On Flaccus,* and notes that the Roman procurator deliberately ignored the very public slight against the Jewish king.[24]

Jesus was returned to Pilate still in the mock costume, and the New Testament accounts tell us simply that "Herod and Pilate became friends with each other that very day, for before this they had been at enmity with each other" (Luke 23:12).

Having failed to pass the responsibility for Jesus on to Antipas, Pilate then resorted to offering to punish him by scourging—in his eyes, a suitably humiliating punishment—and then to release him. His misgivings were increased when, at some stage in the proceedings while he was sitting on the judgment seat, his wife sent a message to him, "Have nothing to do with that righteous man, for I have suffered much because of him today in a dream" (Matthew 27:19). Like all Romans, Pilate would have taken such a dream seriously as an augury. It would have reinforced his sense of insecurity over how to act. His fears of doing the wrong thing were intensified when the Jewish leaders called out, "If you release this man, you are not Caesar's friend. Everyone who makes himself a king opposes Caesar" (John 19:12). The reference to not being a "friend of Tiberius" directly alluded to the issue of Sejanus. Around this time, the spring of A.D. 33, those closely associated with the dead Sejanus were still being executed or punished. Citizens of Rome were anxious to be seen as friends of Tiberius rather than of Sejanus. The civic leaders of Jerusalem knew that Tiberius had been directly involved in Pilate's recent removal of the offensive shields from Jerusalem to Caesarea Maritima. He could not afford to incur Tiberius's displeasure again. They were signaling that if Pilate let Jesus go, Tiberius would hear about it. They may not have known that Pilate had probably been recruited as prefect by Sejanus. If it were so, Pilate would have been acutely aware of it. The reference to being no "friend of Caesar" helps to explain Pilate's uncharacteristically wavering behavior.

Pilate's final tactic was to offer to release Jesus as an act of clemency at the feast, according to all the Gospel accounts.[25] As prefect, Pilate had power of life and death over those he governed and no doubt liked to remind them of this. When Barabbas, one of the condemned insurrectionists, was preferred to Jesus, Pilate handed the innocent man over for crucifixion, after having him scourged, a brutal flogging that lacerated the flesh and left Jesus seriously weakened. (Some considered a severe scourging a mercy, as the crucified victim thereby died more quickly.) In Eastern fashion Pilate had three times declared him innocent, the number of finality. We are told that the time was now about 9 a.m. (the third hour, using Jewish reckoning). His public washing of his hands of Jesus was probably a superstitious act rather than one of moral virtue. He typically used the occasion to mock his Jewish subjects, while keeping to the letter of the law, by having the charge written down. In Aramaic (the local language of Judea and Galilee), Greek and Latin he ordered the inscription "Jesus of Nazareth, the King of the Jews." The prisoner had this tag tied around his neck as he carried the horizontal beam of the cross to the place of execution near the northern city wall. When Jesus was crucified, the label was placed on the cross above his head.

The New Testament narrators are understated about the details of the scourging and crucifixion. Readers at the time would have been all too familiar with this form of execution and the suffering involved. It was designed as a public spectacle to instill fear of breaking Roman law. Some of their friends in the new Christian community might have suffered it. We do not therefore know the exact way Jesus was crucified; there were variations of method, depending on how quickly it was intended the victim should die. (Death could be postponed for two or three days.) In 1968, however, the body of a crucified man about twenty-six years old was found at Giv'at ha-Mivtar, just north of Jerusalem. It was quite likely that Jesus was executed in a similar fashion. The prisoner would have been stood against the cross. Nails were hammered to the crossbeam, being first placed through the extended forearms between the two bones, the idea being that the nails would slowly tear up the flesh to the wrist joint under the weight of the hanging body. The legs were forced up off the ground and doubled back, and nailed to the upright of the cross using one nail that penetrated the heel bones. The condemned man then had to push himself up in order to breathe, and eventually died of suffocation. The method was designed to inflict maximum torture. It is easy to see why Jesus, already weakened by his horrific scourging, died quickly. The Gospel accounts make it clear that the two insurgents who remained after Jesus Barabbas's release were hung on crosses on either side of Jesus. They died more slowly; there is no mention of scourging in their cases.

The last three hours in which Jesus hung dying coincided, the New Testament narratives tell us, with a period in which the sun failed and there was darkness. This could not have been an eclipse of the sun, because of the position of the moon on April 3, A.D. 33. (There had been a total solar eclipse a few days before, on March 19, but in the southern hemisphere, visible in Africa.) The most likely cause was a dust storm in the nearby desert. Whatever the cause, it would have been seen as portentous by both the native population and the Romans in Jerusalem. Peter would refer to it a few weeks later, on May 24, when Jesus' followers came out and publicly spoke of his crucifixion and resurrection. In the same breath Peter spoke of the moon turning to blood, an apocalyptic image. Later this same day there was a substantial eclipse of the moon at its rising, visible from Jerusalem. Such an eclipse characteristically took on a blood-red appearance in the umbral shadow. This eclipse would have been portentous—it often signified the death of a king or other important person, or a disaster. The moon would have risen at 6:20 p.m. this day, marking the beginning of the new Jewish day, the Passover and also the sabbath. All eyes in Jerusalem would have seen the eclipse, the moon turned to blood, as they watched for the appearance of the moon to signify the start of the sacred day.[26]

◆ ◆ ◆

As Jesus hangs dying, the narratives largely shift from political players such as Pilate, Caiaphas and the authorities to his everyday followers. Of his band of disciples, most had deserted him at Gethsemane the night before; Judas had probably by now committed suicide out of guilt for his betrayal; Peter was broken with remorse for his own failure; and only John was there at the cross, watching, with Jesus' mother by his side, if the Gospel accounts are to be believed. With him were other disciples, mainly women—Mary Magdalene (a disciple who had come from Galilee for the Passover), Jesus' aunt (Mary, wife of Cleopas), Salome (John's mother, and another aunt of Jesus, who may well have lived in Jerusalem), and probably Joanna, from Herod's household. Joseph of Arimathea and Nicodemus were also present. There were other unnamed disciples, men and women, and well-wishers. Jesus' uncles were perhaps there, Cleopas and Zebedee. Jesus' brothers were absent; they had probably come to the Passover with their mother, but fled because of perceiving danger in being associated with Jesus. His friends had to suffer the verbal abuse thrown at him from those watching who had conspired in his execution. At one point his friends came closer to where Jesus was, and he asked John to take his mother away to his home in the city. John returned later after taking her, accompanied by Salome.

From the Gospel accounts Jesus died soon after 3 p.m., the time when the slaughter of lambs for the Passover began.[27] Later this timing was seen as heavily symbolic, as he was the Lamb of God, according to the prophecy of John the Baptist: "Behold, the Lamb of God, who takes away the sin of the world!" (John 1:29). Jesus appears to have hung lifeless for a considerable time before the Roman executioners were asked to dispatch the dying so that their bodies could be disposed of before sunset and the sabbath—a particularly sacred day as it was also the Passover. This was done by the simple expedient of smashing their legs so that they could no longer push themselves up to take breaths. As Jesus was clearly dead already, a spear was thrust into his chest to make sure. John, who had returned by this time, vividly records: "At once there came out blood and water." (John 19:34).[28] The spear thrust is presented as an eyewitness account. Physiologically, this has been seen to indicate that the body had been lifeless long enough for the blood left in the heart to separate.

Nicodemus and Joseph of Arimathea realized that Jesus' body was destined for a common criminal's grave, along with those of the two insurrectionists. Joseph happened to have a newly cut grave in a garden he owned near the scene of execution. He hurried to Pilate to request the body for proper burial. Perhaps Pilate was oppressed by the darkness that had hung over the city for so many hours, or maybe it was simply Joseph's rank that inclined him to grant the surprising request. Thus it came about that hurried preparations were made to bury the body before nightfall, presumably after it was extricated efficiently from the cross by the soldiers. Two of the women at the scene, Joanna and an unnamed disciple (possibly Susanna), helped Nicodemus and Joseph in the task. Mary Magdalene and Mary, wife of Cleopas, watched the burial from nearby. Joseph procured a linen cloth to wrap the body in, and Nicodemus a large quantity of spices to apply to slow down the corpse's decomposition. John possibly helped in carrying the heavy spices (more than an astonishing 70 lbs. in weight). A smaller cloth would have been tied around the head to prevent the jaw falling open. The women who helped with the hasty burial, and those who watched, agreed to return immediately after the sabbath to anoint the body properly. Before the women left, they saw Joseph's servants roll a great stone over the entrance, as was the custom. Then they returned to their dwellings and hastily bought and prepared burial ointments before moon-rise.[29] That should have been that.

Later that evening, however, after the sabbath began, the Jewish author-ities made a surprising move, according to the account in the Gospel of Mat-thew. They were so concerned about the possibility of the body of Jesus be-ing stolen (based on well-known claims that Jesus would rise again to life) that they asked Pilate's permission to seal the tomb and post a guard on it. Presumably they had to disturb the prefect at Herod's sumptuous palace during his lengthy evening meal. It is likely that he and his wife would have discussed the fate of Jesus, given her dream. In any event, Pilate conceded to their wishes.

6

THE GLORY OF THE TEMPLE

THE EVENTS OF A.D. 33 ARE DOMINATED by a Jewish man who spent most of his life in Galilee, a backwater in relation to the spiritual and cultural center of Judaism—Jerusalem and its splendid temple. Nevertheless, Jesus was fully versed in the Torah and other Scriptures, and in many ways had affinities with one of the many and probably largest parties within Judaism in his day—the Pharisees. Like their teachers, he was concerned about purity of life, and like them he submitted to the authority of the Scriptures, carried immense personal authority and was popular with the people. Unlike them, he emphasized inner, subjective purity, or what we might today call holistic purity, rather than external, ritual practice, bolstered by what he saw as their irrelevant traditions and systems of interpretation. Unlike them, he saw the temple cult as secondary, a means to the end of worshiping God and enjoying his presence, not an end in itself. Jesus can also be understood against his full Jewish context, in all its varieties, especially in terms of his titles, such as Messiah (Christ), Son of Man, and Teacher.[1] Most of all, he can be understood in relation to the temple, as the defining center of Judaism—the place of the indwelling presence of the Most High God. His attitude toward the temple condemned him to destruction by the Jewish authorities of Jerusalem. That same temple defined Jesus for the predominantly Jewish members of the church in its first generation, who saw him as the new temple of God.

To get an idea of the diversity of the Jewish context in Jesus' time, before the catastrophic fall of Jerusalem and the destruction of the temple, it is necessary to look at some of the groups and movements of the time. Much of the information that would provide this mix of aspirations and beliefs was destroyed in that catastrophe, so scholars and archaeologists have had to try to build up what is quite a conjectural picture. The kind of Jewish orthodoxy that slowly emerged after A.D. 70—called rabbinic Judaism—may not represent the heartbeat of lay and professional doctrine before that year, even though, it seems, it developed from Pharisaism. The prevailing climate was able to accommodate what appeared at the time to be a distinctive group within Judaism—an element we now call the Christian church. One New Testament scholar, D. A. Hagner, judges that "It may fairly be said . . . that there is no Christianity in the N[ew] T[estament] that is not Jewish. All of the writers of the NT, with the exception of Luke, were themselves Jews who had believed in Jesus Christ and the gospel. Even Paul's Christianity, often categorised as reflecting 'Gentile Christianity,' remains deeply Jewish in character."[2]

Even more fundamental than the temple to Jewish identity is the notion of being a chosen people. This notion existed before the establishment of a land of Israel and continued after the Jews were effectively dispossessed of their nation in the second century. It was this idea of God's covenant with his chosen people that made messiah figures so attractive in the time of Jesus. Jews were not content to see their land merely as a province of Rome. Its destiny was to play a dynamic part in world history that its size belied. The notion of a chosen people goes back to the time of Abraham and his migration from Ur of the Chaldees to the holy land, a time that predated the writing of the Torah and the establishment of the law. It was an idea that sustained Jewish people through the Babylonion exile and during the possession of Israel by the Ptolemies and then the Seleucids in the aftermath of Alexander's empire. It continued to sustain them under the Romans in the time of Jesus, and later when an event occurred far more terrible than the desecration of the temple by the Seleucid Antiochus Epiphanes in 167 B.C. That was, of course, the destruction of the temple itself.

It may have been the strength of the ideas of the temple (made real by the splendid temple in Jerusalem) and of being chosen that provided a unity of belief that allowed a great diversity of convictions and movements in the time of Jesus. This period of radical diversity belongs to "Second Temple" or "early" Judaism, and was inaugurated by Antiochus's desecration of the temple in 167 B.C., referred to by Jesus as the "abomination of desolation." Even before that there were competing interests under the restored Israel following the exile.

In the Jerusalem of Jesus' day was a reminder of a strong strand of the "early Judaism," the Hasmonean palace, in which Antipas was likely to have stayed during the Passover festival in the spring of A.D. 33. The palace reflected the old royal as well as priestly powers enjoyed by the Hasmoneans. They were originally "the faithful," who resisted Antiochus and kept to the proper temple practices. One of them, Judas Maccabaeus, introduced their powerful priestly rule. The high priestly power in Jerusalem in Jesus' day was a vestige of this institution. The high priesthood remained under Hasmonean control until the period of Roman rule. Many Jewish people were unhappy about this priestly rule, and there were other contenders for the priesthood who felt that their claim was stronger and more scriptural.

A faction called the Essenes, still active in the time of Jesus, had marked their opposition to the Hasmonean priesthood by establishing their own system of purification and other religious practices, using their own calendar and secluding themselves in their own communities, which might be in towns and cities or in isolated places like Qumran.[3] Like many, they looked to an apocalyptic future deliverance from oppressive conquerors rather than to temporal power. At such an end time, they believed, they would be given the use of Jerusalem and the temple, where they could worship according to their interpretation of the law of Moses.

Another faction, the Pharisees, was distinct from the Hasmonean priestly families and the Essenes. The Pharisees were conservatives rather than activists, focusing on the theory and practice of purity of life and the practicalities of being distinctive in faith and life. They defined purity by a highly detailed oral tradition as well as by the Scriptures. The Pharisees were attractive to the majority of people, who were neither Hasmonean nor Essene. Unlike the Essenes, the Pharisees were able to accommodate the predominately priestly rule in Jerusalem out of expediency. Their reliance on the authority of oral tradition as well as Scripture ultimately prepared the way for rabbinic Judaism, developed after the fall of Jerusalem, with its Mishnah and Talmud.

The oral emphasis of the Pharisees may account for their popularity and growing influence during the period of Roman rule, which began in 63 B.C. At this time the use of memorization and recitation was more common than written communication among Jewish people. Their teaching and guidance about how to live (Judaism is a faith that encompasses all of life) did not require literacy. It meant that ordinary people received Scripture through an interpretative framework that was Pharisaic, presented by charismatic teachers. Because the rabbis were prepared to earn their living by a trade, they could move around easily, teaching as they went, as Jesus did in the towns and villages of Galilee (though evidently he was supported by disciples). Their influence was stronger in the countryside than in Jerusalem, which was dominated by the priests.

The Roman administration, with its encouragement of local government and judiciary, encouraged the growth of scribes, essentially men who could read and write. Most of these were, likely enough, Pharisees. Certainly, in the New Testament accounts, scribes are often lumped together with Pharisees. The written law of Moses, in the Scriptures, was the foundation of the legal system and religious practice, and favored the employment of scribes, supplementing the work of priests, teachers and leaders of worship in the synagogues. There must have been lively debates and disputes between scribes, judges, Pharisees, priests and elders, as they worked together in town and village communities, about the interpretation and application of the Torah. Though little is known of the extent of debate and disagreement, the very much later rabbinic literature speaks of disputes between the schools of notable Pharisees Shammai and Hillel. The young Saul, being taught by the popular rabbi Gamaliel, would have been exposed to disputes with rival interpretations of points of law and religious practice. Bruce Chilton writes that "Because they lacked any central leadership in the period before A.D. 70, Pharisees differed from movement to movement, town to town, rabbi to rabbi, and even day to day."[4]

The variety of Judaism in A.D. 33 is demonstrated by the strands that are evident, such as the Pharisees and the Essenes. There were many other interrelated strands, all of them interacting dynamically with the others. Some were revolutionary, wishing to intervene in the destiny of Israel by force, and others were quietist. Some sided openly with the Roman administration and were active in local government, notably the priests and elders of Jerusalem and the temple administration.

The complexity and ambivalence of relations with the Roman rule is demonstrated in the priesthood. Some priests, especially those belonging to the wealthy elite of Jerusalem, were, like the leadership there, pro-Roman. The high priest himself was a Roman appointee, which was necessary given the importance to the Romans of establishing local government wherever possible. Josephus and 1 Maccabees have stories of sons of the high priest having surgery to give the appearance of having a foreskin when they practiced gymnastics (which took place in the nude). Sadducees predominated among the wealthy families of Jerusalem associated with the priests. Our knowledge of this group comes mainly from sources who disliked them (the New Testament Gospels, Josephus and rabbinic traditions). It appears that they did not believe in the resurrection of the body—this characterization of them may have come from their emphasis on material prosperity here and now. They no doubt saw their wealth as a blessing coming from proper practice in the temple ceremonies, justifying this from the Torah. The importance of priests in upholding this comfortable status quo led to many being called "high priests" by both the Gospels and Josephus. Though literally there was only one high priest in A.D. 33, Caiaphas, it reflected reality to speak of "high priests." It was the interests of this wealthy elite that were so severely challenged by Jesus, in his teaching, condemnations and his cleansing of the temple shortly before the Passover.

Not all priests, however, were Sadducees. Some had affinities or sympathies with the Pharisees or the Essenes. Some were involved in revolts against the Romans. Josephus was a priestly nationalist who got caught up at the end of the 60s in the major rebellion that led to Jerusalem's downfall. Some no doubt were sympathetic to Jesus and even his disciples. The Sanhedrin in Jerusalem had members who were Pharisees, such as Nicodemus. Even though he was not a priest, it reveals the diversity of the political leaders in Jerusalem. The term *Sanhedrin* itself is an anachronism from the second-century Mishnah and the descriptions it gives of the local council in Jerusalem may not be accurate for events and institutions in A.D. 33. Along with Josephus and the Gospels, however, the Mishnah indicates that the ruling council in Jerusalem was quite diverse. Though dominated by Sadducean priests and presided over by the high priest, elders and the wealthy elite of the city were involved. Among them would have been Pharisees and also scribes, who might not always have been Pharisees, priests or elders. It is not known for certain if there were seventy-one members of the Sanhedrin, as described in later rabbinic literature. As local administrators the Roman overlords gave the council considerable powers, including, probably, limited powers of capital punishment for serious sacrilege. The authority of the Jerusalem Sanhedrin, however, did not automatically apply in the countryside. There the Pharisees were a modifying influence in their teaching and interpretation of the law. Pharisees also taught within Jerusalem, in the temple courts. The Pharisees of Jerusalem were the most significant in the movement. We read, for instance, of the influential Gamaliel, teacher of Saul (later Paul), in the book of Acts (Acts 5:33-40). He was "a Pharisee of the council."

In the diverse mix of movements and factions in Jesus' time, there were many revolutionary currents. In the Gospel accounts the nervousness of the

Jewish leadership about Jesus' teaching and popularity, and the danger of a Roman crackdown, which would threaten or destroy their power, is entirely plausible. The first century is one of the most violent in Jewish history, climaxing in the rout of Jerusalem in A.D. 70 and the mass suicides of Masada soon after.

Many factors contributed to political ferment in Palestine. Not only was there the foreign (and Gentile) occupation by Rome but also a vast gulf between rich and poor—the rich benefiting from and often exploiting Roman rule. It is easy to see that, in religious terms, wealth and power were easily associated with unfaithfulness to the divine law of Moses, the Torah. The Pharisees, earning their own upkeep while teaching, powerfully distanced themselves from the contamination of benefiting from the regime. Jesus too regularly took the side of the poor, exploited and marginalized, even though he won over many of the rich. The gulf between rich and poor was exacerbated by the heavy Roman taxation necessary to support its administration.

The circumstances bred insurgency and other revolutionary activity, ranging from banditry to the rise of those claiming to be messiahs and deliverers. In addition, Israel had a tradition of prophets, interpreting the times (sometimes like modern journalists) and urging religious remedies. Related to prophecy were visions of the end time, offering the hope of divine intervention in historical events. In Jesus, many of these elements were present: he was a prophet, a messiah and offered a vision of the end times. Most notably, he prophesied the fall of Jerusalem, according to the Gospel narratives of Matthew, Mark and Luke, the Synoptics.

It is by the title of "Messiah" that Jesus is best known. Early on he was called Jesus the "Christ," *Christ* being in the Greek text of the New Testament the Greek *Christos,* translating the Hebrew word for *Messiah.* From very early in the history of the church, the followers of Jesus were called "Christians" (Messiah people). The book of Acts tells us that the nickname was first used in Antioch, one of the first Christian churches outside of Palestine (Acts 11:26). Later, the Roman historian Tacitus refers to Jesus as "Christ," being executed under Pontius Pilate.[7] Although he took this as a person's name, not a title, it reveals that it was the common way of speaking about Jesus. A controversial passage in Josephus calls Jesus the Christ (Messiah). For many years this was dismissed by scholars as it clearly showed the mark of later Christian additions. Many scholars now, however, believe that some of the passage is authentic, backed up by an Arabic version that lacks the Christian gloss. What may be the authentic version indicates that Jesus was considered by his followers to be the Messiah. Another indication of some authenticity is that elsewhere Josephus refers to the death of James, the brother of Jesus, marking the latter's status among his followers by recording that "he was called the Christ." I have numbered Josephus's sentences to aid comparison of the two versions. (The likely Christian insertions or modifications are indicated in brackets.)

The Greek version of Josephus's account of Christ:

(1) At this time there appeared Jesus, a wise man [if indeed one might call him a man]. (2) For he was a doer of startling deeds, a teacher of people who receive the truth with pleasure. (3) And he gained a following both among many Jews and among many of Greek origin. [He was the Messiah.] (4) And when Pilate, because of an accusation made by the leading men among us, condemned him to the cross, those who had loved him previously did not cease to do so. (5) [For he appeared to them on the third day, living again, just as the divine prophets had spoken of these and countless other wondrous things about him.] (6) And up to this very day the tribe of Christians, named after him, has not died out.

The Arabic version of Josephus's account of Christ:

(1) At this time there was a wise man who was called Jesus. (2) And his conduct was good, and he was known to be virtuous.[6] (3) And many people from among the Jews and other nations became his disciples. (4) Pilate condemned him to be crucified and to die. And those who had become his disciples did not abandon his discipleship. (5) They reported that he had appeared to them three days after his crucifixion and that he was alive; accordingly, he was held to be the Messiah concerning whom the Prophets have recounted wonders. (6) And the people of the Christians so-called after him, has to this day not disappeared.[7]

In Jesus' day, there was considerable variation in the way a messiah was understood to function. Linking such a role to divinity was distinctive to the Christian community, though the early Christians found substantiation for such an identification in the Hebrew Scriptures. What was universal, however, was the view that the death of any who declared themselves a messiah was certain proof that they were not such a figure. The understanding by his followers that Jesus was Messiah was predicated on the belief that he had risen from the dead. In ancient documents we have the names of several failed messiahs, all eliminated by death. The actual title "Messiah" does not seem to have been in common use in writings before A.D. 70, but this does not mean that there was not a widespread expectation of a Jewish leader, anointed by God, even if the expectations varied in scope. In the Scriptures known and interpreted at the time there were indications of a messiah. Many of these are linked to a descendant of ancient King David. A "branch" of David would be raised. Isaiah 11:1-9 speaks of the "shoot from the stump of Jesse" who "with righteousness . . . shall judge the poor." The prophet Micah located Bethlehem as the home town of the Messiah (Micah 5:2). The Dead Sea Scrolls, from a first-century community in Qumran, seem to suggest two anointed figures. One was a high priestly messiah, and the other a royal "prince of the congregation," head of a community of the faithful at the end times. After the death of Herod the Great, there were several messianic movements recorded in Josephus's *Antiquities of the Jews:* those of Judas, Simon, servant of King Herod, and Athronges. According to Josephus, all these pretenders aimed to become king of Israel. Their followers were primarily uneducated and from the countryside. As well as fighting the Romans for sovereignty of Israel, the insurgents also attacked the homes of the wealthy. Apart from these rebellions after the death of Herod and the revolt that led to the destruction of the temple in A.D. 70, there are no surviving records of messianic movements other than that among the followers of Jesus. His was the only one which aimed to inaugurate the kingdom of God (the rule of God on earth) without using armed force. Implicit in this notion of the kingdom was that it applied to all nations, making the idea of forcefully establishing a Davidic reign in Israel unnecessary.

Over the temple, the diversity of Jewish movements and beliefs in the time of Jesus is not so evident. At the festivals, pilgrims from Galilee and throughout the Diaspora poured into Jerusalem to celebrate at the temple, offering sacrifices. It is true that some groups among the Pharisees disagreed over processes to do with animal sacrifice, but overwhelmingly the temple cult defined the heart of Jewish worship. The temple was the house of God. The inmost holy of holies contained no figure—it was empty except for a small rock upon which the high priest made his annual offerings of incense and sprinkled the blood of atonement. It was unfurnished because the God worshiped was the Maker of heaven and earth, and to depict him was idolatrous. Nevertheless, his presence was there. It was his exclusive dwelling place among humankind. His people could offer sacrifices in that place.

It is likely that the ideal of the temple was more important than the actual temple. Some groups with strong apocalyptic leanings downplayed the actual temple in favor of a new temple and new Jerusalem at the end of time. Jesus expressed strong disapproval of temple practices that had overwhelmed the courts with trading, eclipsing its purpose as a place of worship and prayer that acknowledged the presence of God in his house. At his last supper, on the eve of the Passover, he made it clear that his wine and bread, as "flesh" and "blood," were more acceptable to God than temple sacrifices. In early Christianity, worship centered on the meal of remembrance was preserved, leading to an understanding of church worship as the replacement of the temple. For a time, however, the temple was still used for worship and as a place for teaching, without the practice of sacrifices. The temple is employed as a God-given symbol for the presence of God with humanity. Jesus was preeminently "God with us" while on earth, and, with his departure, God was present as Holy Spirit in the symbolic temple of the church. The apocalyptic book of Revelation has the New Jerusalem as the denouement of human history, with God ever after dwelling with humanity, with his perfect rule over all the world. "Its temple is the Lord God the Almighty and the Lamb" (Revelation 21:22).[8] Thus the imagery of the temple was as central to early Christian belief as the physical temple was to Judaism in the days of Jesus.

FIFTY DAYS

PRELUDE TO CHANGING THE WORLD
(APRIL 5-MAY 23)

IN THE SAME PLAIN UPSTAIRS ROOM, most likely, where Jesus held his farewell supper, about 120 people are gathered. They sit on every available space of floor. It has become their regular custom since the return from Galilee to meet daily here. The group includes the remaining Eleven of Jesus' inner band of followers and many other disciples, including women. Mary, mother of Jesus, is with them and also his brothers, James, Joses, Simon, and Judas, who for long had been skeptical about him. Having seen him alive after his death, and with Jesus making a personal appearance to James, they no longer disbelieve in their brother's astounding claims. Indeed, James will become a leader in the Jerusalem church and will write a letter that would be preserved in the New Testament documents, in a style that recalls his brother's manner of teaching. It is likely that Mary, Martha and Lazarus of Bethany are here, together with the women who witnessed the burial and came to anoint the body following the sabbath a few weeks before—Mary of Magdala, Mary, wife of Cleopas, Joanna, and an unnamed woman.

Through the glassless windows the sun glances into the room, still cool in the early morning. It is only a matter of days since Jesus bade a second, and this time final, farewell to the Eleven on the slopes of the Mount of Olives, near Bethany. He was taken into a cloud—that was the best way it could be described—and lost from view.

The group in the Upper Room remain overwhelmed by Jesus' resurrection, in which he had appeared a number of times both in or near Jerusalem and in Galilee. Their minds are still taking in the implications—their world is changing before the rest of the world follows. For one thing the resurrection has made them read, interpret and understand the Scriptures in a new way. Now the familiar books seem full of the promise of the coming of their Lord. Their natural response is to turn to fervent, sustained prayer, in which the women participate freely.

They also recall the events and teachings of Jesus. As they do so, the narratives, parables and discourses begin to fall into a pattern, more easily remembered in their predominantly oral culture. This is rather like the way a loved one is remembered and talked about after a funeral. Here, however, they talk of someone who had died, but, contrary to all expectation, has done the unthinkable and unimaginable: returned to life. True, he has now left them once again, after sharing their bread and fish, and remaining substantial when clung to in the wonder of his resurrection. But it is not, this time, the departure of death—more that of a friend leaving who will one day return.

The noisy hubbub of prayers and conversations is interrupted by a booming voice with a broad Galilean accent. Silence is eventually established among the excited people. The speaker is Peter, unrecognizable as the defeated figure of a few weeks before, full of remorse at his public denial of Jesus. "Brothers and sisters," he says, "Judas, who betrayed our Lord, died at his own hand. To replace him we need to choose one of the men who have accompanied us during all the time that the Lord Jesus went in and out among us, beginning from the baptism of John until the day when he was taken up from us—one of these men must become with us a witness to his resurrection."

◆ ◆ ◆

The scenario above is largely drawn from the account of the gathered disciples at the beginning of the New Testament book of Acts, part two of Luke's narrative of the life of Christ and the birth and early expansion of his church. I have added my speculation that the 120 rehearsed the events and teaching of the life of Jesus, because it is unimaginable that they would not. For well over a century scholars have posited that there was some kind of early tradition of teaching that formed the core of the three written Synoptic Gospels—Matthew, Mark and Luke—so called because of their similarity of view. One scholar's title for it, "Q," has been universally accepted, as mentioned in chapter one. The fourth and latest Gospel—John—supplemented the other three Gospels.

The belief in Jesus' resurrection by his disciples so soon after his execution by the Roman authority, Pilate, in Jerusalem, is the central causal factor for the subsequent dynamic spread of the Christian faith. The world would not have changed without this belief. J. M. Roberts comments that "To find something which has had an impact comparable to that of Christianity we have to look not to single events but to big processes like industrialization, or the great forces of prehistoric times like climate which set the stage for history."[1] What made Christian faith unique in changing world history was its conviction that Jesus had returned from the dead. His existence as a Jewish lay teacher born late in the reign of Augustus, no matter how charismatic, is not enough to account for his impact on history. J. M. Roberts points out:

> Whatever may be thought of the Gospel records, it cannot plausibly be maintained that they were written by men who did not believe these things, nor that they did not write down what they were told by men and women who believed they had seen some of them with their own eyes. Clearly, too, Jesus' life was not so successful in a worldly sense that his teaching was likely to survive because of the impact of his ethical message alone. He had, it is true, especially attracted many of the poor and outcast, as well as Jews who felt that their traditions or the forms of behavior into which they had hardened were no longer satisfactory. But these successes would have died with him had his disciples not believed that he had conquered death itself and that those who were saved by being baptized as his followers would also overcome death and live for ever after God's judgment. Before a century had passed, this message was being preached throughout the whole civilized world united and sheltered by the Roman empire.[2]

Familiarity with Christianity has made us forget how strange it is that its main symbol is a cross, a means of execution particularly but not exclusively employed by the Romans. This is rather like a group of people today incorporating an image of an electric chair, gallows or firing squad into their logo. The potency of such a gruesome image as the cross was the implicit belief that Jesus had overcome it—the cross is bare not simply because Jesus' body had been removed from it, but that, his followers claimed, he had suffered and then defeated death. One of the most beautiful poetic treatments of the symbolism of the cross (early English, *rood*) is the medieval English poem *The Dream of the Rood*. Not only in literature, but in painting, architecture and sculpture, the theme of the cross has been present in the centuries after Christ.

Almost immediately after Jesus drew his last, hard-won breath on the cross, the fate of his body became an important issue. The Jewish authorities

asked Pilate's permission to seal Jesus' tomb in case his body was stolen and
his disciples claimed that he had risen from the dead (Matthew 27:64). Later,
on the following Sunday morning, when the guards went to the same authorities with confused stories of blinding lights, earth tremors and the body
gone, they were bribed, according to Matthew's account, to tell people "His
disciples came by night and stole him away while we were asleep" (Matthew
28:13).[3] The authorities promised to keep the soldiers out of trouble if the
incident came to the governor's ears (who clearly would have been unhappy with their statement that they had fallen asleep). Matthew's narrative
adds that "this story has been spread among the Jews to this day" (i.e., the
time that he was writing, possibly as late as A.D. 75-80 if he made use of the
Gospel of Mark, as many scholars believe). A ruling by the emperor Claudius may shed light on this story of the body being stolen, though it is not
possible to be certain about this.

In 1932 an inscription originating from the emperor Claudius was found
in Nazareth.

> Ordinance of Caesar. It is my pleasure that graves and tombs remain undis-
> turbed in perpetuity for those who have made them for the cult of their an-
> cestors or children or members of their house. If however any man lay
> information that another has either demolished them, or has in any other way
> extracted the buried, or has maliciously transferred them to other places in or-
> der to wrong them, or has displaced the sealing or other stones, against such
> a one I order that a trial be instituted, as in respect of the gods, so in regard
> to the cult of mortals. For it shall be much more obligatory to honor the buried.
> Let it be absolutely forbidden for anyone to disturb them. In case of contra-
> vention I desire that the offender be sentenced to capital punishment on
> charge of violation of sepulture.[4]

Claudius's decree about violating tombs seems to follow from Christian
preaching about the resurrection of Jesus and the counterstory that his body
had been stolen. It may correlate with Claudius's expulsion of Jewish people,
including their Christian elements, from Rome in A.D. 49. Suetonius, recording the event over half a century later, says that the riots and troubling of the
peace of the city was "at the instigation of one Chrestos." He was almost certainly referring to Christ, probably confusing two similar Greek words whose
only difference is in a vowel. *Christos* is Greek for "Christ" or "Messiah." If
so, Suetonius mistakenly thought that Jesus was there in person.[5] It seems
that the trouble may have come from conflict brought about by the claims of

the Christians within the Jewish community there about Jesus Christ.[6]

When the New Testament writers refer to the resurrection of Jesus, they refer to his state of having a physical human body that is alive and capable of eating, being touched, speaking, and so on after a period in which his body had started to decompose in the usual natural process after death (such as the destruction of brain cells a few minutes after death due to lack of oxygen, rigor mortis, and the internal devastation caused by bacteria in the digestive system consuming the system itself). They were not speaking of some kind of mere spiritual vision. The actual moment when the heart began beating again, air was sucked into the lungs and Jesus rose up from his lying position in the tomb was not witnessed. Jesus' resurrected body had new physical properties as well as the normal ones—witnesses claimed to see him passing through walls and suddenly disappearing. This, Paul later reasoned, pointed to a new creation that Jesus had inaugurated with his resurrection. Such new properties had been hinted at before, in Jesus' evident control over nature, such as when he told the professional fisherman Peter where to fish or when he was seen walking on water or making a storm cease. These qualities of Jesus are the stuff of Christian theology through the ages, affirming his dual nature of full humanity and full divinity.[7]

The oldest existing documentation of the resurrection of Christ is in the apostle Paul's letter to the church at Corinth, in the New Testament, written about A.D. 54. Paul assumes knowledge on the part of his audience (the letter would have been read out loud) of the life and teaching of Christ. Paul gives an early credo, which includes an important sequence of resurrection appearances, which he says were witnessed by various groups, small and large, and individuals (including himself—probably the year following the other appearances, i.e., A.D. 34 or the year after).

> For I delivered to you as of first importance what I also received: that Christ died for our sins in accordance with the Scriptures, that he was buried, that he was raised on the third day in accordance with the Scriptures, and that he appeared to Cephas [Peter], then to the twelve. Then he appeared to more than five hundred brothers at one time, most of whom are still alive, though some have fallen asleep. Then he appeared to James, then to all the apostles. Last of all, as to one untimely born, he appeared also to me. (1 Corinthians 15:3-8)

The sequence is that Jesus was seen by Peter, then the Twelve (adding in Matthias, who was chosen to replace Judas Iscariot), then a group of about five hundred disciples (or a larger group, if Paul is only indicating the males in the group), then James the brother of Jesus, and last of all Paul, at his dramatic conversion on the way to Damascus. It is notable that Paul does not include the women who were the first to see Jesus after he was raised from the dead. This may simply be because women at this time had no status as witnesses, and Paul is pointing out the historical veracity of Jesus' postdeath appearances. Nor does he include Jesus' appearance to two disciples in Emmaus (see p. 131). This indicates that Paul is giving a selection, and there are other appearances he does not mention in making his case. For Paul, there would be no basis for Christianity without Christ's full physical resurrection as a living, breathing human being (1 Corinthians 15:14).

SUNDAY, APRIL 5 (NISAN 16)

According to the New Testament Gospels the first resurrection appearances took place very early on the Sunday morning of April 5. We must picture the women who had witnessed Jesus' hasty burial making their way back to the tomb to anoint his body in the customary manner. Such a picture would try to reconcile the various Gospel accounts. Some scholars see the narratives as too contradictory to make this a worthwhile exercise; others see variations as inevitable in relatively independent accounts of events (even where a core of shared material is used). The anointing would usually be done immediately after death but of course the sabbath, and with it the Passover, had intervened. They may have come in two groups, having arranged to meet up at the tomb. Mary Magdalene and Mary the wife of Cleopas made their way from the place where they were staying in Jerusalem, perhaps John's house. Salome may have joined them. From another direction Joanna and an unnamed woman (possibly a disciple called Susanna) may have set out from the Hasmonean palace near the temple mount, where Joanna was part of Herod's household. Putting together the various New Testament accounts we get an idea of the possible sequence.

As the two Marys and Salome approached the burial area they may have felt earth tremors. This was relatively unremarkable, as such things were common close to the Rift Valley through which the River Jordan flowed. What was more pressing for them was the fact that they suddenly realized that they would not be able to roll away the heavy stone in front of the tomb. As they approached, however, they noticed that the tomb had already been opened. Mary Magdalene, assuming the body had been taken, ran off to inform Peter and John, the two disciples who had remained in

Jerusalem, leaving the two older women at the spot. At this point they were joined by Joanna and her companion. They decided to enter the tomb to see what might have happened. There, we are told, they were surprised to see two young men whose white robes were dazzlingly bright. (This is a normal depiction of angelic beings or divine messengers in Scripture; they look like men, wearing the usual clothes of the period, not airy beings with wings.) One of the men told them that Jesus had risen, as he said he would. They were to inform the disciples and Peter that he was going before them to Galilee. At this the four women fled from the tomb and ran to tell the disciples. A great deal of running went on in those early hours, as a result of the extraordinary events which were presumably almost too much for the mind to grasp.

Meanwhile, Mary Magdalene had found Peter and John in the city and blurted out, "They have taken the Lord out of the tomb, and we do not know where they have laid him." Immediately the two men started running to the tomb, with Mary following behind. In the crowded Jerusalem streets, offering several routes north to the tomb outside the city wall, Peter and John did not intercept the other women on their way from the tomb to tell the disciples, as instructed by the angel. John, probably younger than Peter, reached the tomb first, but Peter was the first to go right in. There he saw the empty grave clothes. When John entered he "saw and believed" that Jesus was risen. He noted "the face cloth, which had been on Jesus' head, not lying with the linen cloths but folded up in a place by itself" (John 20:7). This simple observation seems to have had a profound impact on his faith. By now Mary Magdalene had reached the tomb and lingered there while Peter and John went back. As she wept, she experienced the first resurrection appearance of Jesus. Probably she dropped to her knees in amazement and joy and wrapped her arms tightly around his legs. He told her not to cling to him. It seems that this was not a shyness of human touch, nor a reprimand, but a signal that his relationships had now changed with his resurrection—he would soon be leaving his disciples. They had to let him go.

While the other women were contacting the various disciples with the angel's message, perhaps on their way to Bethany, they were hailed by Jesus. Thus both his first and second appearances were to women, who had no legal status as witnesses. It is only after this that Jesus appeared later in the day to the band of disciples, who seem to have gathered together in Jerusalem as a result of the women's unlikely stories and were having a meal. Before this appearance, two of the larger group of disciples, Cleopas and an ✔ unnamed person, set off for a village called Emmaus, several miles away. As they walked they were joined by a third person, whom they did not recognize at first. They told him about the events surrounding Jesus' crucifixion and how "some women of our company amazed us" with their stories of an empty tomb and visions of angels (Luke 24:22-24). Later, as they pressed him to stay with them, they recognized him as Jesus. This slowness to recognize him may well have been because of expectation. After all, you may see someone in the street who looks like a friend who has died, but you quickly dismiss the idea. It may also have been that Jesus was ordinary looking and that his head was covered—it is usually his teaching, his inherent authority and his relationships with a diversity of people that are noted in the New Testament.

We are given no further description of appearance, this time to Peter alone, later that day. Around this time too Jesus appeared to his brother James, as mentioned by Paul. However, the New Testament documents do tell us in some detail that Jesus appeared to Peter and the other immediate disciples (with the exception of an absent Thomas) as they talked at a meal about the overwhelming events of the day. The occasion was recorded in Luke's memorable words:

> As they were talking about these things, Jesus himself stood among them, and said to them, "Peace to you!" But they were startled and frightened and thought they saw a spirit. And he said to them, "Why are you troubled, and why do doubts arise in your hearts? See my hands and my feet, that it is I myself. Touch me, and see. For a spirit does not have flesh and bones as you see that I have." And when he had said this, he showed them his hands and his feet. And while they still disbelieved for joy and were marveling, he said to them, "Have you anything here to eat?" They gave him a piece of broiled fish, and he took it and ate before them. (Luke 24:36-43)

Some time later, when Thomas rejoined the others of the Eleven, he was skeptical about the stories of Jesus' resurrection and the visions of the women. When the others told him, "We have seen the Lord," his no-nonsense response was, "Unless I see in his hands the mark of the nails, and place my finger into the mark of the nails, and place my hand into his side, I will never believe" (John 20:24-25). He referred very specifically to Christ's horrific wounds from the crucifixion.

SUNDAY, APRIL 12 (NISAN 23)

It is clear from the New Testament documents that the disciples stayed on in Jerusalem at least a week before following Jesus' instruction to go to Galilee to meet with him there. This may have been in keeping with the custom of pilgrims to remain in or near Jerusalem for the six days of unleavened bread that followed the Passover. We are not told the location of the mountain where they were to meet him. Many steep hills butt onto the shore around the Lake (or Sea) of Galilee. John records the appearance of Jesus to Thomas, together with the ten who had already seen him, the following Sunday in Jerusalem. As usual, the doors of the room in which they were meeting were locked, for fear of the city and temple authorities, so it is likely that they met in the Upper Room that may have been the property of the parents of John Mark. Once again Jesus suddenly appeared. This time, after his familiar greeting of "Peace be with you," he invited Thomas to touch the scars on his body. The quick-minded disciple responded with "My Lord and my God!" Perhaps more than the others, he had thought through the deep implications of what was happening. His new conviction would soon carry him, according to credible tradition, to India and possibly also Parthia, where he would tell the story many times.

It was such convictions about the resurrection appearances of Jesus that provided the impetus and dynamic for the dramatic expansion of Christianity in the thirty years after these events.

BETWEEN WEDNESDAY, APRIL 15 (NISAN 26), AND MAY 13 (IYYAR 24)

If the Eleven and other disciples from Galilee had set out the next day, Monday, April 13, they may have reached the vicinity of the Lake of Galilee by that Wednesday. They would have descended the steep Roman road from Jerusalem to Jericho, then headed north along the broad Jordan Valley. It was in the area around the Lake of Galilee that several appearances took place. One of them is recorded in extraordinary detail in John's Gospel and concerns a group from among the Eleven who are taken by surprise by a meeting with Jesus. Another is the occasion mentioned by Paul, in his letter to the church in Corinth, in which a very large number congregate. Because of the large number, this may be the meeting that Jesus had specified in Galilee. It is likely to have been the occasion when Jesus commissioned his disciples, men and women, to go and make new disciples in all the nations of the world (Matthew 28:19-20). This commission is the heart of the expansion of the church, which began just weeks later. Though the church was initially entirely Jewish, its leaders eventually began to realize that the good news about Jesus was equally for Gentiles.

The meeting with Jesus, recorded only in the Gospel of John, began with a group from among the Eleven—Peter, John, James his brother, Thomas, Nathaniel and two unnamed disciples—going out fishing on the lake one night. They caught nothing, but spied a figure on the shore as day was breaking. He called out to them to fish on the right side of the boat, and the result was a huge haul. Peter suddenly realized that it was Jesus and jumped overboard and swam to him. The others followed with the catch. It was a numinous setting—in the freshness of morning Jesus had a wood fire burning and called them to have a breakfast of bread and fish. For the Gospel writers the ordinary and the sacred were the same. The occasion was important in publicly restoring Peter after his failure on the night of Jesus' trials. Echoing Peter's three denials, Jesus three times asked Peter if he loved him. After each affirmation Jesus said, "Feed my sheep." Peter thereafter was restored and acknowledged as a leading pillar of the church among the apostles, as the Eleven became known, other evident pillars being the brothers James and John, Jesus' brother James, and, eventually, Paul.

During the appearances in Galilee it seems that Jesus then directed his close disciples to return to Jerusalem. The purpose of the Galilean appearances appears to have been to demonstrate his resurrection to a large number of disciples in the area in which he had done most of his teaching in the past three years of his ministry. He also included them in his commission to go throughout the world with his Gospel. Undoubtedly the Galileans were more amenable to the spread of the message to the Gentile world than many in Jerusalem. Nevertheless it was to Jerusalem that he directed his immediate followers, where the church would be centered for a considerable time. Judaism in the period before the fall of Jerusalem and the destruction of the temple in A.D. 70 was varied and many-colored. Some scholars believe that the distinctive Jewishness of Jesus may have owed much to the Galilean context, which was less rigid, to all appearances, than in Jerusalem and Judea. If this were so, the history and development of the church would have been very different had it been centered in Galilee—where most of Jesus' ministry took place—rather than in Jerusalem.

THURSDAY, MAY 14 (IYYAR 25)

In obedience to Jesus the Eleven had returned to Jerusalem, accompanied by many close disciples from Galilee, including women. Either this day or the evening before, Jesus appeared to the Eleven in the Upper Room in Jerusalem. It is not recorded how long they spoke. According to the account in Acts, Jesus referred to the baptism of water offered by John the Baptist, which had signified a decisive repentance and a desire for inward as well as external purity. They would, he said, be baptized by the coming of the Holy Spirit "not many days from now" (Acts 1:4-5; see Luke 3:16). They probably asked him many questions. One was about the issue of the nature of his kingdom. The book of Acts records them asking, "Lord, will you at this time restore the kingdom to Israel?" This was a leading "messianic" question. At that time there were various concepts of what a messiah would do. Popular with some groups was an apocalyptic or eschatological messiah, who would decisively change the world order by supernatural means. Jesus deflects the question, suggesting that this is not the main concern. Rather he focuses on a task for which they would be agents, using their hard work and resourcefulness in the here and now but drawing on a divine supernatural power that was unprecedented in scale: they would "receive power when the Holy Spirit has come upon you, and you will be my witnesses in Jerusalem and in all Judea and Samaria, and to the end of the earth." At some point, perhaps at daybreak, he led them out of Jerusalem, over the Mount of Olives toward Bethany. It was here that he left them for the final time. They described the manner of his disappearance afterward as being taken into a cloud. Luke says that, on the Mount of Olives, "lifting up his hands he blessed them. While he blessed them, he parted from them and was carried up into heaven" (Luke 24:50-51). He had instructed them to remain in Jerusalem until the mysterious Holy Spirit came. After Jesus had gone they returned to the city, overwhelmed with joy.

FRIDAY, MAY 15 (IYYAR 26), TO SATURDAY, MAY 23 (SIVAN 5)

Each day for the next ten days the apostles, the Eleven, were continually to be found in the temple "blessing God." They also met throughout the day in the Upper Room, where, one day during this period, they chose by lots a successor to Judas Iscariot, called Matthias, so that they became the Twelve once more. They were accompanied in the Upper Room by a large body of disciples, men and women, many from Galilee. They devoted themselves to prayer with great fervor and, I suggest, went over the events of recent days and, further back, of the most memorable incidents and teachings in the three years of Jesus' ministry. The church was about to be born and an unstoppable force created that would over the next thirty years, despite resistance and brutal persecution, spread through the eastern Roman empire and into the western, and, to the east, reach India via the trade routes. This group of about 120 Jewish people, together with those remaining in Galilee, would shape the character of the future Europe, and their message would be carried to the utmost parts of the earth, as Jesus instructed.

A sculptured head of Agrippina the Elder who starved to death in A.D. 33, after being banished to an island northwest of Naples by the emperor Tiberius. *(Réunion des Musées Nationaux/Art Resource, NY. Used by permission of Art Resources.)*

Head of Emperor Tiberius depicted on a coin. *(From* Life of Christ, *F. W. Farrar, Cassall and Company, 1903. Public domain.)*

Shops would have lined this remarkably preserved thoroughfare in Pompeii. Roman engineering in roads, bridges, aqueducts and buildings expressed confidence in and reinforced the empire's values of civilization, law and peace. *(Ruth Brown. Used by permission of the author.)*

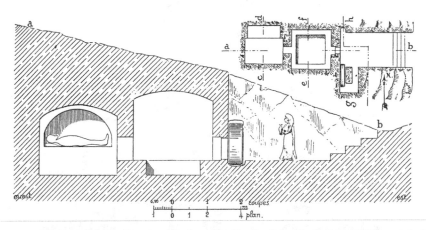

Reconstruction of the rock-cut tomb described in the Gospels. Peter and John are said to have entered the tomb chamber, possibly through a low entrance (see p. 130). There may not have been a fully formed antechamber, as represented in this diagram, as not all rock tombs had this. *(Drawn by Pére Vincent, after Vincent and Abel 1914, ii, fig. 53. Public domain.)*

A rolling stone in its groove: the entrance to the tomb of Queen Helena of Adiabene ("The Tombs of Kings"), Jerusalem, mid-first century A.D., looking southeast. The stone that was rolled over to close the entrance to the tomb of Jesus may have been a cruder one, lacking a precise groove. *(Martin Biddle. Used by permission of Martin Biddle.)*

A Celtic snake etched on a rock in Galicia, Spain. Discovered in a high Castro settlement near Vigo, the snake could have represented water, rivers, healing, fertility and prosperity. It may have symbolized the connection between river and sea, and between heaven and earth. *(Author's collection)*

"Street of the Dead" at Teotihuacán, Mexico. The street is the ceremonial center of the city. The architecture of the city embodies a highly developed cosmology and belief system. The position of the huge avenue appears to align with local sacred geography and star movements. *(Werner Forman/Art Resource, NY. Used by permission of Art Resource.)*

Jerusalem seen from Mount Josaphat. *(Erich Lessing/Art Resource, NY. Used by permission of Art Resource.)*

This nineteenth-century engraving of Bethany (modern 'el-'Azariyeh, named after Lazarus) gives an impression of the ancient village surrounded by olive groves. The village still exists, at the distance from Jerusalem indicated in John's Gospel (11:18). *(From Life of Christ, F. W. Farrar, Cassell and Company, 1903. Public domain.)*

Reconstruction of Jerusalem in the time of Christ: bird's-eye view looking northeast. The temple dominates the city. Beside the near wall is Herod's Palace, with the Hasmodean Palace midway between it and the temple. Jesus' execution took place on the slopes above the city wall, near where the wall turns east in the foreground. The Mount of Olives lies in the distance, beyond the temple and the Kidron Valley. *(Leen Ritmeyer. Used by permission of Leen Ritmeyer.)*

THE WIDER WORLD

THE WESTERN EMPIRE

THE WESTERN EMPIRE, LIKE THE EASTERN, comprised a vast area: Hispania (Iberian peninsula), Gaul (France) and Germania. The south of this area tended to be urban and the north rural. Two centers founded in the north, however, remain important to this day: Bonna (Bonn) and Lutetia (Paris). The northern parts, Gaul and Germania, were in relation to Rome a wilderness world, populated by Celtic peoples, with Germanic tribes farther north and east. The Celtic tribes had a well-developed culture that fascinated Roman invaders such as Julius Caesar. Theirs was an oral culture. It was left to Greek and Roman historians and geographers to document it. Britannia at this time was unoccupied by the Romans, but there were strong trade links between the island and the continent, facilitated by the fact that many of the British tribes were Celts. Tiberius took an active interest in the Roman administrations throughout the western empire, and during the year A.D. 33 he was behind a large-scale project of road building that soon enhanced trade between Hispania, Gaul and Italy, as well as increasing security. One such road initiated by Tiberius crossed the Pyrenees, connecting northern Spain with Burdigala in Gaul.[1]

To all these regions Romanization brought peace and wider trading possibilities, creating a new economic infrastructure. The empire itself benefited from the trade and from a supply of slaves and conscripts to the legions. The soldiers were essential not only for policing and putting down insurrectionists and invaders but also for the building of roads. In A.D. 33 or 34 the Moesian legions (Moesia was an ancient province in today's Serbia and Bulgaria) were engaged in constructing a strategic road along the River Danube. The project required considerable resourcefulness and determination. One of the many challenges was in some stretches to cut the road into the face of cliffs overhanging the river.[2] The infantry practiced a diversity of skills, and carried a variety of tools for building, hunting and setting up camp.

As Roman culture was adopted in the west, new cities were established,

with streets following a grid pattern and baths and temples created. Amphi-
theaters were constructed, and in the southern towns theaters were set up
to entertain the literati with plays. Brilliantly engineered aqueducts supplied
cities with fresh water for drinking and the all-important baths. The legions
were particularly strong along the Rhine, which marked the northeast frontier of the empire, because of the strategic importance of Germania for
Rome's security. Lentulus Gaetulicus, who survived the downfall of Sejanus
despite his friendship with the former deputy of the emperor, commanded
powerful legions in upper Germania. Tiberius, as a former military commander in this region, was aware of the importance of retaining the allegiance of his legions there. He had served in German campaigns nine times
for Augustus.

Before the Roman conquests of Gaul and Germania the Celts had dominated Europe. They were a family of tribes who had settled across western
and northern Europe. Classical writers, including Virgil (70-19 B.C.), Julius
Caesar (104?-44 B.C.), Diodorus Siculus (first century B.C.), Arrian (c. A.D. 96-
180) and Strabo (64 B.C.-A.D. 21), have described the Celts, remarking on
their appearance and "barbarian" characteristics.

> After Iberia, we come to Celtic territory, which reaches eastwards as far as the
> Rhine. Its entire northern edge is bathed by the British Channel. (Strabo *Ge-
> ography* 2.5.28)

> Their hair was of gold, their clothing was of gold and light stripes brightened
> their cloaks. Their milk-white necks had gold collars around them, a pair of
> Alpine spears glinted in each warrior's hands, and their bodies were protected
> by tall shields. (Virgil *Aeneid* 8.659-62)

> They wear amazing clothes: tunics dyed in every color and trousers that they
> call bracae [breeches]. (Siculus *World History* 5.30)

> The whole nation that is nowadays called Gallic or Galatic is war-mad, and
> both high-spirited and quick for battle although otherwise simple and not un-
> couth. (Strabo *Geography* 4.4.2)

> They [the charioteers] . . . combine the mobility of cavalry with the solidity of
> infantry in battle, and become so skilled in their use through training and daily
> practise that they can even control galloping horses on steep and dangerous
> inclines, make them slow down very quickly, and turn them around. (Caesar
> *Gallic War* 4.33)

> The women of the Gauls are not only like men in their stature but they are a

match for them in courage as well. (Siculus *World History* 5.32)

The Gauls are tall and have a high opinion of themselves. (Arrian *Anabasis of Alexander* 1.4.6)

In conversation, the Gauls' speech is brief and enigmatic, proceeding by allusions and innuendo. . . . They have a threatening, boastful, tragic manner, and yet their minds are sharp and not without aptitude for learning. (Siculus *World History* 5.31)

The Celts displayed inventive brilliance, having wheeled transport and a well-developed plough long before their exposure to Roman influence. Their metalworking resulted in elegant and beautiful works of art. In fact, they achieved the highest level of culture in the western world outside of the Mediterranean region. They originally came from the east and settled in the western Alps, and to the south of the upper Danube. As well as moving into the British Isles, Spain, most of France and northern Italy, they spread eastward down the Danube and even into Galatia in Asia Minor. They seemed to retain a sense of unity with other Celts that transcended their individual tribes, though they sometimes fought among themselves. They apparently had a physical resemblance (Boudicca, who was a young girl in A.D. 33, fitted the stereotype in being tall with long red hair) and Celtic artifacts and culture were distinctive.

Though they did not practice writing, they had highly developed oral abilities, with associated powerful memories. They lived in towns, which of course required advanced social organization. They had kings to rule them. As tribes, lacking a national or state identity, they were not able to unite adequately to resist Roman occupation successfully. The Romans, however, were also scared of their savagery in battle. They were noted for hunting human heads as part of their religious practice. Severed heads would be nailed on the gateway or on posts around hill forts. The heads would serve to display military prowess and also to exert magical protective power. Diodorus Siculus recounts how heads were nailed by Gauls onto their houses or embalmed in oil.[3] The prospect of becoming a human sacrifice in a Druidic ceremony after capture was also unattractive to Roman soldiers engaged in conquering the Celts.

A Celtic religious symbol that in some ways is as potent as the cross in Christianity is the severed human head. It encapsulates Celtic faith at this time. The head was seen as the seat of human power. The displayed heads of warriors would protect homes and fortresses from evil. Good luck and success would be guaranteed by their presence. Not only were heads displayed as trophies or charms, but even adapted into drinking cups, being adorned with gold. A good head count from battle also indicated valor and prowess. As the seat of the human soul, the head was also a potent symbol of divinity. Heads were fashioned in wood or stone, and many have survived to be discovered by archaeologists.

In Celtic religious systems, Druids held an integrating role. They were the elite of an elaborate hierarchy, which included bards and soothsayers, and had an extensive education. Theirs was a varied social role, concerned with the nature of the Celtic deities, morality and legislation as well as astrology and divination. Their mystique of knowledge was associated with the oak tree, a symbol of the divine. The mistletoe was also of great significance, perhaps associated with fertility. Julius Caesar wrote that "the Druids were concerned with divine worship, the due performance of sacrifices, both private and public, and the interpretation of ritual questions."

North and west of the Celtic territories conquered by the Romans were Germanic "barbarians." The Roman historian Tacitus vividly describes the geography and ethnology of Germania in his book of that name.

> Their country, though somewhat various in appearance, yet generally either bristles with forests or reeks with swamps; it is more rainy on the side of Gaul, bleaker on that of Noricum and Pannonia. It is productive of grain, but unfavorable to fruit-bearing trees; it is rich in flocks and herds, but these are for the most part undersized, and even the cattle have not their usual beauty or noble head. It is number that is chiefly valued; they are in fact the most highly prized, indeed the only riches of the people. . . . The border population . . . value gold and silver for their commercial utility, and are familiar with, and show preference for, some of our coins. The tribes of the interior use the simpler and more ancient practice of the barter of commodities. They like the old and well known money, coins milled, or showing a two-horse chariot. They likewise prefer silver to gold, not from any special liking, but because a large number of silver pieces is more convenient for use among dealers in cheap and common articles.[4]

Tacitus is describing Germanic tribes. The Romans called the Celts Gauls and named France after its Celtic inhabitants as "Gaul." The Rhine was perceived as a significant boundary between the Germanic tribes and the Celts. The first accounts of the inhabitants of France are in the records of the

Greeks and Romans. In the sixth century B.C. the Greek colony of Massilia (or Marseilles) was founded. In the first century B.C. Caesar brought Gaul under Roman rule and memorably recorded his exploits in his *The Conquest of Gaul,* which also includes the earliest eyewitness account of Britannia and its inhabitants, which he failed twice to conquer. Caesar, however, was able to conquer the whole of what today is France, Belgium and Switzerland, and parts of the Netherlands and Germany.

The conquest of Gaul was relatively easy because Celts had never formed an organized army. They were a loose federation of tribes. Some tribes for political reasons welcomed Roman military support. Some needed help to protect them from German invaders from the north and east. Resistance to the Romans effectively ended with the strategic defeat of Vercingetorix in 52 B.C. by Caesar. Romanization of Gaul quickly followed. The policy of Roman occupation was liberal and permissive. For the occupied, as in many other parts of the empire, the benefits of Roman civilization usually outweighed the burden of taxation. The Gauls replaced their breeches with togas and cropped their long hair. They named themselves and their cities with Roman names. Today's Provence was Rome's first southern province in Gaul (known as Gallia Narbonensis). The new Roman roads, in the words of one historian, were like "stone arteries" through the country.[5]

The acquisition of Gaul was very strategic for the survival of the Roman empire. Not only did the millions of people provide a market for trade and a supply of soldiers, but the securing of Gaul also weakened the threat from the barbarian north. The legions protecting Rome's frontiers from barbarians in the north and northeast were swelled with recruits from Gaul. Later, Gauls were allowed to serve on the Senate as consuls. The future emperor Claudius was a native of Lyon (Lugdunum), born in 10 B.C., son of Drusus, Tiberius's brother.

In his *Conquest of Gaul,*[6] Caesar remarks on the superstitious nature of the Gauls:

> The nation of all the Gauls is extremely devoted to superstitious rites; and on that account they who are troubled with unusually severe diseases and they who are engaged in battles and dangers, either sacrifice men as victims, or vow that they will sacrifice them, and employ the Druids as the performers of those sacrifices; because they think that unless the life of a man be offered for the life of a man, the mind of the immortal gods cannot be rendered propitious, and they have sacrifices of that kind ordained for national purposes.

Others have figures of vast size, the limbs of which formed of osiers they fill with living men, which being set on fire, the men perish enveloped in the flames. They consider that the oblation of such as have been taken in theft, or in robbery, or any other offense, is more acceptable to the immortal gods; but when a supply of that class is wanting, they have recourse to the oblation of even the innocent.

What was true of Gaul was also true of Britannia, to the northwest across the narrow sea. Many Celtic tribes lived here with close connections with fellow tribes on the continent, in Gaul and what is now Belgium. The geographical isolation of Britannia from the rest of Europe was reflected in A.D. 33—it was not part of the empire. Its temperate lands, warmed by the Gulf Stream, made the land an attractive prize for the Romans, though they were only ever to conquer part of the islands.

Before humans arrived, much of Britain was forest. In lowland England a great deal of the woodland was cleared by around 700 B.C., the start of the Iron Age, as the demand for wood intensified. Dwellings and farms were constructed to keep away animals such as foxes and wolves. In a rich diversity, bears were to be found and also eagles and kites. Change was slow, and by A.D. 33 much of England was still marsh or swamp. Extensive drainage was not to come in until the Romans occupied much of Britannia.

In his *A History of the English-Speaking Peoples* Winston Churchill describes pre-Roman Britannia as an island world,

> not widely sundered from the Continent, and so tilted that its mountains lie all to the west and north, while south and east is a gently undulating landscape of wooded valleys, open downs, and slow rivers. It is very accessible to the invader, whether he comes in peace or war, as pirate or merchant, conqueror or missionary. . . . Caesar's landing at Deal bridged the chasm that nature had cloven. For a century, while the Roman world was tearing itself to pieces in civil war, or slowly recovering under a new Imperial form, Britain remained uneasily poised between isolation and union with the Continent, but absorbing, by way of trade and peaceful intercourse, something of the common culture of the West.[7]

The area now called England had a long history before the Romans invaded, which is slowly being uncovered by archaeologists. Our knowledge of Britannia in A.D. 33 and its earlier centuries is hampered by the fact that the Celts kept no written records. We know that trees of elm, oak, lime and ash had joined those of colder climes—hazel, pine and birch—as Britain had slowly warmed after the ice receded and disappeared. Plant and animal life became rich, encouraging nomadic hunter-gathering and then agricultural settlement as forests were cleared. With settlement and more complex social organization came the development of crafts and utensils, and eventually jewelry and metalwork. After the cultivation of domestic animals, such as sheep and cattle, came wheeled vehicles. Trade along rivers, coasts and across seas developed. By A.D. 33 the skills of iron smelting and forging had been practiced for over seven hundred years. The impact of an increasing and sophisticated Celtic influence on the native population—such as the influx of "Belgic" peoples from northern France—was felt in the concept of definite groups or kingdoms, such as the Trinovantes of what is now Essex, the employment of coins and the establishment of towns like Seaford, Wheathampstead, Hengistbury, and the capital of the Trinovantes, Colchester. This impact was particularly evident in the south of Britain. As is typical of the Celts, there was nothing like the developed urban civilization of Rome—the idea of the city. There was also no concept of nation, like "England," "Wales" or "Scotland."[8] Because of this lack of a national consciousness, little would have been remembered of Julius Caesar's failed attempts to conquer Britannia, even though trade continued with countries under Roman rule across the narrow stretch of seaway to the continent. An increase in trade afterward was, in fact, the main impact of Julius Caesar's invasions.

"Jerusalem," the familiar poem by William Blake, begins, "And did those feet in ancient time." It is sung in Britain today in Women's Institute meetings, Rugby matches and the Last Night of the Proms.[9] The stirring words create a feel-good vision of Jesus visiting Britain some time during his short lifetime. The poem was first sung publicly as what is in effect a secular hymn at a 1916 "Votes for Women" concert, reflecting Blake's radical and visionary spirit. Jesus' visit has, of course, no foundation in fact. To be pedantic about the visit, it would be recorded in the Gospels and mentioned in his teachings had it occurred. It certainly does not fit his focus and the particularity of his existence as a Jewish man in first-century Palestine, unlikely to have even heard of Britannia. His excursions were limited to his parents' asylum-seeking in Egypt—probably Alexandria—and visits to Gentile towns near his native Nazareth.[10]

An important Celtic tribe in southern Britannia was called the Iceni. They possessed the fens, from the Wash south across present-day Norfolk and Suffolk. As trade flourished across the British Channel with the Roman empire, the merchants and rulers of the Iceni prospered, so much so that they issued their own coins from about 65 B.C. Boudicca, a young girl in A.D. 33, may have belonged to another tribe and married into the Iceni when she became Prasutagus's queen. Dio Cassius describes the adult Boudicca as very tall and "in appearance most terrifying. Her glance was fierce, her voice harsh, and a great mass of the most tawny hair cascaded to her hips."

The Trinovantes started to grow rich by controlling trade abroad. Among goods traded were imports of wine from the Mediterranean and Roman silverware and quality pottery from Gaul. With growth in trade before the Roman occupation the social and economic structure of the whole southeast changed. Towns developed and a money-based economy spread.

The Catuvellauni, also a significant tribe, occupied the central part of England, encompassing the modern-day area of London, Hertfordshire, Bedfordshire, Buckinghamshire, Cambridgeshire, Oxfordshire, parts of Essex, and Northamptonshire. When Claudius invaded Britannia ten years after A.D. 33, the Catuvellauni were the most dominant tribe in Britain, having taken control by force of much of southeast England. The tribe had a strong leadership and were well organized as a military force. This enabled them to control the land occupied by the Trinovantes and other tribes. The famous King Cunobelinus reigned over both his Catuvellaunian people and the Trinovantes from about A.D. 10. He was the father of Adminius, Togodumnus and Caractacus. He ruled from Camulodunum (Colchester), the main British settlement in the southeast. Cunobelinus was a powerful opponent of the Romans and financially aided the Druids of Anglesey, who at the time were strongly anti-Roman. He also gave refuge to warriors from Gaul.

Cunobelinus is also famous under the name given him by Shakespeare—Cymbeline. The play of that name is based on opposite and legendary accounts of the king in Geoffrey of Monmouth's *Historia Regum Britanniae* (composed before 1147) and Raphael Holinshed's *History of England* (1587), where he ruled a Britain that was under Roman political control. Cymbeline, in Monmouth, Holinshed and Shakespeare, was raised in the courts of Emperor Augustus and his country. When he returned to Britain, which was equipped with Roman weapons, Cymbeline was very friendly with the emperor's court.

According to Holinshed:

Cymbeline was brought up at Rome, and there made knight by Augustus Caesar, under whom he served in the wars, and was in such favor with him, that he was at liberty to pay his tribute or not. Cymbeline ever showed himself a friend to the Romans, and chiefly was loth to break with them because the youth of the Briton nation should not be deprived of the benefit to be trained and brought up among the Romans, whereby they might learn both to behave themselves like civil men, and to attain to the knowledge of feats of war. Little other mention is made of his doings, except that during his reign the Savior of the World, our Lord Jesus Christ the only son of God, was born of a virgin about the 23 year of the reign of this Cymbeline. He reigned 35 years, leaving behind him two sons, Guiderius and Arviragus.

Shakespeare's own version of the legend finishes with a happy view of the relations between Britain and Rome, as Cymbeline proclaims at the end of conflict between his forces and the Roman:

> Laud we the gods;
> And let our crooked smokes climb to their nostrils
> From our bless'd altars. Publish we this peace
> To all our subjects. Set we forward; let
> A Roman and a British ensign wave
> Friendly together. So through Lud's Town march;
> And in the temple of great Jupiter
> Our peace we'll ratify; seal it with feasts.
> Set on there! Never was a war did cease,
> 'Ere bloody hands were wash'd, with such a peace.

The "Pax Romana" was hard won and stretched across many nations and ethnic groups. Within ten years of A.D. 33, it would begin taking in Britannia. There were many other countries beyond the boundaries of the empire, however, nearly all of the historically significant ones of which at this time had trade links with the empire, as Britannia did.

PAST THE
BOUNDARIES OF EMPIRE

IN A.D. 33 THE WORLD POPULATION might well have been around 250 million (less than five times the population of present-day Italy). Half of earth's peoples lived within the three major empires of Han in China, Parthia and Rome. These, together with emerging kingdoms at this time in India and southwest Asia, meant that an arc of urban civilization existed from what is now Korea in the east to the Iberian peninsula in the west. At one end of civilization lay the Roman empire in the west, and at the other was the vast Han dynasty of China to the east. Each empire at the extremities of east and west was dimly aware of the other through the artifacts of trade. Trade, however, was filtered through middlemen, and in this the kingdom of Parthia played an important role. As a legacy of Alexander's conquests, Greek was a common language as far east as India. There were direct sea routes from the Red Sea to India that were busy with trading vessels. The spikenard that Mary anointed Jesus with in the spring of this year had traveled from India on some of those vessels and passed through Alexandria. It would have changed hands a number of times as trading transactions took place before it passed into Mary's possession.

The overland Silk Route from China to Parthia and the Mediterranean region, together with the discovery of maritime routes utilizing the winds across the Indian Ocean, led to a new and stimulating contact between cultures and empires. Trading brought new goods and knowledge of distant worlds. Roman artifacts appeared in India and even China, and wealthy Roman citizens enjoyed wearing Chinese silk. Pliny the Elder complained of Roman wealth being drained by the purchase of luxuries from the east.

The pattern of winds that made trade across the Indian Ocean possible was discovered by Hippalus, who between A.D. 14 and 37 sailed through the Red Sea and across to the Indus. The Romans were quick to exploit the possibilities of trade, establishing trading stations on the Indian coast. This was not a simple one-way process. Indian traders expanded eastward to southeast Asia, setting up trading stations on the lower Mekong and elsewhere. Shipping from the Roman empire may have confined itself to west coast ports, so as not to risk the contrary winds of the Indian cape. The important trading center of Arikamedu (Pondicherry, south of Madras) may have been reached overland.

A fascinating contemporary picture of the trade routes down the Red Sea and along the east African coast, and of the newly discovered route across the Indian Ocean, is given in the anonymous *Periplus Maris Erythraei* (or *Voyage Around the Erythraean Sea*). It may have been written around a decade after A.D. 33, so it gives an accurate picture of the time. Ptolemy's *Geography* in the second century added more detail. The author of the *Periplus* seems to have been an Egyptian merchant, writing in the Koine Greek that was used throughout the territory of Alexander's ancient conquests, that is, eastward as far as India. The last sections of the *Periplus* describe the route around the Arabian Peninsula and past the Persian Gulf on to the west coast of India. It reads like an eyewitness account of the author himself rather than being made up of secondhand accounts. The pace of a sea voyage, dependent on prevailing winds, and then the slow progress from port to port, is captured beautifully. It ranks with Luke's account of the sea voyage he undertook with the apostle Paul and the shipwreck at Malta (Acts 27) as a vivid piece of first-century travel writing. It is a trader's rough guide to new worlds. The seafarer chronicles the east coast of India as far north as the mouth of the Ganges. He includes information helpful to traders and seafarers to India from Alexandria and Red Sea ports, such as the distances (in Roman stadia) and conditions of the routes, the trading posts and least hazardous anchor points, the local inhabitants, and the exports and imports of a particular region. Interestingly, the narrative includes reports of little-known lands beyond to the fabled east, where the land of China is called "This," and includes a description of people apparently from the Steppes:

> After this region under the very north, the sea outside ending in a land called This, there is a very great inland city called Thinae [China], from which raw silk and silk yarn and silk cloth are brought on foot through Bactria to Barygaza [modern Broach, in India], and are also exported to Damirica [Limyrike] by way of the river Ganges. But the land of This is not easy of access; few men come from there, and seldom. The country lies under the Lesser Bear [that is,

Ursa Minor], and is said to border on the farthest parts of Pontus and the Caspian Sea, next to which lies Lake Maeotis; all of which empty into the ocean.

Every year on the borders of the land of This there comes together a tribe of men with short bodies and broad, flat faces, and by nature peaceable; they are called Besata, and are almost entirely uncivilized. They come with their wives and children, carrying great packs and plaited baskets of what looks like greengrape-leaves. They meet in a place between their own country and the land of This. There they hold a feast for several days, spreading out the baskets under themselves as mats, and then return to their own places in the interior.[1]

This opening up of the distant lands from the Roman empire, with the seizing of trading opportunities, allowed the dissemination of ideas. Not only did it ease the spread of the new Christianity but also the eastward expansion of Buddhism. More permanent than national boundaries or those of empires were the domains of world religions, such as Judaism, Confucianism and Buddhism. Far to the east, the Han empire was shaped by a long Chinese tradition of Confucianism, which it officially adopted, and the ethos of which made possible its administration and paid civil service. This was a school of ethical, political and religious teachings associated with Confucius (c. 551-479 B.C.). It was concerned with the cultivation through ritual of virtues like kindliness, humanity and gentle behavior. Such ideals held the expanding empire together, despite tensions and conflicts of interest among administrators. India too, at this time, had been dramatically molded by religious beliefs, in this case the teachings of the Buddha. The great ruler Ashoka (273-232 B.C.) had unified a vast area by force. He ruled over a kingdom—the first Indian empire—that stretched from Kashmir and Peshawar in the north and northwest to Mysore in the south and Orissa in the east. Everything changed for him after he had experienced the waste of human life at the battlefield of Kalinga in Orissa (269 B.C.). He embraced Buddhism and was called the "Prince of Peace." His empire was morally strong and tolerant of other religions, and had an extensive administrative machinery. His conversion to Buddhism and renunciation of war influenced succeeding generations, but made India vulnerable to the invasions that took place from the north and west. In the subsequent centuries, after the Ashoka empire fell apart, India experienced wave after wave of invasion, and frequently suffered the rule of foreign rulers—Indo-Bactrians, the Scythians (Sakas) and others. The apostle Thomas, according to tradition, later preached in the dominions of one Saka king, Gondopharnes, who reigned

A.D. 20-48. Furthermore, Hinduism, shaped by Vedic values and the sway of the Brahmans, was subverted by the spread of Buddhism. Hinduism is primarily defined by the authority of its religious writings called the Vedas and the Upanishads. John Keay writes, in *A History of India,* that this period is steeped in obscurity and uncertainty. "Between the death of Ashoka in 231 B.C. and the advent of Gupta power in A.D. 320, India's ancient history plummets again to a murky obscurity."[2]

Some clearer but very patchy facts emerge in the almost forgotten period. In Tengnoupal, in the eastern Himalayas, Pakhangha established a dynasty in A.D. 33 that lasted right up until integration with the Indian union in 1947. Coins that have been discovered indicate names of a plethora of otherwise forgotten kings, such as Luwaang Punshiba, Meithei King of Manipur, whose reign ended at this time. The Meithei were a people related to Tibetans and Burmese. Archaeological discoveries and other inscriptions yield information about religious establishments and guilds. Texts from India, the Roman empire and China allude to links with a wider world and provide evidence of the significance of trade. The picture, however, is still incomplete. There was no national, unifying king or dynasty recording its history and documenting its conquests.

There were intermittent bursts of cultural innovation and some integration, particularly in peninsular India. A devout merchant class were patrons of the sculptural reliefs of the Bharhut, Sanchi and Amaravati stupas, round, usually domed buildings, erected as Buddhist shrines. These depicted scenes of popular devotion. To this period also belong the distinctive "rock-cut cathedrals" or "cave temples," cut into rock, sometimes expanding natural caves. These could contain intricate networks of prayer chambers, halls, tall stupas and cells for meditation. In the north of India some of the smaller sculptures reflected the influence of the Greek world. The famous *Kama Sutra* of Vatsyayana was in development at this time.

There were evidently three kingdoms in the south of India in this period—Kerala, Pandy and Cola. In south India, Tamil poetry dates from around this time in the Sangam period. It was composed and recited originally at marathon arts festivals or assemblies (called sangam, meaning "academy" or "fraternity"), organized by the Pandyan court. It was collected in anthologies and put into writing much later. Sangam literature shows knowledge of the Aryan and Sanskrit epics (e.g., the Mahabharata, a vast and enormously influential work then in oral form) as well as Buddhism. The south kingdoms were also exposed to the wider world through trade as well as an influx of people from the north. Sri Lanka (Ceylon) to the far south was particularly associated with Buddhism, a legacy of Ashoka's missionary activity.

At this point in the first century, when India was still greatly divided, Buddhism was poised to spread from there via the Silk Route to China, where its impact would be profound. One manifestation of Buddhism, the Mahayana, was influenced in its visualization of its beliefs by Greek art, portraying a hint of an incarnation of the divine in a human Buddha. Buddha was an iconic figure of enlightenment. The other school—the Hinayana—was purist and essentially ethical, presenting the enlightened presence typically in a tree, a footprint, a throne or an umbrella rather than as a human figure.

It was not only in the east that religions were important. To the west the Roman empire, like the earlier Greek, was deeply religious—the emperor was effectively the sacred head of its domain. Augustus, Tiberius's predecessor, had been deified, leading to an emperor cult. Numerous gods were worshiped, from Isis to Jupiter, many of them from the Greek pantheon. What at first seemed a sect within Judaism, Christianity would within a generation percolate through all classes of Roman society in every province of the eastern empire and would soon pass farther west. The apostle Paul may have visited Spain not long before his imprisonment and death under Nero. Within the same period Christianity would reach India via the sea routes and establish some of the world's earliest churches.

The Silk Route was opened up from the east as a result of campaigns by the Qin emperor, Shi Huangdi, and his successor from the Western Han dynasty, Wudi, in the second century B.C. They fought to push back the nomadic Xiongnu. Steppe people to the north and west of China were a constant trouble to the Chinese, whose people were largely to the north of the country, where lay the capital, Luoyang, established with the restoration of the Han dynasty in A.D. 26.[3] The Silk Route was a series of routes that networked across central Asia. For centuries it persisted as the main east-west trade route. From China the route ran north of Tibet, passing through Sinkiang and eventually down the Oxus river (today called the Amu Darya, or Amu river) through Bactria to Bakhara, Parthia and the Roman territories. It linked Anxi in the east with Samarkand in the west. The summer route went north of the Tien Shan range. The main route divided to bypass the Takla Makan desert, one of the largest sandy deserts in the world, where some dunes reach three hundred feet in height.

The history of China, over several millennia, makes it unique in its longevity as a civilization. Antiques and monuments from very ancient times were documented as early as around 100 B.C. (by Sima Qian, historian at the court of the Western Han, in his important *Historical Records*). The first Han emperor, whose reign began in 221 B.C., brought order to the land. He instituted a new system of administration, made possible by the Confucian beliefs of the people. The country was divided into prefectures and districts. These were managed by civil servants paid by the central government. Roads were built to allow troops to be moved easily. Laws were introduced and writing systems were simplified. In the time of the first emperor the initial sections of the Great Wall were constructed to challenge the marauding tribes to the north. It was this first emperor who was responsible for the terracotta warriors in his mausoleum.[4] The Han dynasty extended its boundaries furthest under the emperor Wu Ti (140-87 B.C.), west as far as Xinjiang and Central Asia, northward to Manchuria and Korea, and south to Yunnan, Hainan island, and even Nam Viet (Vietnam). The Han dynasty established an enduring pattern of imperial order and eventually instilled a national consciousness that survives today. The Chinese still see themselves as the "Han people."

In the year that concerns us, China was still rebuilding stability after a brief interregnum, before which the Han dynasty had ruled (known as the Western Han empire). Between A.D. 9 and 23 Wang Mang had gained the throne of emperor. There were unsuccessful attempts at political reform. The loss of Central Asiatic provinces, combined with natural disasters, spurred many uprisings. Most significant was the revolt of the "red eyebrows," large numbers of peasants who carried a distinct marking. Their political naivety, however, prevented a sustained revolution.

In A.D. 25 the Eastern Han dynasty was founded by Liu-Hsiu (Liu-Xiu), a descendant of the Han emperors. He had had a dream one night of mounting a red dragon (in the east, dragons are seen as friendly creatures) and ascending into the sky. When he became emperor he took on the name of Guangwudi (Kuang Wu-ti). Then followed a flourishing period in which overseas trade became centered on Nan-hai (Canton). Trade in silk to the Roman empire flourished. The rule of Guangwudi and successive emperors relied on support from powerful landowners, who tended to look to their own interests, and thus hindered reforms. Nevertheless, Guangwudi was determined to reunify the country under his sole control. The political influence of southern and eastern China began to increase. Moving the capital

to Luoyang meant that it had a superior strategic position to the earlier capital to the west. It was well sited for communications with the various regions of the vast empire and also was protected by the Yellow River to its
south and mountains to its north. Its city walls, which had twelve painted
gates, were between fourteen and twenty yards thick and almost ten yards
in height. A moat surrounded the city, whose streets were set out in a grid
pattern. Guangwudi strengthened the fortifications and improved the capital. One such improvement was the establishment of an imperial academy,
the Tai Xue. Before long more than thirty thousand students were housed
there, with access to a wide-ranging collection of classical texts. Separate
wards were established for foreigners, usually traders from distant lands.
The population soared and in time became nearly half a million, making it
one of the world's largest cities.

By A.D. 33 the civil war was nearing its end, Guangwudi having system-
atically eliminated most of his rivals. This was helped by their individualistic
refusal to unite against him. He was also successful in promoting the idea
that he was chosen by heaven, backing up his claim by spreading news of
prophecies and omens, such as his vision of riding the dragon in the sky.

Bridging the distant western fringes of Chinese influence and the guarded
borders of the Roman empire were Parthia and Bactria. These had been
shaped by Alexander's expansion in earlier centuries, one that had extended
into India. Bactria (today's Afghanistan) was a significant force affecting India at this time. Greek settlements established following Alexander's conquests became independent kingdoms around the middle of the third century B.C. Around the middle of the second century they expanded forcibly
into India, controlling Taxila, the Punjab and Gandhara. In this way Indian
art and craft were influenced by Hellenism through the Asian Greeks. In
Gandhara this led to powerful sculptures, inspired by Hellenism and Buddhism. In the Indus Valley region Bactria established kingdoms where there
was a syncretism of Greek and Indian elements.

Like Bactria, Parthia seceded from Seleucid rule in the mid-third century
B.C. By early in the first century B.C. the Parthian empire included Mesopotamia and extended from Syria to Bactria. Parthia was significant enough to
halt Rome's expansion eastward. The Parthian empire in fact was to last five
hundred years. It gained many economic advantages through controlling the
western end of the Silk Route from China.

Another force was forming at this time, as the Eastern Han dynasty in

China reestablished the Han empire. Nomadic peoples, the Yuezhi or Yueh-chi, were forced westward from the Chinese borders. These Kushans united the other tribes and would soon pass into Bactria, and from there move into northern India, forming Peshawar as a new capital. Like the Parthians, the Kushans would gain wealth from controlling east-west trade routes. They would also facilitate the spread of Buddhism overland via the Silk Route to central Asia and China, just as new trade routes would facilitate the spread of Christianity eastward from the Roman empire to India.

BEYOND THE
ENDS OF THE EARTH

IN THE FIRST CENTURY THE AMERICAS had no contact with the great land-mass made up by Europe, Africa and Asia. It would be many centuries later that explorers established sea routes between them. Settlements and cultures in the Americas had developed independently of the rest of the world ever since nomadic human beings had crossed via the frozen Bering Strait from far northeastern Asia. The Americas perhaps are for the study of the human race what animal species isolated on the Galapagos Islands were for the study of natural development for nineteenth-century biologists. In the Americas the isolated development of civilization, writing and culture is played out in a somewhat parallel way to the civilizations of the Mediterranean, Near East and China.

The chronology of civilizations in Central and South America has been very difficult to determine. Archaeologists and historians have used a combination of radiocarbon dating, a study of the strata of archaeological remains and the systems of chronology, where known, to try to determine dates.[1] It is impossible to know in deep antiquity in the Americas what was happening in a particular year such as A.D. 33, especially at the level of individual people and notable historical events. It is possible only to give the most general picture of the early part of the first century. This differs markedly from what we know of events within the Roman empire for instance in A.D. 33, where what happened on a number of particular days can be known in some detail. For most people in the Americas the pattern of life had changed very little over thousands of years.

Human beings first reached North America from Siberia perhaps as long ago as thirty thousand years. There was then a land bridge across the Bering Strait.[2] Hunters searched for food in northern forests and steppe areas. In time, fishermen were at work harvesting the north Atlantic. Because of the wealth of food in North America and the small population, settled agricultural society only developed in scattered places. Agricultural settlements slowly began to the south as some groups became sedentary. With increasing settlement came the beginnings of higher cultures—for example the development of burial and temple mound cultures on the basins of the Ohio and lower Mississippi. In most areas, however, hunting and gathering persisted. The enormous river basin of the Mississippi, between the Appalachians and the Rockies, proved to be an ideal habitat for more settled agricultural communities.

As people penetrated further into the vast continent, some eventually made their way through Central into South America. By the first century, in the Mexican highland, the sacred city of Teotihuacán was close to becoming one of the world's main population centers, in a class with Rome, Athens, Alexandria in Egypt, and Luoyang in Han China. It eventually may have become the sixth largest city in the world. Teotihuacán was located in the northeastern part of the Basin of Mexico, a plateau over six thousand feet high, the height creating a temperate climate.

Archaeological work over the last century has uncovered a great deal about the structure and life of this once-great city.[3] Teotihuacán became established as a new religious center about the time of Christ. The city had developed over the previous two centuries, but little is understood of these early stages. In the first two centuries A.D. there was a huge burst of construction, when Teotihuacán quickly became larger and more populous than any other settlement in the Americas. Its urban complexity and social organization seem to have been linked to its popular religious system. Its influence gradually spread all over the area between North and South America. The name "Teotihuacán" was used of the city several centuries after its sudden fall. Its original name is unknown, as is the language or languages used by its population and the ethnic groups who built the city.

Cutting through the city dramatically was a thoroughfare called by archaeologists "The Avenue of the Dead," more than 1.2 miles in length. The river San Juan, which had been modified into a canal, intersected it. At its peak, the city may have had as many as two thousand apartment compounds surrounded by high walls. The city was dominated by huge monuments with religious significance, mainly concentrated in its northern sector. The Avenue of the Dead led to the west-facing Sun Pyramid, the dominant pyramid in the north of the city. An associate Moon Pyramid was also important. In the south of the city the Feathered Serpent Pyramid dominated other structures. This featured large sculpted heads. Also in the south city was the Ciudadela ("Citadel") and the Great Compound, which may have enclosed the city's principal marketplace. Excavations, which are still in process, have made it clear that Teotihuacán was the largest and most highly planned center of religious ceremony in the Americas. It is possible that in the early first century, Teotihuacán was already in contact with many other centers in the region between North and South America—Mesoamerica. Trading systems were developing in Mesoamerica, and Teotihuacán was establishing economic, political and religious communication with many regional centers far beyond the Basin of Mexico. It eventually controlled the production and supply, throughout Central America, of obsidian—a semi-precious stone also used ornamentally for carvings.

It may have been as early as 15,000 B.C. that humans arrived in the Andes region of South America. An Andean civilization eventually developed that spread along the western coast and then inland into the high Andes, penetrating regions of what are now called Peru, Ecuador, Bolivia and northern Chile. Because this civilization persisted over centuries and was marked by outstanding technological and artistic achievements, it is referred to as a single, Andean, civilization.

In the Peruvian areas many ancient cultures were found. Here the cultures of Nazca and Moche were significant. The Moche culture centered on the northern coast of Peru and grew by means of aggressive military conquest. Its distinctive temples were built of solid adobe brick. Artifacts and ruins from the area suggest that Moche was a military state using irrigated agriculture in arable valleys. In the first century Moche was establishing itself as the dominant civilization of the area, a dominance that was to last until the eighth century A.D.

The name comes from the chief city or capital, Moche, which was built in the river valley of the same name. Moche settlements extended along the coast for more than 215 miles. Excavations of the capital have found two immense structures, given the names "The Temple of the Sun" and "The Temple of the Moon," though their Moche names are not known. The Temple of the Sun was a causeway and stepped pyramid. Nearby, the Temple of the Moon was a terraced platform built against a natural hillside. There is evidence that it had large rooms and courtyards. Remains of crowded buildings surrounding the temples indicate that Moche was a city as well as a religious center. Elaborate tombs have been found in the extensive coastal area of Moche settlement.

The Moche people utilized the copious streams that flowed down from the Andes into an extensive system of canals that were used to irrigate crops of corn (maize), beans and other produce. An abundance of urban centers were supported by this intensive agriculture. Political authority was fragmented, however, with each river valley being relatively independent, having its thread of towns and villages, with its own royals and warrior priests. The Moche crafted fine pottery that portrayed animals, plants, buildings, demonic beings and fantasy figures, and, in a later period, heads of real people. Painted scenes on some vessels pictured ceremonial and everyday life. Images included human sacrifice and ritual drinking of the victim's blood.

Another longstanding culture important in the first century was based on the southern coast of what is now Peru. It is named the Nazca, after the Nazca Valley where it was found, but it encompassed other important valleys in the region. Nazca pottery was simply prepared, but was polychromic and could employ four or more colors. The people, animals, birds, fish and plants portrayed were distinctly stylized and symbolic. Features from Nazca's religious beliefs and mythology were used in the design of the pottery, and it is likely that the representations of humans and natural beings had religious significance.

The Nazca culture is most famous today for its so-called Nazca lines, which have a great imaginative attraction. They became obvious with the advent of flight, for they are not visible as meaningful shapes from ground level. The lines are large "geoglyphs," vast drawings etched onto the earth's surface. There are figures of fish, monkeys, birds, a whale, spiders and plants. Some of the figures extend twelve miles. The line art is found on the ground over more than eight hundred miles. The purpose of the geo-drawings has been lost, but it is thought to be related to the economy and beliefs of the Nazca. Anthropologist Johan Reinhard argues that the drawings reflect a belief that mountain gods protected humans and controlled the weather.[4] They were associated with lakes, rivers and the sea, and thus influenced water sources and fertility of the land. The flow of water was of immense significance for human life and survival. It is astounding that the Nazca were able to draw such accurate representations of natural forms over these vast areas. Even if sophisticated templates were used, the creation of the figures

was an extraordinary communal effort, taking hundreds of years and involving many people. The Nazca lines are another of the mysteries of these
times. Perhaps they are mysteries to us because we have grown so far away
from the people who walked the earth then.

JERUSALEM

SIMON PETER

THE BIRTH OF THE CHURCH
(PENTECOST, MAY 24)

THE CONVICTION THAT JESUS HAD RETURNED FROM DEATH, which required a paradigm shift in the perception of the disciples, was not the whole story of what ignited the church's expansion. To find this final factor, we have to go back to the group of 120 disciples who were gathered expectantly after Jesus' departure—his ascension. They were not sure what they were waiting for. According to the account in the Gospel of John, the evening before his death Jesus had said that after he had gone a spiritual Paraclete (the Comforter or Helper) would come. This was to be the presence of God, not in visible, human form, as in Jesus, but as the mysterious Holy Spirit. There were, it is true, glimpses in the Scriptures that they knew so well of the Spirit of God descending upon individuals so that they prophesied, sometimes ecstatically, giving instruction or warning to those who had set themselves apart to follow God and to live holy lives in the commonplace world of work, meals, family life and celebration. But what Jesus had promised, they realized, was not a peripatetic spirit but a permanent presence that would be the secret life of the church and would persist until Christ returned at the end of the age.

After centuries of Christian theology, working out the relationship of Trinity in the divine being—Father, Son and Holy Spirit, it is difficult for us today to imagine what those 120 people expected. What is clear is that their expectations and knowledge would have been based on the Jewish Scriptures and varieties of interpretation around at the time. Most important to them, of course, was Jesus' own interpretation of the Scriptures. He had claimed that he was equal with God as Son of his Father, according to the Gospel accounts.[1] To the two disciples on the road to Emmaus, he had pointed out his presence in the Scriptures in terms of allusion and prophecy, so that they saw the sacred writings with new eyes (Luke 24:13-35; Mark 16:12-13). With the promise of the coming presence of the Holy Spirit, a further member of the Godhead was introduced. The monotheism of true Jewish belief was much more complex and many-layered than the interpretations of Scripture allowed by Pharisees, Sadducees, Essenes and other groups. Given this, however, the Holy Spirit was not an alien concept in their Scriptures. Philo, a contemporary, identified the Spirit of God in the Scriptures with knowledge (following his Platonic orientation, which denigrates the value of the material world and the body [see his *On the Giants* 5-7]).

It may be that the idea of the Spirit of God was seen by many at the time as tied up with the central Jewish scriptural idea of humanity being in the image of God, so that the coming of the Holy Spirit would be a radical factor in the restoration of that image in a pure inward and outer human life, hence the link to baptism in the idea of a baptism of the Holy Spirit.

However it was understood, this mysterious, spiritual factor is unavoidably part of the causality of the birth and dynamic expansion of the church in its first generation, taking it up to Nero's pogrom of Christians in the 60s of that first century. The other main factor was the conviction that Jesus had risen from the dead in bodily form. Through this initial generation the church would remain centered in Jerusalem and be predominantly Jewish, though the number of Gentile believers steadily rose through the missionary activities of the apostle Paul and others.

The coming of the Holy Spirit is recorded precisely in the book of Acts as the beginning of the Feast of Pentecost, which in A.D. 33 was Sunday, May 24. At a particular location, probably the Upper Room in Jerusalem, and at a specific time, early in the morning of that day, the Spirit came and remained. Something mysterious and yet real entered the spectacle of world history. Can this mysterious something be recounted as a part of the history of this year? Luke, thought by many scholars to be the author of the book of Acts in the New Testament, attempted, he says, a historical description based on accounts he had gathered from among those assembled in that room.[2]

> When the day of Pentecost arrived, they were all together in one place. And suddenly there came from heaven a sound like a mighty rushing wind, and it filled the entire house where they were sitting. And divided tongues as of fire appeared to them and rested on each one of them. And they were all filled

with the Holy Spirit and began to speak in other tongues as the Spirit gave them utterance. (Acts 2:1-4)

The coming was marked by wind (breath) and fire, traditional emblems of the Spirit, and also by a healing of the separation of human languages at Babel. The new "babble" was understandable to those who spoke the foreign languages of the Jewish Diaspora, as the anointed disciples were soon to discover. The coming marked the healing of the barriers of ethnicity, gender, culture and social standing, as the apostle Paul was to point out in his letters to the cosmopolitan churches in Ephesus and Galatia. In other words, the pouring out of the Holy Spirit was seen as a sign by the New Testament writers that God's kingdom was now inaugurated. The early Christians, who did not even have this name in A.D. 33, but were known as "followers of the Way," believed that the coming of the Holy Spirit was the culmination of Christ's life, death, resurrection and ascension.

Many scholars are doubtful that we have a clear idea of what the earliest Christians believed, preferring to conjecture that later Christian developments were anachronistically projected back to that period of the initial expansion. Other scholars have instead embarked on a fruitful examination of the book of Acts in its historical, geographical and sociopolitical context.[3]

It was significant that the coming of the Holy Spirit occurred at Pentecost, also known as the Feast of Weeks, so called because it occurred fifty days after Passover. This was a major festival in the practice of Jewish belief. The holiday was established to celebrate the wheat harvest. In particular, the feast celebrated the first produce of the Promised Land after the return there from slavery in Egypt by the Hebrews. In some Jewish traditions it was also linked with the giving of the ancient law and the renewal of the covenant between the people and God. The celebration of a new kind of harvest and covenant renewal was about to be instituted, taking in the old thanksgiving.

◆ ◆ ◆

So it was that a noisy and large group of men and women emerged from the Upper Room and on to the busy early morning streets of Jerusalem, making their way up to the temple courts. The city was teeming with pilgrims there to celebrate the feast. The crowds they passed or who were also heading toward the temple were astonished to find that in the babble of voices they heard familiar languages. Some, however, simply mocked and said that the noisy Galilean group had been drinking. The pilgrims, as usual, were from across the Jewish Diaspora, from Bactria and Parthia in the east to Libya and Rome in the west. Several languages other than the usual Koine Greek and Aramaic were therefore filling the air. The first expression of the new church as a body of people was not a Sunday-suited one.

The Diaspora of Jewish communities was widespread at this time. They had been established in almost every part of the civilized world, from Spain in the west to India in the east. There were few major cities or regions that did not have a community of Jews in residence. These communities reflected a spectrum of Judaism from strictly orthodox to more Hellenized forms, and all looked to the temple in Jerusalem and the festivals associated with it as definitive for their identities. Whether communities were in Palestine or in the wider world, they were shaped by their social and political context. Pilgrims would travel great distances to attend major feasts such as Pentecost. The Diaspora had initially begun through deportations by conquerors of Palestine (for instance, to Babylonia where, after the period of exile, many chose to remain) but later many people voluntarily migrated. These communities played an active role in society and culture. Interestingly, during the reign of Nero a high priestess of the imperial cult, Julia Severa, built a synagogue for the Jewish community in Acmonia, located in Phrygia Pacatiana, in Asia Minor, and now known as Ahat-Keui. It lay on the road between Dorylaeum and Philadelphia.[4]

Luke records pilgrims at the festival who were "Parthians and Medes and Elamites and residents of Mesopotamia, Judea and Cappadocia, Pontus and Asia, Phrygia and Pamphylia, Egypt and the parts of Libya belonging to Cyrene, and visitors from Rome, both Jews and proselytes, Cretans and Arabians" (Acts 2:9-11). It was a kind of catalog of nations, perhaps deliberately harking back to the list of nations separated on earth after the curse of Babel in the Scriptures (Genesis 11). All these, says Luke, recognized their own native languages (except for the cynics, who interpreted the sound of these languages as gobbledygook, the result of too much wine).

When the disciples reached the bustling temple court, packed with thousands of pilgrims, Simon Peter began to speak, his voice booming confidently.[5] His usual Galilean dialect, which people from other territories sometimes found hard to make out, had smoothed out temporarily into a clear and distinct voice.

Peter's speech in the book of Acts is quite lengthy and, so near the beginning of Luke's account of the genesis of the church, signals that his narrative belongs to the genre of ancient history. This structuring may have been for the benefit of the person to whom the book is addressed, one "most excellent Theophilus," evidently a high-ranking Roman official and a Gentile, who would be familiar with the genre (Luke 1:3). Acts is distinct from the four Gospel narratives, even though it is part two of one of them— the Gospel of Luke. The Gospels belong to the genre of ancient biography (although it could be argued that biography is a form of history).[6] Peter's speech is one of several recorded in Acts. As is characteristic of ancient histories, the gist of important speeches is recorded, but in the style of the speaker and reflecting the occasion of the speech. The accounts may be based on notes taken from the recollections of those who heard the speeches—in a predominantly oral culture, retention of speeches was high (presumably so long as speakers employed the rhetorical devices of the time effectively!).

Peter's speech was a successful and direct piece of communication, explaining why the large group of men and women was so excited, why they were miraculously speaking in a number of recognizable languages, who Jesus of Nazareth was, and accusing those who had unjustly executed Jesus just a few weeks before.

For Peter the languages spoken in the Spirit were a sign that needed explanation. In doing so he cites scriptural passages, interestingly including one from the prophet Joel that links to the eclipse of the moon, with its blood-red appearance, on the day of Jesus' crucifixion, just over seven weeks previously (April 3). The passage also refers to the darkening of the sun and seismic activity. All these features would have been in the recent memory of many in the listening crowd (Acts 2:19-21; Joel 2:28-32).

Peter, furthermore, with typical directness, apportioned blame for Jesus' death. In doing this he referred to the recent event of the crucifixion, while standing less than half a mile from where the event took place. "Jesus of Nazareth . . . you crucified and killed by the hands of lawless [wicked] men" (Acts 2:22-23).

On the face of it, Peter seems unclear whether "lawless men" refers to the Jewish leaders or to the Roman administration, but his Jewish audience probably would have understood it to mean the Romans. He spreads the moral guilt for Jesus' execution between the civic and temple leaders of Jerusalem, the mob who, notoriously, howled for Jesus' blood, and Pilate.[7] This is made even more explicit after Peter and John were arrested and brought before the Jewish Council, probably a few weeks later. Peter on that later occasion prayed after that interrogation, "there were gathered together against your holy servant Jesus, whom you anointed, both Herod and Pontius Pilate, along with the Gentiles and the peoples of Israel" (Acts 4:27). It is not true, as some have said, that the Gospels are anti-Semitic, blaming Jesus' death on the Jews (seeking to justify persecution of Jewish people). This is patently absurd, as the church for its first generation was predominantly Jewish. Peter's comment helps to balance out a text that historically has been wrongly used as a basis for anti-Semitism, where the mob, crying for Christ's crucifixion, called upon his blood to be on them and on their children (Matthew 27:25).[8]

Peter summarizes his speech in a powerful conclusion: "Let all the house of Israel therefore know for certain that God has made him both Lord and Christ, this Jesus whom you crucified" (Acts 2:36). His final focus, according the account in Acts, evokes a massive response from the crowds in the temple courts, as around three thousand become disciples.[9] This dramatic number of conversions indicated what would follow in the weeks, months and years ahead, as "the Way" spread geographically through the empire and beyond to Parthia, Bactria and India, and socially from slaves to the Roman upper classes. Some scholars have been skeptical of this number of conversions, but the figure (obviously rounded) does correspond with the remarkable expansion and spread of Christianity during this period. Furthermore, the population of Jerusalem was greatly swollen by pilgrims.

As that first day of Pentecost passed and the momentous events associated with Christ's death became more distant, what seemed in effect a group within Judaism had to structure itself. Its members were Jews or Jewish proselytes and included Hellenized Jews. They would continue to practice their beliefs as any Jew would, attending the synagogues and using the temple as a kind of giant synagogue, a place for prayer and teaching. Yet they also met in large houses, where there were facilities for preparing what was an essential feature of their congregation—the shared meal. It may be that the Upper Room, where Peter and John had been able to prepare the pre-Passover meal the day before Jesus' death, which became known as "the Lord's Supper," was the model for their gatherings. This pattern was universal for Christian gatherings across the empire and beyond, as there does not appear to have been any formal basilica or church building until the fourth century, when Christianity became the official Roman religion, supplanting emperor worship and the veneration of gods. Before the fourth century, however, houses were adapted internally and unobtrusively to function as meeting places. Robin Lane Fox suggests that "it was through the household and the house church that Christianity and its other-worldly 'assembly' first put down its roots, then grew to undermine the old civic values and the very shape of the pagan city."[10] Meetings of Christian worship in the home would have been patterned on the synagogue, with prayer and hearing the Jewish Scriptures read and expounded. It also featured a "love feast," where followers of the new faith would eat and share food together. Baptism in water was an important initiation rite for new converts. In the Jerusalem church, the temple precincts were used as a place of prayer and teaching. The Psalms and other parts of the Scriptures, such as the Torah and the Prophets, would have been interpreted in the light of belief that Jesus was the Messiah promised in the Scriptures. There was also, evidently, a kind of hymn singing in addition to the psalms. Some later passages in the letters of the apostles to various churches may reflect or hint at early liturgies used in worship, and perhaps sung. One such possible passage is the closing of the letter of James (who was associated with the church in Jerusalem). An ancient document from the end of the first century and called the *Didache* may reflect church order and discipline in early church congregations.

Many of the three thousand converts, as they were pilgrims, would have soon returned to their homes throughout the Roman empire and eastward to Parthia and perhaps even to Bactria as well as nearer to Galilee. Therefore, within weeks of Jesus' great commission, the news about what had happened to him was starting to spread far and wide. But there were also many new disciples who lived in Jerusalem and its satellite villages or who chose to remain in the city. In concise terms, Luke describes the aftermath of Pentecost and the early weeks of the fledgling church: "They devoted themselves to the apostles' teaching and fellowship, to the breaking of bread and the prayers. . . . All who believed were together and had all things in common . . . selling their possessions and belongings and distributing the proceeds to all, as any had need" (Acts 2:42, 44-45). Luke adds that daily they attended the temple together and met in their homes.

Luke's brief words encapsulate the characteristics of the new community: it is confessional, immersing itself in the narrative and doctrinal teaching of the Twelve, burning hot in its formation; it is voluntarily communitarian (clearly not an oxymoron in A.D. 33), directed to social welfare and care; it meets daily in the temple courts and in some of the larger houses of disciples, presumably in the afternoon, after working hours; and it is recognizable in its celebration of the Lord's Supper, the Eucharist, in its worship and its prayer. Its spontaneous primitive form, in the days, weeks and months after Pentecost, was to be seen in later centuries by reforming and revivalist movements in the church as an ideal to be restored. It is worth observing that the communitarianism of the early church is not ideological; that is, property is not the integrating factor. Rather, the importance of property is relative in relation to the law of love, based on Jesus' famous command to his disciples to love one's neighbor. This radical sharing of food and property was echoed in a contemporary sect called the Essenes, a group that had a monastic community at Qumran (made famous by the discovery of the Dead Sea Scrolls in 1947).

The social impact of the new church is elaborated further in Luke's narrative, as some months have passed. One person, who becomes an important figure in the early church, is recorded as selling a field and giving the proceeds to the common purse. This was Barnabas, cousin of John Mark. As mentioned earlier, the Upper Room, which figured so prominently in the events leading up to Christ's death and the weeks following it, may have been in John Mark's home. Luke tells of the experiment in voluntary communitarianism, which was based on the practice of the band of disciples, men and women, who had followed Jesus in Galilee over the three years before his death. This is to prepare the way for his account of a couple who chose to deceive the church, with dire consequences:

> Now the full number of those who believed were of one heart and soul, and no one said that any of the things that belonged to him was his own, but they had everything in common. . . . There was not a needy person among them, for as many as were owners of lands or houses sold them and brought the proceeds of what was sold and laid it at the apostles' feet, and it was distributed to each as any had need. (Acts 4:32, 34-35)

The extraordinary sequel tells of a wealthy city couple, Ananias and Sapphira, who sell property and cynically keep back some of the proceeds. They give the remainder to the church, pretending that it is the complete amount. The event is a significant test of the integrity of the new movement. The outcome is that the couple are, in the view of the book of Acts, divinely judged for their action in a way that makes it clear that their deaths are not coincidental. This is church discipline of an extraordinary and terrifying kind, as Luke points out, but, importantly, not administered by its leaders. They of course had no legal power to punish any such wrongdoing. The wrong, Peter made clear, was not in holding back some of the money. The couple were entitled to this, and even to the whole amount. The giving to the church was voluntary. What was insidious was the compromising deceit, presumably to buy standing and prestige in the church. Peter (who would have been aware that Jesus had described him on one occasion as the agent of the prince of darkness over a particular matter) pointed out to Ananias,

> Why has Satan filled your heart to lie to the Holy Spirit and to keep back for yourself part of the proceeds of the land? While it remained unsold, did it not remain your own? And after it was sold, was it not at your disposal? Why is it that you have contrived this deed in your heart? You have not lied to men but to God. (Acts 5:3-4)

As well as this important internal moral conflict in the new church, it faced continuous opposition from the civic and temple leaders, as Jesus Christ had done earlier in the year. This opposition did not have a figure like Jesus to focus on, with his witty retorts and devastating demolition of their sly, incriminating questions. It soon became clear to the authorities, however, who the leaders of the troublesome movement were. The inner core of the original twelve disciples who had surrounded Jesus, Galileans all of them, had become the main leaders of the new church—Peter, John, James and Andrew. Peter and John particularly were much in evidence around Jerusalem. According to Luke, they practiced signs and wonders reminiscent of Jesus, such as the healing of a lame man at the Beautiful Gate soon after the Feast of Pentecost. They uttered stinging words of accusation about the crucifixion of Jesus that undermined the standing of the city and religious leaders. It was not surprising, then, that opposition continued.

The crippled beggar used to squat each day at the Beautiful Gate of the temple. The book of Acts tells us that Peter healed the man as Peter entered the gate with John. The beggar, overjoyed with his new mobility, went with them into the temple courts where Peter addressed the astonished crowd. This is a second major speech recorded by Luke, in the fashion of ancient histories. As he spoke, Peter reminded them that they had denied Jesus his life "in the presence of Pilate" in favor of a known murderer (Barabbas). He and John, he said, were witnesses that God had raised him to life. Jesus' "name—by faith in his name—has made this man strong whom you see and know, and the faith that is through Jesus has given the man this perfect health in the presence of you all" (Acts 3:16). Interestingly, Peter added, pointing out how Jesus' death was all in God's plan to save humanity, "I know that you acted in ignorance, as did also your rulers." Here he echoed Jesus' dying words, perhaps related to him by John, "Father, forgive them, for they know not what they do." As a result of this sensational event and its impact, and Peter's driving speech, Peter and John were arrested by the temple guards. The authorities had become increasingly disturbed by the apostles' teaching, and particularly their teaching that Jesus had returned from the dead. Proclaiming such a triumph subverted their recent hard work in displaying Jesus publicly as an abject failure—a would-be messiah hanging shamefully on a Gentile cross. The two were detained overnight. Next day they were questioned by Annas, Caiaphas the high priest and others. Examining the two confirmed the worst fears of the religious leaders, according to the author of Acts. Because they could not deny that the lame beggar was now standing beside them, they were forced to release Peter and John with a threat to keep quiet. The opposition that faced Jesus had started to transfer to his followers, particularly the apostles and leaders. Josephus, the Jewish historian, records the tragic consequences of this opposition some years later (A.D. 62) in the death of Jesus' brother, James, the leader of the Jerusalem church, an execution instigated by the high priest Ananus (Annas the younger), son of Annas and brother of Caiaphas, former high priest. Josephus reveals that the act received widespread condemnation among influential people in Jerusalem.

> Ananus . . . assembled the sanhedrim of judges, and brought before them the brother of Jesus, who was called Christ, whose name was James, and some others; and when he had formed an accusation against them as breakers of the law, he delivered them to be stoned: but as for those who seemed the most equitable of the citizens, and such as were the most uneasy at the breach of the laws, they disliked what was done; they also sent to the king [Agrippa], desiring him to send to Ananus that he should act so no more, for that what he had already done was not to be justified; nay, some of them went also to meet Albinus [Roman procurator], as he was upon his journey from Alexandria, and informed him that it was not lawful for Ananus to assemble a sanhedrim without his consent. Whereupon Albinus complied with what they said, and wrote in anger to Ananus, and threatened that he would bring him to punishment for what he had done; on which king Agrippa took the high priesthood from him, when he had ruled but three months.[11]

ROME

AGRIPPINA

SUNDAY, OCTOBER 18

SPARE A THOUGHT FOR AGRIPPINA, granddaughter of Augustus, widow of the great Germanicus (named after his military service in Germania) and mother of nine children, including the future emperor Gaius Caligula. Agrippina died of starvation on October 18 in exile on the tiny island of Pandateria, west of Italy. Whether the starvation was voluntary or induced on Tiberius's command we do not know, but murder is plausible. Of the six of her children who survived infancy and childhood, only four survived her. Two sons had been murdered in prison, one—Drusus Caesar—gnawing at the straw of his mattress in hunger just months before. Nero Caesar had died in A.D. 31 in a dungeon in Rome's Palatine. Her husband, Germanicus, may have been poisoned to clear the route to the throne of Tiberius's son Drusus. Agrippina certainly believed so. Of the four children still alive on this autumn day in A.D. 33, Caligula became renowned for his inventive cruelty and terrifying unpredictability, eventually and inevitably being assassinated. His sister, Agrippina the Younger, mothered the future emperor Nero, the antichrist of the young church. Later she married her elderly uncle, the emperor Claudius, whom she poisoned to gain Nero's succession.

Agrippina was a person of fierce will and ambition, particularly on behalf of her politically vulnerable children. She was ruled by strong moral principles and suffered intensely during the forty or so years of her life. Her sufferings were undeserved, one of many examples of blatant injustice, even though she lacked the insight to avoid danger in the Roman jungle. On his deathbed Germanicus was reported to have urged his wife, in vain as it turned out, to "lay aside her intractable temper" to avoid conflict in Rome.

The day of her death happened to coincide with the second anniversary of the execution of Sejanus. This was not lost on Tiberius, with his heightened and compulsive awareness of dates and numbers. In response to the end of the woman he loathed, he set up an annual holiday for October 18, devoted to Jupiter. He was worshiped as the god of rain, storms, thunder and lightning, perhaps a grim joke to allude to Agrippina's temperament.

Agrippina was the youngest daughter of Marcus Vipsanius Agrippa, a close friend of Augustus, and of Julia, the daughter of the emperor. Augustus was particularly attached to her. She was born some time before 12 B.C., and married Tiberius's nephew, Germanicus, by whom she had the nine children. In his old age the emperor Augustus proudly included the two oldest, Nero and Drusus, in the royal box during games. Agrippina was admired as fulfilling classical ideals. One eminent Victorian scholar described her as

> gifted with great powers of mind, a noble character, and all the moral and physical qualities that constituted the model of a Roman matron: her love for her husband was sincere and lasting, her chastity was spotless, her fertility was a virtue in the eyes of the Romans, and her attachment to her children was an eminent feature of her character. She yielded to one dangerous passion, ambition.[1]

Tacitus describes her as rather excitable, and prone to being imperious.[2]

Agrippina's mother, Julia, married her stepbrother Tiberius at the instigation of Augustus, and there was no love lost between the unhappy couple. It was a marriage of political convenience. Julia was eventually banished to the island of Pandateria by Augustus, due to her sexual activities. Agrippina was never to see her mother again, only to be incarcerated on the same island. On Tiberius' orders, Julia was starved to death. Agrippina was to share her mother's fate. Perhaps Agrippina reminded Tiberius of her mother, Julia, whom he despised, accounting in part for his obsessive antipathy to his step-daughter, who was also his adoptive daughter-in-law.

When the emperor Augustus died in A.D. 14, Agrippina was on the Lower Rhine with Germanicus, who commanded the legions there. It was very unusual for Roman wives to accompany their husbands in a theater of potential war. Convention expected them to stay at home. The soldiers devoted to Germanicus were dissatisfied with Tiberius's accession and made known their intention of proclaiming their idol, Germanicus, as Princeps of the state. Because the new emperor feared the popularity of Germanicus and intensely loathed Agrippina, the intention of the troops put the two in grave peril. Germanicus and Agrippina saved themselves by acting immediately and effectively. Backed up by his wife, Germanicus quelled the outbreak and threw his troops into a rigorous offensive against the German barbarians east of the Rhine.

Although the campaign achieved successes for the Roman legions, they were exhausted by the difficult terrain and other hardships. They often faced the threat of ambush by bands of Germans. In time a rumor gathered that a large force of Germans was approaching the Roman defense at the River Rhine in order to invade west into Gaul. Part of the Roman army under Caecina—who had thrust eastward into enemy territory—was in retreat before the threat, heading for the Rhine and safety. Germanicus was absent at this time, leaving Agrippina and their children behind. In panic, those in command proposed to destroy the bridge over the Rhine. Had the bridge been crippled, the retreat of Caecina's army would have been cut off. It was only the firm resistance of Agrippina to such a cowardly measure that saved the bridge. When the retreating troops approached, Agrippina went to the bridge. Acting as a general would, she received the soldiers as they crossed it. She presented clothes to the wounded among them and personally gave them everything necessary to relieve their wounds. Tacitus records "that brave woman [Agrippina] took on the duties of a general throughout those days. . . . It is said that . . . she stood at the front of the bridge and gave thanks and praise to the returning legions."

Tiberius recalled Germanicus from the north. The children all took part in his triumphal parade in May. Later that year, A.D. 17, Tiberius transferred him to Asia Minor, giving him a special command (*maius imperium,* "greater power") to settle affairs there. Agrippina and the children accompanied her husband. It was in the east that the couple came under the baleful influence of Gnaeus Calpurnius Piso and his wife Munatia Plancina. Piso was the new governor of Syria and had been elected to his post by the Senate at Tiberius's instigation (some governors were chosen by the Senate and others directly by the emperor). It seems that Tiberius was behind the appointment; he may have wanted Piso to keep his eye on Germanicus as potential heir to the Princeps. Piso seemed determined to insult Germanicus, perhaps reflecting Tiberius's attitude to his adopted son. One task of Germanicus's was to travel to Armenia. Here he established the popular Zeno as king, who was acceptable to the neighboring Parthians. Most of Cappadocia was established as a new Roman province, and it proved a lucrative source of revenues. Tensions between Germanicus and Piso were revealed when the former visited Syria late in A.D. 18. At a banquet given by Aretas, king of the Nabateans, Piso was given a smaller gold crown than his rival. In disgust Piso threw his gift to the floor, saying that the occasion suited a king of Parthia more than a Roman prince.

Tacitus writes of another event which evoked Tiberius's anger and no doubt incensed Piso and Munatia Plancina:

> Germanicus set out for Egypt to study its antiquities. His ostensible motive however was solicitude for the province. He reduced the price of corn by opening the granaries, and adopted many practices pleasing to the multitude. He would go about without soldiers, with sandalled feet, and appareled after the Greek fashion, in imitation of Publius Scipio, who, it is said, habitually did the same in Sicily, even when the war with Carthage was still raging. Tiberius having gently expressed disapproval of his dress and manners, pronounced a very sharp censure on his visit to Alexandria without the emperor's leave, contrary to the regulations of Augustus.[3]

Germanicus died in the east, in Antioch, in A.D. 19. The circumstances evoked suspicions that he had been murdered, and it may be that Piso and Munatia Plancina did away with him to please Tiberius, who wished his natural son Drusus rather than the adopted Germanicus to inherit the throne of Rome. Marks on the corpse, such as foam around the mouth, suggested poisoning. It was generally believed that the immensely popular and affable Germanicus would have become emperor, especially as Augustus had arranged his adoption by Tiberius for this purpose. Agrippina herself was certain that Tiberius's mark was on her husband's death.

Agrippina returned to Italy with her children and Germanicus's ashes. She stayed some days at the island of Corcyra (Corfu) to overcome her grief. It was then but a short voyage to Brundusium (modern Brindisi) on the Italian mainland. There she disembarked, accompanied by two of her children, and gripping in her arms the urn holding the ashes. When news spread of her arrival, the harbor, the walls and even the roofs of the houses were filled by crowds anxious to see and to greet her. The widow was solemnly received by the officers of two praetorian cohorts, which the emperor had dispatched to Brundusium to accompany her in honor to Rome. (With the threat of Germanicus's succession removed, Tiberius could afford to be generous with his honor.) The urn containing the ashes of Germanicus was solemnly borne by tribunes and centurions. The funeral procession was received en route by Drusus, Tiberius's son, and by Germanicus's brother Claudius, and lastly, close to Rome, by the consuls, the Senate, and crowds from the capital. Germanicus's ashes were placed reverentially in the Augustan Mausoleum.

Piso, the chief suspect in Germanicus's death, was charged with treason.

The accusation of murdering Germanicus could not be substantiated, but Piso had tried to reenter the province of Syria by force. In the face of this charge, the outcome of which was clear both to him and to his wife Plancina, Piso committed suicide. He had time to prepare a document (perhaps with his wife's help) addressed to Tiberius that was read to the Senate and that helped to acquit Plancina and their children. The rumor passed around that Piso did away with himself in order to avoid revealing Tiberius's complicity in a murder plot. Graffiti appeared all over Rome shouting the words "Rendite nos Germanicum" ("Give Germanicus back to us").

The acquittal of Plancina was a grievous blow to Agrippina, and the two women remained enemies for the rest of their lives. Plancina did not survive long after Agrippina, dying late in A.D. 33. It was said that Tiberius only spared her so as not to give Agrippina the satisfaction of knowing that her enemy was dead. Suetonius records, "Besides Agrippina, Munatia Plancina was slain; up to this time, it would appear, Tiberius, though he hated her (not on account of Germanicus, but for another reason), nevertheless had permitted her to live, in order to prevent Agrippina from rejoicing at her death."

Despite Germanicus's warning, Agrippina did become involved in Roman politics, furthering the cause of her children as heirs over against the claim of Drusus, Tiberius's natural son. The death of Drusus in A.D. 23 brought Agrippina's sons into the direct line of succession. She therefore became the target of attacks by Sejanus, carried on with subtlety. For some years after Germanicus's death Tiberius also concealed his antagonism to Agrippina, but secret accusations and intrigues were soon under way. When she asked the emperor's permission to choose another husband, probably the distinguished and controversial senator Asinus Gallus, Tiberius prevaricated and mentally stored Gallus's name for future condemnation. Tiberius probably saw Agrippina's request as an attempt to protect her children, vulnerable because of their potential as heirs to the emperor. Tacitus narrates the event, the account of which, he records, came from memoirs of her daughter, Agrippina the Younger (now lost):

> Agrippina in stubborn rage . . . when the emperor came to see her, wept long and silently, and then began to mingle reproach and supplication. She begged him "to relieve her loneliness and provide her with a husband; her youth still fitted her for marriage, which was a virtuous woman's only solace, and there were citizens in Rome who would not disdain to receive the wife of Germanicus and his children." But the emperor, who perceived the political aims of

her request, but did not wish to show displeasure or apprehension, left her, notwithstanding her urgency, without an answer. This incident, not mentioned by any historian, I have found in the memoirs of the younger Agrippina, the mother of the emperor Nero, who handed down to posterity the story of her life and of the misfortunes of her family.[4]

The malice of Sejanus then entered the equation of factors that would destroy Agrippina. He persuaded her that the emperor intended to poison her—a very plausible story. Alarmed, she refused to eat an apple that the emperor offered her from his table. Tiberius in turn was offended at being regarded as a poisoner. Tacitus tells the story:

> Sejanus . . . yet more deeply alarmed the sorrowing and unsuspecting woman by sending his agents, under the guise of friendship, with warnings that poison was prepared for her, and that she ought to avoid her father-in-law's table. Knowing not how to dissemble, she relaxed neither her features nor tone of voice as she sat by him at dinner, nor did she touch a single dish, till at last Tiberius noticed her conduct, either casually or because he was told of it. To test her more closely, he praised some fruit as it was set on the table and passed it with his own hand to his daughter-in-law. This increased the suspicions of Agrippina, and without putting the fruit to her lips she gave it to the slaves. Still no remark fell from Tiberius before the company, but he turned to his mother and whispered that it was not surprising if he had decided on harsh treatment against one who implied that he was a poisoner.[5]

Tiberius's suspicions of Agrippina appear to have been unfounded, but Sejanus eventually had her exiled after the death of Livia, widow of Augustus, who would not have countenanced such an unjust act against her granddaughter.

Shortly after Livia's death a letter from Tiberius emerged, which she may have held back. It accused Agrippina's son Nero of homosexuality with equals, and attacked Agrippina. According to Tacitus, "It contained expressions of studied harshness, yet it was not armed rebellion or a longing for revolution, but unnatural passions and profligacy which the emperor imputed to his grandson. Against his daughter-in-law he did not dare to invent this much; he merely censured her insolent tongue and defiant spirit."[6] The letter was enough, however, to have Nero exiled and soon executed.

Sejanus then had rumors passed around that Agrippina, relying on the good will toward her because of Germanicus's memory, planned to flee from Rome and seek refuge with the army. In A.D. 29 he had her banished to the small island of Pandateria (modern Ventotene), where her mother Julia had died in exile. Her other son, Drusus, was imprisoned in Rome. Agrippina was beaten so badly by a centurion, apparently with the acquiescence of Tiberius, that she lost the sight of one eye.

Her son Drusus was also abused in his prison before being starved, not long before his mother. Tacitus claims that he died "having prolonged life for eight days on the most wretched of food, even chewing the stuffing of his bed." After his death Tiberius vilified him. Spies had noted Drusus's every word and declamation against the emperor in prison, and, said Tacitus, "what seemed most horrible of all, he ordered a daily journal of all that he said and did to be read in public."[7] Even his dying curses against Tiberius were read out to the Senate, including the elaborate "As he had slain a daughter-in-law, a brother's son, and son's sons, and filled his whole house with bloodshed, so might he pay the full penalty due to the name and race of his ancestors as well as to future generations."

The news of Drusus's death may have been communicated to Agrippina. Soon after she refused food, or was denied it on Tiberius's orders, and died the lingering death of starvation. According to both Tacitus and Suetonius, Tiberius boasted of his clemency in not having her strangled and thrown on to the Gemonian Steps.[8] Tacitus believed that, with the downfall of her enemy Sejanus, Agrippina lived in hope for some time that she would be released from her captivity. The death of her friend and lover Asinus Gallus, he thought, might have been a significant factor in her decision to end her life; even so, he considered it likely that suicide was a fiction put about to cover her murder by starvation.[9] The same doubt was raised by the starvation in prison of Gallus.

Gallus had been consul of Rome in 8 B.C. and was noted for his forthright and sometimes tactless speeches in the Senate. Augustus found him too free in what he said, and observed that Gallus wished to be the first man in the Senate but that he had not the talent for it. Tiberius developed a hatred of him, partly because he was so opinionated, but particularly because he had married his former wife, Vipsania, after Augustus had forced him to divorce her in favor of Agrippina's mother, Julia. With Sejanus's collusion, Tiberius had got the Senate to sentence Gallus to death, but kept him alive another three years to make him suffer and perhaps to torment Agrippina. Gallus went hungry for these years of imprisonment before finally starving not long before the woman he had wanted to marry.

The impact of their mother's death on the four surviving children can only be guessed. The notoriety of two of them, Gaius Caligula and Agrippina the Younger, has gone down in history. The latter had married. The two other sisters were married off within the year. These were Livilla and Drusilla. Suetonius records that Tiberius got very near to Rome for the occasion (he would not enter the capital, because of the prophecy he feared): "Tiberius now approached the capital and sojourned in its environs; but he did not go inside the walls, although he was but four miles away, and bestowed in marriage the remaining daughters of Germanicus and of Julia, the daughter of Drusus. Hence the city, on its part, did not hold any festival in honor of their marriages, but everything went on as usual, even the senate convening and deciding judicial cases."

There seemed no end to the family sorrow. Tacitus records that even the citizens of Rome felt grief over the arranged marriage of Julia, who was the daughter of Drusus (and hence Tiberius's niece) and late wife of the unfortunate Nero, son of Agrippina. She was married off to the lower-born Gaius Rubellius Blandus, whose grandfather, Tacitus remarked snobbishly, was remembered by many as a Roman knight from Tibur.[10] Gaius Caligula was also married this year. He had turned twenty-one on August 31, which allowed him to hold a quaestorship, giving him access to the Senate. His marriage, which followed, was an arranged one, to Julia Claudia, linking him to a powerful Roman family. This arrangement was part of an orchestrated build-up to his eventual naming as an official heir of Tiberius.

Tiberius's main concern in the last years of his life was the succession. As with the choice of Augustus's heir, it was not an easy matter. His son Drusus had been dead ten years in A.D. 33. His rival Germanicus, adopted son of Tiberius, was gone, probably poisoned fourteen years before. The unsuitable oldest sons of Agrippina, Nero and Drusus, had been violently removed. The field was now looking rather empty. Tiberius was becoming more and more settled on two young men who seemed the least offensive of the choices. The older was Gaius Caligula, and the younger was Tiberius Gemellus, Tiberius's nephew by Drusus and Livilla (whom, some later thought, might have been sired by Sejanus). Caligula had as strong a claim as any, being Augustus's great-grandson. His marriage to Julia Claudia strengthened the lineage.

Caligula had been taken to Capreae in the early autumn of A.D. 31 for his own safety, while Sejanus was still active. There he experienced court life, and, if the accounts of Tacitus and other later historians are founded in fact, he also witnessed the sexual excesses and banal cruelties of his step-uncle. There too he would have heard news first of the killing of his brother Nero, then of his brother Drusus, and, most crushing of all, the starvation of his mother, Agrippina. It would have been impossible for him in the circumstances to express grief or, worse, anger at the deaths. Tiberius, it seemed, was pleased with his promising protégé. At some stage he famously remarked, "I am nursing a viper in Rome's bosom." It was later remarked that, in Caligula, there was never a better slave or a worse master.

There is a later conclusion to the story of the ill-fated and remarkable Agrippina. When emperor, Caligula brought the ashes of his mother and those of his brother Nero from Pandateria and the Pontian islands to Rome, and he struck a number of medals in honor of his mother. In one the head of Caligula is on one side and that of his mother on the other. On one side is a person remembered for her principles and morality, and the injustices perpetrated against her. On the other is someone notorious in history for his cruelties (even in company with hard-to-beat twentieth-century tyrants), though some believe his excesses were the result of madness or a severe illness that struck him during his reign and changed his personality. He would succeed Tiberius in A.D. 37 and reign only four years until he was assassinated before the age of thirty. He saw to it that the other heir established by Tiberius, the unfortunate Gemellus, was eliminated. He also saw the decline and death of his much-loved (and perhaps incestuously abused) sister Drusilla. Truly he was a deadly viper in the bosom of Rome, as Tiberius had predicted.

JERUSALEM

NEW CONFLICT IN JERUSALEM

STEPHEN AND SAUL

MANY MONTHS HAVE PASSED SINCE THE DAY OF PENTECOST. The inhabitants of Jerusalem have grown accustomed to the sight of Peter, John or others of the Twelve, people of the Way, preaching fervently in the temple courts, surrounded by a knot of listeners. Their preferred location is Solomon's Portico, the colonnade on the east side of the vast temple courts, where Jesus had taught just months before. They are not alone in addressing the people. There are other teachers around the courts, each with their own audiences. For not only are the apostles of Christ teaching but, as is customary, also devout scribes, who tend to align with the fundamentalist and conservative Pharisees. But what is distinct about Peter, John, Andrew and the other apostles, according to Luke in Acts, is not only their teaching about Jesus of Nazareth and his resurrection but also their signs and wonders. Relatives and friends of the sick and disabled have even begun putting out cots or mats for them to lie on, in the hope that the healing shadow of Peter might fall on them.

The number of disciples continues to grow, stretching the new church to its limits as the welfare needs of those widowed or too ill or too young to work are met out of the common purse. After the lesson of Judas Iscariot, the purse is administered more carefully. The oft-repeated story of the fate of Ananias and Sapphira continues to overawe both those giving and those receiving, helping to prevent abuses of the remarkable social experiment. The large numbers of people drawn into the community are generally happy, but those who emphatically are not happy are the Pharisees (who normally enjoy a good popularity with the people) and those who predominate in the ruling elite of Jerusalem—the worldly wise Sadducees. Shared concerns about the fast-growing sect bring the old rivals together, the fundamentalists and the secularists, the Pharisees and the Sadducees.

Finally, those associated with the ruling council have had enough. At the instigation of Joseph Caiaphas, the high priest, the chief priests, elders and Pharisee faction have the Twelve arrested. Luke tells of what happens, plausibly basing his account on the recollections of his acquaintances, John Mark and Mark's cousin Barnabas. The young Saul of Tarsus—the future apostle Paul—may also have witnessed these events and told Luke of them. Luke tells of the authorities arresting the apostles and putting them in the public prison. But during the night a mysterious man, an "angel of the Lord," opens the prison doors and brings them out. He says, "Go and stand in the temple and speak to the people all the words of this Life." Obediently, they enter the temple first thing in the morning and begin to teach.

Belief in angels and supernatural beings is common at this period. A mural in Pompeii depicts what may be an angel, complete with iconic wings. A strong messianic strand that is also expectant of the imminent arrival of the end times has a passionate interest in divine messengers and supernatural intervention in the course of human affairs. What is striking about Luke's account is its naturalistic, nonsensational portrayal of such a supernatural intervention, extending even to the description of the angel. Luke seems to imply that while supernatural activities underlie the reality of God's kingdom on earth through the church (the new community of Jesus' followers), such activities are far from apocalyptic events. Life continues firmly in the here and now: the world of work and worship, feeding the poor, teaching, and family and social life.

Meanwhile the high priest arrives at his administrative rooms in the temple complex, with his close associates, and they call together the council once more, sending to the prison to have the apostles brought out. But when the officers arrive they are astonished to find them gone. They return and report back something even stranger: "We found the prison securely locked and the guards standing at the doors, but when we opened them we found no one inside." When the council hear these words, they are at a loss, wondering what this will lead to. Just then someone comes and tells them, "Look! The men whom you put in prison are standing in the temple courts and teaching the people." At this, the captain of the temple, with the guards, goes to bring them, but not by force, as they are afraid of being pelted with stones by the people who have been listening attentively to the preaching of the apostles (Acts 5:18-26).

They set the Twelve before the council. Caiaphas, the high priest, who is ex officio leader, questions them. He begins acidly, very angry, "We strictly charged you not to teach in this name, yet here you have filled Jerusalem with your teaching, and you intend to bring this man's blood upon us." He cannot say the name of Jesus Christ, so angry is he. But Peter and the apostles answer, "We must obey God rather than men. The God of our fathers raised Jesus, whom you killed by hanging him on a cross. God exalted him at his right hand as Leader and Savior, to give repentance to Israel and forgiveness of sins. We are witnesses to these things, and so is the Holy Spirit, whom God has given to those who obey him." Luke, as is the custom with such accounts, gives only the gist of their reply, as is their entitlement as the accused in the religious court.

When they hear this bold reply, many in the council are enraged and want to kill the apostles. At this point, however, a much-respected and distinguished Pharisee on the council stands up and urges caution and coolheadedness. He is named Gamaliel, a teacher of the law who is held in high esteem by all the people.

◆ ◆ ◆

Gamaliel was a liberal Pharisee. His best-known pupil has been famous all the centuries since those far-off days: Saul of Tarsus, better known as the apostle Paul, a man of formidable intellect and learning. At this time Saul's zeal was for the purity of the Pharisees, and he lacked the irenic attitude of his eminent teacher. If he was observing the actions of the council, or was at least in touch with what was happening, Saul would have shared the general outrage against the disciples of Jesus. Gamaliel ordered that the apostles be put outside for a while before he addressed the Sanhedrin. What he said to the assembled council reflected his liberalizing influence and also his devout belief in divine providence, characteristic of the Pharisee party. It also gives a rare insight into the thinking and character of the Pharisees. There was sufficient political realism in what he said also to appeal to the Sadducee majority on the council.

> Men of Israel, take care what you are about to do with these men. For before these days Theudas rose up, claiming to be somebody, and a number of men, about four hundred, joined him. He was killed, and all who followed him were dispersed and came to nothing. After him Judas the Galilean rose up in the days of the census and drew away some of the people after him. He too perished, and all who followed him were scattered. So in the present case I tell you, keep away from these men and let them alone, for if this plan or this

undertaking is of man, it will fail; but if it is of God, you will not be able to overthrow them. You might even be found opposing God! (Acts 5:35-39)

Theudas and Judas were insurrectionists who may have risen up in Galilee in the vacuum after the death of Herod the Great in 4 B.C.[1]

Gamaliel's advice was taken, and the apostles were merely given a sound beating. The Twelve were charged not to speak in the name of Jesus, and released. It was a brief respite from the repression of the temple and civic authorities. The apostles, Luke tells us, continued to teach and exhort every day in the temple courts and in the home meetings that had become an essential feature of church life. The substance of their teaching and preaching, according to Luke, was Jesus as the long-promised Messiah (Acts 5:42), a message still addressed exclusively to Jewish people or to Gentiles who had fully converted to the Jewish religion.

The young church was now suffering from its own speedy success. The growing numbers required the establishment of an infrastructure. The issue had become urgent because the welfare needs of a significant section of the new community were being overlooked. This was a group Luke calls the "Hellenists," in contrast to the main body of "Hebrews." The Hellenists were apparently those believers who had come to Jerusalem from the Jewish dispersion and whose first language was probably Greek rather than Aramaic, and who had adopted Greek customs. As well as the Christian house services, they may well have attended a synagogue or synagogues in the city that used Greek for Scripture reading and prayer rather than the usual Aramaic. (The Scriptures had been translated into Greek between the third and first centuries B.C. in Alexandria.) They were also more likely to be cosmopolitan in their outlook than the more conservative Hebrew Christians. One synagogue in the city is later mentioned by name—that of the Synagogue of the Freedmen. Freedmen were former slaves who had been manumitted or otherwise released. In the recent past large groups of Jewish people had been consigned to slavery as punishment by the Romans, as at the fall of Sepphoris after the rebellion by Judas, following the death of Herod the Great.

In response to this neglect of the needy, particularly widows, among the Hellenist group, the Twelve acted decisively. They knew that they should be giving their full attention to what Christ had charged them to do, that is, to preach and teach using their authority as eyewitnesses who had been with him from the beginning of his own teaching and healing after his baptism by John in about A.D. 29. It would be better to delegate financial and other administrative tasks. Their choice is instructive. They chose seven men who were Hellenists. All their names were Greek, and one was specifically identified as a proselyte—that is, a Gentile convert to Jewish faith. The Twelve would have been aware that this group of men, some of whom would be teaching as well as administering, would not have had the rigidly exclusive views regarding Jewish identity as many of the majority Hebrews in Jerusalem. The decision to appoint these administrators turned out to be an important new phase in the life of the church, which was soon to allow mission to Gentiles. Among the seven was an outstanding and charismatic teacher, Stephen, who would soon make a deep impression on the fervently separatist and antagonistic Pharisee Saul of Tarsus, set to become one of the foremost shapers of world history.

Stephen's powerful reasoning and teaching particularly rankled members of the Synagogue of the Freedmen and other Jews from the countries of the Diaspora now resident in Jerusalem. At the same time the numbers of the followers of Christ swelled, with even "a great many of the priests [becoming] obedient to the faith" (Acts 6:7). At this time the new Christian faith had a wide acceptance in the Jewish community, where it was evidently perceived as part of the variety of Judaism that existed before the cataclysmic fall of Jerusalem in A.D. 70. There was also, of course, opposition, as there had earlier been to the ministry of Jesus. The growth in the early years was mainly in the Jewish communities here and in the Diaspora. To account for the dramatic rise of Christianity by the time of Nero's oppression in the 60s, we should expect the large numbers of conversions recorded in the early chapters of Acts. Stephen seemed to have a profound insight into the way things would go, and the resistance to him by the Hellenists anticipated the later conflicts that the apostle Paul faced on his missionary journeys through Asia Minor and Greece.

The irritation with Stephen developed over a period that probably brings us toward the end of A.D. 33. No one knows the exact date at which Stephen was martyred. The fact that Saul was associated with the proceedings as a young man, fiercely opposed to the new cult of Christ, means that the event clearly took place some time before his conversion. This momentous turnabout was quite likely to have been in A.D. 34, even though the chronology of Paul's life is complex. Pentecost in May A.D. 33 began with a dramatic number of conversions to faith in Christ, and that enormous growth continued, the growth alone affecting strongly those with vested interests in its suppression, that is, most of the civic and religious leaders on the council. It is plausible, therefore, that we are looking at the events only of a few months between Pentecost and the execution of Stephen.

The elimination of the popular leader and speaker began with a plot against him by fellow Hellenists who followed the formula that had been used against Jesus in his Jewish trial. It is possible that Stephen was seen as a dangerous man in terms of the fragility of the status quo upheld by the Jewish authorities, in uneasy partnership with Rome. This time, however, they could not claim that Stephen was seeking political power against Rome, as they had with Jesus. Therefore they had to rely on the limited allowance there was for capital punishment imposed by the Jewish court, relating to the charge of blasphemy. The blasphemy was seen in relation to the temple as the place inhabited by the invisible God. The plot was to show Stephen as a threat to the authority of the temple, which was the foundation of the authority of the Jewish faith and for its political leadership, including all the interest groups within the ruling council.

According to Acts it had proved impossible to defeat Stephen's position by debate and argument. Stephen fluently refuted their objections when they disputed with him in public, to the satisfaction of the listening crowds. In fact, the weak objections fueled the swing to Stephen's faith. His disgruntled opponents secretly instigated distorted legal charges against him. Luke narrates that they set up false charges, such as "We have heard him speak blasphemous words against Moses and God" and "This man never ceases to speak words against this holy place and the law, for we have heard him say that this Jesus of Nazareth will destroy this place and will change the customs that Moses delivered to us" (Acts 6:11, 13-14).

When the charges were brought against Stephen in open court at the council, he was allowed the customary right of reply. This reply is another of the major speeches represented by Luke in digest form in Acts. His speech before the Sanhedrin infuriated the council members, particularly his implication that God was building a new temple not made with human hands (further seeming to imply the transitory nature of the order of Moses). The speech followed a typical pattern of early Christian preaching and teaching, which included stories of Abraham, Joseph and Moses, as befitted a primarily Jewish audience. Stephen surveyed Israel's history from the age of the founding fathers Abraham, Isaac and Jacob onward. His main point was that God's presence is not confined to one holy land or to one sacred spot, such as the temple. His secondary, and biting, theme was that those who recently rejected Jesus follow an all-too-familiar pattern of repudiating messengers from God. The speech before the council represented the themes he had been preaching and teaching in the temple courts, which had provoked his detractors. Stephen's message was more radical than that of the Twelve about the lack of need for the temple order. Interestingly, however, the apostles were evidently entirely happy to let him preach it. They recognized and endorsed his gifted teaching, even if perhaps they did not see the full implications then of what he was saying. According to F. F. Bruce, Stephen "plainly advanced far beyond the position of the Twelve with regard to the traditional Jewish institutions, and saw more clearly the inevitability of a break."[2] Ironically, it would be left to Saul, then a young man seething with anger at Stephen's message, to argue and implement his conclusions. Although he was from the province of Cilicia in Asia Minor, Saul was not, like Stephen, a Hellenist, but a devout Hebrew, a Pharisee of Pharisees, as he later described himself.

Stephen's words were intended to inflame the council, as he was challenging them on a matter of principle, and there was no way that they would change their position, though a minority among them would have favored the accused. They were deeply offended, as they had been by Jesus a few months before. By justifying his view of the redundancy of the temple, Stephen in effect was determining his fate. Not all Hellenists held Stephen's view. Most venerated the temple; its existence was foundational to their Jewish identity. Among these was Philo of Alexandria. On one occasion, quite probably before this year, he made a pilgrimage to the temple in Jerusalem to offer prayers and sacrifice.[3] When Stephen went on to denounce the council for continuing the tradition of rejecting God's messengers, in particular Jesus, events moved swiftly. By implication, he was also accusing them of rejecting his own prophetic witness. He was sentenced to death for blasphemy, which, under the religious jurisdiction of the council court, meant stoning. He was taken outside the city walls, where there were many steep drops and a plentiful supply of rocks for the means of execution. Under religious law those who witnessed against him and who convicted him had to participate in the execution.

The Mishnah, compiled very much later, provides a description of such a procedure.

Four cubits from the place of stoning the criminal is stripped. . . . The drop
from the place of stoning was twice the height of a man. One of the witnesses
pushes the criminal from behind, so that he falls face downward. He is then
turned over on his back. If he dies from this fall, that is sufficient. If not, the
second witness takes the stone and drops it on his heart. If this causes death,
that is sufficient. If not, he is stoned by all the congregation of Israel, as it is
written: 'The hand of the witnesses shall be first against him to put him to
death, and afterward the hand of all the people [Deuteronomy 17:7]."[4]

From Luke's account of the stoning in Acts 7, it is clear that Stephen was
not killed by the initial fall, when he was pushed face forward over a drop,
presumably with his arms bound behind him so that he could not protect
himself from the impact. He stood up after being pushed over the drop (assuming proper procedures were followed). Luke records: "As they were
stoning Stephen, he called out, 'Lord Jesus, receive my spirit.' And falling to
his knees he cried out with a loud voice, 'Lord, do not hold this sin against
them.' And when he had said this, he fell asleep" (Acts 7:59-60). For his account Luke could draw on the eyewitness account of the apostle Paul (originally known as Saul), with whom he later traveled for many years. In fact,
Luke tells us, "The witnesses laid down their garments at the feet of a young
man named Saul. . . . And Saul approved of his execution" (Acts 7:58; 8:1).

Luke presumably selects this incident of the first martyrdom because of
its momentous impact on the early church. By linking the event with the future apostle Paul, he is signifying that Stephen's influence passed on to the
great shaper of early Christianity, who turned to the Gentile world as his
mission. It does seem that Stephen's teaching and death were important elements in the process by which Gentiles could be accepted as Christian converts without first having to become Jewish proselytes, that is, in particular,
if male, having to submit to circumcision and other elements of ritual purification, such as avoiding certain foods. The account of Stephen naturally
leads on in the narrative of Acts to the apostle Peter's own paradigm shift,
when he embraces the Gentiles as potential Christians.

At this time, therefore, perhaps at the end of A.D. 33, the names of
Stephen and Saul become linked. In less than a year, after a period of fervent
attempted suppression of the followers of Jesus Christ—what we now know
as the church—Saul himself would become convinced of their message at a
dramatic conversion. The violence of that suppression, which even attempted to track down believers who had fled Jerusalem, was instigated by

this landmark execution of Stephen. Saul, as the apostle Paul, would become the chief advocate of preaching and teaching the message to Gentiles, without the requirement to be proselytes of the Jewish religion. He would convince the leaders of the mother church in Jerusalem, who had already allowed the radical teaching and preaching of Stephen. Saul had seen Stephen die as a criminal; within months he would perceive him as a prophet of God and feel an agonizing remorse over his death. The execution of Stephen is one of the pivotal events that shaped the future of the church and thus the world. At the end of the year A.D. 33 the church was still tied to its Jewish roots and to the holy city of Jerusalem, but with the seeds deeply planted for its worldwide expansion. The visionary New Jerusalem, an important motif in New Testament writings, would encompass all nations, languages, cultures and social divisions.

A WORLD IN
THE MAKING

WHAT HAPPENED NEXT?

THE YEAR A.D. 33 IS SUCH A MOMENTOUS YEAR, historically, that it is impossible to do more than give the briefest of indications of some of the consequences of its significant events. These will mainly focus on some of those people known to be active in this year. To name just one sequel that is too huge to cover in this chapter, it is the very history of Europe over the following centuries. At the end of this year the new Christianity is poised to spread through the Roman world and beyond.

ROMANS

Tiberius, the emperor, continued to live and hold what was effectively his court on the little island of Capreae. Gaius Caligula remained there with him, under his protection, watched over by Macro, the Roman commander who had helped to depose Sejanus. In A.D. 35 Caligula was named jointly with Gemellus as Tiberius's heir. One of the many visitors to Villa Jovis was Agrippa, the future Jewish king, who had a long association with the family of Antonia, Tiberius's sister-in-law. Agrippa was a friend of Gaius Caligula, who lived in Antonia's household before being brought to Capreae in A.D. 31.

Tiberius grew increasingly frail. In the spring of A.D. 37 he took part in a ceremonial game in which he threw a javelin. He strained his shoulder, and the pain forced him to rest. He then became ill and lapsed into a coma. Proud of his physical strength, the emperor had refused doctors for many years. Now that they could examine him they decided that he was on the verge of death. Caligula was summoned, and the praetorian guard, controlled by Macro, declared their support. The story went that news of the succession was proclaimed prematurely. Tiberius at this point regained consciousness, sat up in bed and demanded food. In the confusion Macro remained calm. On the next day he hurried to Tiberius's bed and smothered the weakened emperor with his bedclothes. This was only one of Macro's favors for Caligula. Another was to let him share his wife, turning a blind eye to the affair.

The year before Tiberius's death, Pilate's heavy-handed misjudgments in Judea took such a serious turn that he was ordered to return to Italy and answer to the emperor. He had been under the watchful eye of exconsul Lucius Vitellius, commander of the eastern legions, who had been appointed legate of Syria. One of the would-be messiahs who emerged from time to time in Palestine caused great excitement when he claimed that he knew where on Mount Gerizim holy relics of Moses were to be found. Large numbers of Samaritans ascended the sacred slopes, convinced that the revelation of these relics would inaugurate a new age free of Roman control. The Jewish historian Josephus tells how Pilate

> blocked their projected route up the mountain with a detachment of cavalry and heavy armed infantry, who in an encounter with the firstcomers in the village slew some in a pitched battle and put the others to flight. Many prisoners were taken, of whom Pilate put to death the principal leaders and those who were most influential among the fugitives.[1]

After a delegation of Samaritan leaders had petitioned Vitellius, he commanded Pilate to go before Tiberius. It is also possible that Vitellius could have heard about how Pilate dealt with Jesus, and knew about the incident of the votive shields. Some accounts say that the emperor died while Pilate was en route, another that Tiberius banished him to the south of Gaul. Pilate simply vanishes from the pages of history. But not from legend. Pilate proved a fertile inspiration for active imaginations, some even seeing him as a convert to Christianity.[2]

As well as being mentioned by Josephus and Philo of Alexandria, and his dramatic presence in the New Testament Gospels, the historian Tacitus refers to the minor Roman official only because of his connection with the death of Christ: "Christus . . . suffered the extreme penalty during the reign of Tiberius at the hands of one of our procurators, Pontius Pilatus." This is from a fuller section where Tacitus describes how Nero, whose cruelties exceeded those of his predecessor Gaius Caligula, made the Christian community in Rome a scapegoat, blaming them for the great fire of A.D. 64. (In this persecution, it is likely Nero also executed the apostles Paul and Peter.) Tacitus records:

> All human efforts, all the lavish gifts of the emperor, and the propitiations of the gods, did not banish the sinister belief that the conflagration was the result of an order. Consequently, to get rid of the report, Nero fastened the guilt and inflicted the most exquisite tortures on a class hated for their abominations,

called Christians by the populace. Christus, from whom the name had its origin, suffered the extreme penalty during the reign of Tiberius at the hands of one of our procurators, Pontius Pilatus, and a most mischievous superstition, thus checked for the moment, again broke out not only in Judaea, the first source of the evil, but even in Rome, where all things hideous and shameful from every part of the world find their center and become popular. Accordingly, an arrest was first made of all who pleaded guilty; then, upon their information, an immense multitude was convicted, not so much of the crime of firing the city, as of hatred against mankind. Mockery of every sort was added to their deaths. Covered with the skins of beasts, they were torn by dogs and perished, or were nailed to crosses, or were doomed to the flames and burnt, to serve as a nightly illumination, when daylight had expired.

Nero offered his gardens for the spectacle, and was exhibiting a show in the circus, while he mingled with the people in the dress of a charioteer or stood aloft on a car[riage]. Hence, even for criminals who deserved extreme and exemplary punishment, there arose a feeling of compassion; for it was not, as it seemed, for the public good, but to glut one man's cruelty, that they were being destroyed.[3]

Another Roman administrator, the tetrarch Herod Antipas, fared much better than Pontius Pilate, but within six years of his brief trial and mockery of Jesus Christ, he too was deposed, and exiled. The "fox" had a moment of glory during Rome's struggles with the Parthians between A.D. 35 and 36, when he negotiated a peace treaty between the two empires. This was during the summer or autumn of A.D. 36. That same year, however, in the autumn, Antipas was defeated by Aretas, the Arab king of Petra, whom Antipas had slighted by putting away his first wife, the daughter of Aretas, in favor of Herodias. His fortunes further declined because of Agrippa's friendship with Gaius Caligula, who took power at Tiberius's death in March, A.D. 37. He granted to Agrippa a kingdom in Palestine, and Antipas was removed from his tetrarchies in the summer of A.D. 39.

Rome continued to hold power for many centuries, officially becoming Christian under Constantine in the fourth century, until it was invaded in A.D. 476, its fall shocking the countries it had ruled and creating a crisis in civilization itself.

OUTSIDE THE EMPIRE

Britannia. Cunobelinus, who held power over much of eastern Britannia in A.D. 33, died between A.D. 40 and 43, according to Dio Cassius. His son

Togodumnus was killed during the Roman invasion of A.D. 43. Another son, Caratacus, continued to resist the invaders for several more years in Wales. Tacitus described the eventual defeat of his forces:

> His deficiency in strength was compensated by superior cunning and topographical knowledge. Transferring the war to the country of the Ordovices, he was joined by everyone who feared a Roman peace. . . . While light-armed auxiliaries attacked with javelins, the heavy regular infantry advanced in close formation. The British, unprotected by breastplates or helmets, were thrown into disorder. If they stood up to the auxiliaries they were cut down by the swords and spears of the regulars, and if they faced the latter they succumbed to the auxiliaries' broadswords and pikes. It was a great victory. Caratacus's wife and daughter were captured: his brother surrendered.[4]

The British warrior was brought to Rome in chains, where he showed great dignity and was released by Claudius. It is possible that his daughter, Cunobelinus's granddaughter, was one Claudia Rufina, wife of Aulus Pudens, a friend of Martial.[5] This Claudia was of British birth and may be the Claudia mentioned by the apostle Paul, prominent in the Christian community in Rome (2 Timothy 4:21). Her husband may have been the Pudens martyred by the emperor Domitian in A.D. 95. There is no definite evidence, however, for any of these connections.

Boudicca, who was a young girl in A.D. 33, became a chieftain and led a major insurrection against the Roman occupiers in A.D. 60 or 61, during the reign of Nero. This was after the Romans had plundered her kingdom following the death of her husband, flogged her and raped her two daughters. She united her tribe, the Iceni, with other Celtic tribes, including the neighboring Trinovantes, against the Romans. The events of her rebellion are told by two historians, Tacitus (in his *Annals* and *Agricola*) and Dio Cassius (in his *Roman History*). Legend has it that she is buried under platform 10 of King's Cross station, but it is more plausible that she died at her own hand somewhere near Coventry after her defeat in battle. Dio Cassius vividly described the warrior queen: "Boudicca was tall, terrible to look on and gifted with a powerful voice. A flood of bright red hair ran down to her knees; she wore a golden necklet made up of ornate pieces, a multi-colored robe and over it a thick cloak held together by a brooch. She took up a long spear to cause dread in all who set eyes on her."

Asia. In Han China, Guangwudi (Kuang Wu-ti), also known as Liu-Hsiu (Liu-Xiu) continued to consolidate his empire and develop the capital,

Luoyang. By A.D. 36 the civil war was over, and Guangwudi had conquered most of the Great Plain of China. During this period and beyond, China underwent a traumatic shift of population from north to south, partly because of the ravages of war, and partly because of major flooding of the Yellow River. With northern lands emptying, the country became more vulnerable to incursions by barbarians. To the south Guangwudi faced a revolt in Nam Viet, beginning around A.D. 40. It started with the execution of a native chieftain. His widow and her sister—Trung Tac and Trung Nhi—led an insurrection that resulted in the overthrow of the capital, Lien Lau, not far from modern Hanoi. Trung Tac was made queen of an independent Viet state. Within a year, the areas under the control of the two sisters extended into southern China. The rebellion was not suppressed until the end of A.D. 43. The Trung sisters were to remain a national symbol of independence for two millennia. The Han empire survived the difficulties to the north and south and existed until A.D. 220.

JEWS

What happened to Peter is hard to trace after the death of James, brother of John, at the hand of Herod Agrippa I around A.D. 44, apart from his role in the Jerusalem council perhaps several years later. Before Pentecost, Peter had taken the lead in the new church community. At Pentecost he was the principal preacher and soon after the spokesman before the Jewish authorities. Among the people of Jerusalem, Peter was singled out for his use of supernatural powers. It is clear that his distinctive leadership continued to be exercised.

The book of Acts has references to him in Joppa, Caesarea and elsewhere. This suggests that he was involved in missions in Palestine, with James, the brother of John, remaining very active in the church in Jerusalem. Later, after being imprisoned again in Jerusalem, he went to an unnamed place and later to Antioch, an important center in the Jewish Diaspora. Possibly he went on briefly to Corinth. He was closely associated with Christian communities in the north of Asia Minor (see 1 Peter 1:1). Contrary to the popular view of a fundamental difference between Peter and Paul, Peter was the first apostle to be associated with missions to Gentiles, although this exposed him to criticism from those in the church who wished to preserve a purely Jewish Christianity (see Acts 10; 11; 15:7-11). Peter clearly recognized that his main mission to Jews and Paul's main one to Gentiles was part of the same commission (see Galatians 2:7-10). At the Jerusalem Council of A.D. 51 or a little earlier, Peter is mentioned as the first to urge the full acceptance of the Gentiles on faith in Christ alone, without the necessity of males undergoing the Jewish initiation of circumcision (see Acts 15:7-12).

Peter's final base was in Rome, serving its young Christian community. His first letter, contained in the New Testament, was written from there (see 1 Peter 5:13). That letter shows marks of being written around the time of Nero's persecution. There may have been strong tensions within the community in the Roman capital, and possibly Paul asked Peter to go there to address this rift. Whether those tensions were responsible for the deaths of Peter and Paul is not known, but they were caught up in the general persecution. It is possible that Peter, not having Roman citizenship, was crucified, as tradition suggests. The account of the history of the early church in the book of Acts ends before the deaths of Peter and Paul.

Saul, the zealous young Pharisee who looked after the clothes of Stephen's executioners, was afterward given official sanction to repress the Christian community, which he did with evident brutality. As a result of Stephen's death, many Christians fled elsewhere. It was on his way to purge those who had taken refuge in Damascus that Saul had his famous encounter with the resurrected Christ, the only appearance after his ascension on May 14, A.D. 33, according to the Gospel accounts. Saul's conversion, when he took on the name "Paul," is one of the most famous among several that stand out in the history of the church, including those of Augustine, John Bunyan, John Newton and C. S. Lewis. This may have taken place as early as A.D. 34. It is so significant that there are in fact three accounts of the conversion in the book of Acts (Acts 9; 22; 26). This witnessing of the resurrected Jesus, central to his conversion, was an essential element in Paul's authority to be an apostle, which meant authority over the church in its practice and teaching, along with the Twelve.

Then followed an interval in the Transjordan desert, after which Paul spent three years preaching in Damascus. He was forced to flee to Jerusalem, where Barnabas, the cousin of John Mark, introduced him to the wary church leaders. Within a couple of weeks some Hellenistic Jews were determined to kill him. Paul therefore returned to Tarsus, in southern Asia Minor, where he had been born. This was an important cosmopolitan center, and he spent ten years there. There is no account of what he did in Tarsus. Eventually Barnabas asked Paul to come to Antioch to help in its expanding Gentile mission. (It was here that the followers of Jesus were first nicknamed "Christians.") Paul eventually visited Jerusalem with Barnabas, carrying funds to help its impoverished church community. After this, commissioned by the church in Antioch, Paul and Barnabas set off on a mission tour of Cyprus and southern Galatia—we do not know if they worked among the Celtic population, who tended to live further north. The success of this mission meant a great influx of Gentiles into the churches, creating a crisis over identity for many Jewish Christians. Some tried to impose practices such as circumcision and observance of the law instituted by Moses on the Gentile converts. In response Paul wrote his powerful letter to the Galatians, emphasizing that salvation was solely "by grace through faith." By this he meant that salvation was freely given, not earned as a result of religious practices and ritual purity. In response to this first great theological crisis in the Christian community, the church in Antioch sent Paul and Barnabas around A.D. 50 to discuss the issues with the "apostles and elders" in Jerusalem (Acts 15). The Jerusalem Council gave their groundbreaking judgment, expressed by the leader of the Jerusalem church, James. "My judgment is that we should not trouble those of the Gentiles who turn to God, but should write to them to abstain from the things polluted by idols, and from sexual immorality, and from what has been strangled, and from blood" (Acts 15:19-20). Gentile believers, that is, should have only the limited burden of abstaining from food offered to idols, meat from strangled animals and sexual immorality (perhaps referring to incestuous marriage). This, no doubt intentionally, endorsed Paul's contention that Gentiles were under no obligation to keep the ritual laws of Moses. This Jerusalem ruling became highly important when the Jerusalem temple was destroyed, where belief in Jesus replaced the cult of the temple for very many Jews. The ruling about Gentiles was seen to have far-reaching implications for Jews too. The limited restrictions addressed local issues and seemed intended to help the relations between Gentile and Jewish Christians.

Following the Council, Paul went on with his mission to the Gentiles, embarking on a number of tours throughout Galatia and into Greece, moving from north to south. At one point he remained two years in Corinth, founding the Christian church there. He also continued working in Asia Minor, moving his base of operations to the strategic city of Ephesus, on the Aegean coast. The period associated with Ephesus and the evangelization of the province of Asia, which lasted from around A.D. 53 to 58, was the most important of Paul's missions. The churches that were established then were important for the church in later years, and at this time Paul wrote many of his letters to various churches, which established the theology of the early church, complementing existing oral and written accounts of the life and teaching of Christ, soon to be incorporated into the four Gospels. (Some scholars believe that Paul developed what is distinctively Christianity, and that these views were projected back on to the life and teaching of Jesus, which in its original form would not have been radical in terms of current forms of Judaism at the time; other scholars dispute this theory.) At the end of this period, after a farewell at the harbor of Ephesus, Paul sailed for Jerusalem—and arrest. In Jerusalem, after observing the temple rituals as a devout Jew, Paul was arrested after pilgrims from Ephesus who recognized him accused him of violating the temple, and they incited a riot. The outcome was that Paul was removed to Caesarea Maritima for his own safety. There, between around A.D. 58 and 60, he was imprisoned for two years. After an appeal for a trial before the emperor, an appeal Paul could make as a Roman citizen, he was shipped under guard to Rome. He made the appeal before the governor, Felix, who was accompanied by guests King Herod Agrippa II and his sister Bernice, who at one stage married the nephew of Philo of Alexandria. Luke's account of his shipwreck en route to Rome is a vivid and unique piece of first-century travel writing.

When Paul finally reached Rome, after wintering in Malta, he was held under house arrest for two years. At this point Luke's account in the book of Acts ends. It is likely that Paul was released by A.D. 63, and he may have visited Spain and the area around Ephesus before his return to Rome and detention and execution under Nero. As a Roman citizen he may have had the quick execution of beheading rather than the lingering torture of crucifixion probably suffered by Peter.

Of the other persons who played a part in the events of A.D. 33 as the disciples of Christ—Mary and Martha of Bethany, their brother Lazarus, Mary Magdalene, Susanna, Joanna, Joseph of Arimathea, Nicodemus and others— we have no further historical record from the time. (The Gospel accounts were written later in the first century.) Once again, active imaginations in later centuries created imaginary sequels. In particular, Mary Magdalene was conflated with Mary of Bethany, and with the disreputable woman who first anointed Jesus.[6] Later Gnostic Gospels (second century and later), which read esoteric meanings into Christ's life and exalted the spirit over matter, venerated Mary Magdalene, not showing the interest in historical context that marks the four Gospels. There has been a serious interest in the Gnostic Gospels and other Gnostic writings since the discovery of the Nag Hammadi Codices in Egypt in 1945, including the *Gospel of Thomas.*

Philo, the wise Jewish writer of Alexandria, continued to compose his scriptural commentaries and philosophical reflections, in the tradition of Plato. He left an account of a deputation to Caligula in A.D. 39/40, in which he participated, in response to mistreatments of the large Jewish community in Egypt by the Roman administration under Flaccus. In two books Philo describes the persecutions that the Jews had to endure (which would have included Jewish Christians). The oppression was particularly marked at Alexandria. His narrative is detailed and vivid. It bears the marks of someone involved in the events. He describes attacks on the Jews in Alexandria inspired by Gaius Caligula's own inhumanity and anti-Semitism:

> They began to crush our people as if they had been surrendered by the emperor for the most extreme and undeniable miseries, or as if they had been subdued in war, with their frantic and most brutal passion, forcing their way into their houses, and driving out the owners, with their wives and children, which they rendered desolate and void of inhabitants. And no longer watching for night and darkness, like ordinary robbers out of fear of being detected, they openly plundered them of all their furniture and treasures, carrying them off in broad daylight, and displaying their booty to everyone whom they met, as if they had inherited it or fairly purchased it from the owners. And if a multitude joined together to share any particular piece of plunder, they divided it in the middle of the market-place, reviling it and turning it all into ridicule before the eyes of its real owners. . . .
>
> When the populace had driven together these countless myriads of men, and women, and children, like so many herds of sheep and oxen, from every quarter of the city, into a very narrow space as if into a pen, they expected that in a few days they should find a heap of corpses all huddled together, as they would either have perished by hunger through the want of necessary food, as they had not prepared themselves with anything requisite, through a foreknowledge of the evils which thus suddenly came upon them; or else through being crushed and suffocated from want of any adequate space to breathe in.[7]

The descriptions are chillingly similar to events in World War II under the Nazis. Philo records the reception given to their embassy by Caligula. He treated the five ambassadors with disdain. The emperor would ask a question and then run on to another room or building, leaving them to follow. He raised laughter among those with him by asking, "Why is it you abstain from eating pig's flesh?" They had no opportunity to put their case properly about the mistreatment of their people in Egypt. In the end, his mood appeared to soften, and he dismissed them firmly with the words, "These men do not appear to me to be wicked so much as unfortunate and foolish, in not believing that I have been endued with the nature of God."

In another treatise, *On Flaccus,* Philo has the satisfaction of recounting the downfall and execution of the former prefect of Egypt under whom the persecution of the Jews happened and was encouraged. Philo uses a vivid narrative style to describe Flaccus's sudden recall in A.D. 38 and his banishment to the island of Andros, where he was soon after executed. The command to do away with him came from Gaius Caligula.

> When the men arrived at Andros, who had been commanded to put him to death, Flaccus happened, just at that moment, to be coming from his farm into the city, and they, on their way up from the port, met him, and while yet at a distance they perceived and recognized one another; at which he, perceiving in a moment the object for which they were come (for every man's soul is very prophetic, especially of such as are in misfortune), turning out of the road, fled and ran away over the rough ground, forgetting, perhaps, that Andros was an island. . . .
>
> The officers . . . pursued him without stopping to take breath and arrested him; and then immediately some of them dug a ditch, and the others dragged him on by force in spite of all his resistance and crying out and struggling, by which means his whole body was wounded like that of beasts that are despatched with a number of wounds; for he, turning round them and clinging to his executioners, who were hindered in their aims which they took at him with their swords, and who thus struck him with oblique blows, was the cause of his own sufferings being more severe; for he was in consequence mutilated and cut about the hands, and feet, and head, and breast, and sides, so that he was mangled like a victim, and thus he fell, justice righteously inflicting on his own body wounds equal in number to the murders of the Jews whom he had unlawfully put to death. . . . Such was the end of Flaccus, who suffered thus, being made the most manifest evidence that the nation of the Jews is not left destitute of the providential assistance of God.[8]

Egypt was the location of a remarkable event the year after A.D. 33, according to Tacitus in his *Annals.* He writes: "During the consulship of Paulus Fabius and Lucius Vitellius, the bird called the phoenix, after a long succession of ages, appeared in Egypt and furnished the most learned men of that country and of Greece with abundant matter for the discussion of the marvellous phenomenon."[9] The phoenix was a mythical bird associated with the sun. Pliny the Elder, the naturalist, and the historian Dio Cassius put the date at A.D. 36, although Pliny, typically, was skeptical of the dazzling bird's existence.[10] The phoenix, a potent symbol of death and rebirth, could more fittingly have appeared the year before, in A.D. 33, as Barbara Levick remarks, as that year was a turning point in the events of the Roman empire.[11] The phoenix was taken up as a Christian symbol of Jesus and his resurrection, and of rebirth, but whether this was influenced by the rumors and debates about the phoenix's reappearance in Egypt around this time is not known.

CHRONOLOGY

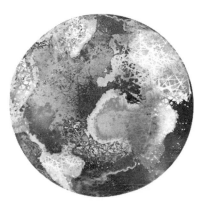

DATING A.D. 33

DETERMINING CHRONOLOGY IN THE ANCIENT WORLD is extraordinarily complex. Some of the best work in this area in is New Testament scholarship, perhaps because here documents with a historical context such as the Gospel narratives and the book of Acts are also revered religious books. This means that they have been easily dismissed or not considered valuable as history. Where careful scholarship has supported the New Testament record, I have used it. In particular, I have relied for my chronology on the painstaking work of Harold Hoehner and Stanley Porter. The collaboration of a scientist and an astrophysicist, Professor Colin Humphreys and W. Graeme Waddington, in determining the likely date of the crucifixion of Jesus Christ has been invaluable. I was surprised to find that they were treading in the venerable footsteps of Sir Isaac Newton in the seventeenth century. From the ancient world Tacitus's *Annals of Imperial Rome* has been indispensable, as by its nature it is annalistic, and Tacitus's section dealing with A.D. 33 has fortunately survived.

In reconstructing a chronology for a period two thousand years ago, the main constraints are whatever facts and evidence have survived over that period, the scarcity of fixed coordinates (such as the birth and death of an emperor or a lunar eclipse), and the reality that the ancients had a different perception of truth. Truth did not equal the measurable but was much richer in its reference; there was no preoccupation with recording time and other abstractions. Science too, as we know it, did not exist, even though there were remarkable scientific developments. There were, nevertheless, means of measuring time—sundials calibrated to their locations and elaborate water clocks. The main tool, however, remained the darkness and the light of each day, and the movement of sun, moon, planets and stars. In determining dates, historians carefully judge a range of evidence from documents, archaeological discoveries and other background data. In the case of A.D. 33, where most of the key players are ordinary people missing from the official records, it is necessary to rely on reconstructions of the dates of events in the life of Christ and the early life of the apostle Paul. It is on the careful work of such historians that the chronology of this book is based.

Not surprisingly, not all scholars agree on pivotal dates. Some place the crucifixion, for example, in the most likely alternative year, A.D. 30. However, the majority of scholars I've consulted in recent work place it in the year A.D. 33, though of course pointing out the difficulties of being certain. It seems to me that the pieces of the jigsaw fit this year very well, and not at all well for the alternative year. For that alternative the mission of Jesus— his teaching and miracles in the Galilee and Jerusalem areas—are tightly compressed into one year, while the events of the early life of the church take place at a leisurely pace. In my view the reverse is much more credible, especially because around three thousand converted when Peter preached for the first time at Pentecost, signaling rapid growth and a dramatic social impact on the crowded confines of Jerusalem.

Let us look first at a construction of the dates of key events in the life of Christ, the timing of the crucifixion and then the early career of the apostle Paul. The dating of the birth of Jesus can only be approximately reckoned. (The dating of A.D. 1 was the result of a calculating error.) A useful coordinate is the death of Herod the Great. (Another coordinate, the census associated in the Gospel of Luke with Quirinius, is too complex to discuss here.) According to accounts in the Gospels, the birth of Jesus preceded the death of Herod. Josephus tells us that there was an omen, an eclipse of the moon, just before his demise.[1] We know that there was an eclipse on March 12/13, 4 B.C. Josephus adds that the Passover was celebrated after the king's death. This would have begun on April 11, 4 B.C. Herod's death occurred therefore between these dates. The birth of Jesus consequently must have been before March or April in 4 B.C. Taking this and other factors into account it is reasonable to suppose that Jesus was born in December 5 B.C. or January 4 B.C. In extrapolating from this date to Jesus' later life it has to be taken into account that there is no zero year between B.C. and A.D.; historical chronology goes from 1 B.C. to A.D. 1.

We have to wait for the beginning of Jesus' mission for chronological data, with the exception of his visit to the temple in Jerusalem with his family when he was twelve years old. This is tied up with the activities of John the Baptist. The Gospel of Luke records that John began preaching and baptizing in the fifteenth year of Tiberius. Calculating dates from the reigns of emperors is not straightforward, but it is reasonable to base Luke's year on either the Julian Calendar used by Rome or from the literal beginning of Tiberius's reign (the usual Roman method). These would give the fifteenth year of Tiberius as between August 19, A.D. 28 and December 31, A.D. 29. We can therefore be safe in assuming that John the Baptist's activities began sometime during this period.

The Gospel accounts imply that Jesus was baptized and began his own mission not long after the beginning of John's ministry. If Jesus was baptized by John in the summer or autumn of A.D. 29, he would have been approximately thirty-two years old. This supposition accords with the statement in Luke's Gospel that Jesus was "about thirty years of age" at this time (Luke 3:23).

John's Gospel documents the first visit of Jesus to Jerusalem, following his baptism, for the Passover (John 2:13—3:21). On this occasion, interestingly, there is a reference to the building of the temple by Herod the Great forty-six years before (John 2:20). Parts of the temple area were still under construction during Jesus' ministry.

Josephus reveals that the construction of the temple began in the eighteenth year of Herod's rule, which was at the same time as a visit by the emperor Augustus to Syria.[2] Dio Cassius indicates that this visit occurred in the spring or summer of 20 B.C.[3] This year of Herod's reign was from Nisan 1, 20 B.C. to Nisan 1, 19 B.C. The building of the temple was in two stages, and it was the first stage that was started in this year of Herod, that is, the inner sanctuary or naos. It took about one and a half years to complete, according to Josephus.[4] The second stage, the complete temple complex, was not finished until A.D. 63—seven years before the temple was destroyed in the Roman siege of Jerusalem. It was the naos that had stood for forty-six years, that is, until A.D. 29 to 30. It follows that the first Passover attended by Jesus was in the spring of A.D. 30. It is reasonable to suppose, therefore, that the mission of Jesus commenced in the summer or autumn of A.D. 29.

The Gospels of Matthew, Mark and Luke—the Synoptic Gospels—give the superficial impression that Jesus' ministry lasted for a year, structured around a journey from Galilee to Jerusalem to die, in which a powerful quest is embodied—no less than the heroic quest to achieve the once-for-all salvation of human beings from the grip of sin, evil and death. John's Gospel provides the chronological clues that in fact point to a longer ministry of three and a half years or slightly more. This fits in well with the supposition that John, in structuring his Gospel, intends to complement and expand at some points the other Gospels, which were written before his. These pointers in John are too complex to go into here, but they include references to three Passovers attended by Jesus and the implication of a fourth (John 2:13; 6:4; 11:55).[5] The argument for the longer ministry is cumulative and strengthened by considerations of the day and year of Jesus' crucifixion.

In coming to a date for Jesus' death it is important to find out the day of the week it fell on, and the day of the Jewish month, as the sources refer to Jewish reckoning. This must therefore incorporate the fact that part of a day is considered a whole day, and that the day begins at sunset in Jewish reckoning. Traditions agree in placing Jesus' crucifixion on the Friday of the week of Christ's Passion. There is no historical reason to challenge this traditional view.

The week of the Passion is described in chapter five, based on a chart such as the following:

- Saturday, Jesus arrives at Bethany (John 12:1).
- Sunday, crowds come to see Jesus, and the "Triumphal Entry" (John 12:9-11; Matthew 21:1-9; Mark 11:1-10; Luke 19:28-44).
- Monday, the curse of the fig tree and cleansing of the temple (Matthew 21:12-19; Mark 11:12-17; Luke 19:45-46).
- Tuesday, the fig tree found withered, the temple controversy and Jesus' discourse on Olivet (Matthew 21:20—23:39; 24:1-25, 46; Mark 11:20—12:44; 13:1-37; Luke 20:1—21:36).
- Wednesday, a quiet day. Jesus warns of his death, and Judas secretly goes to the authorities (Matthew 26:1-5; Mark 14:1-2, 10-11; Luke 22:1-6).
- Thursday, the Last Supper, and Jesus' betrayal and arrest (Matthew 26:20-56; Mark 14:17-52; Luke 22:14-53; John 13:1—18:12).
- Friday, Jesus tried by Annas and Caiaphas, Pilate and Herod Antipas, crucified and buried (Matthew 26:57—27:61; Mark 14:53—15:47; Luke 22:54—23:56; John 18:12—19:42).

Having established the day of Christ's death, the year of the event can be determined with some certainty by considering those officials involved in Jesus' trial, astronomical data, Jesus' ministry and the context of political events in the Roman empire.

The main players in the trial of Jesus (see chap. 5) were the high priest,

Caiaphas, the Roman prefect Pontius Pilate and Herod Antipas, tetrarch of Galilee and Perea, who was in Jerusalem at the time. Joseph Caiaphas was high priest from A.D. 18 to 37, Pilate was prefect of Judea from A.D. 26 to 36 and Antipas governed Galilee and Perea from 3 B.C. to A.D. 39, until he was replaced by Agrippa I. The trial of Jesus therefore occurred between A.D. 26 and 36.

The movements of the sun and the moon are known for every day in the

LUNAR ECLIPSES, A.D. 30-33

(For day of crucifixion, see April 3, A.D. 33.)

Local circumstances at greatest eclipse: 0030 to 0033

Date	UT Greatest Eclipse	Type	Saros #	Gamma	Pen. mag.	Umb. mag.	S.D. par	S.D. tot	GST (0 UT)	Moon RA	Moon Dec
									h	h	
6 May 0030	03:18	Ne	41	1.537	0.032	-0.928	–	–	14.8	14.72	-14.3
4 Jun 0030	10:03	P	79	-0.949	1.115	0.148	41m	–	16.7	16.57	-23.2
28 Nov 0030	20:20	N	84	1.450	0.279	-0.850	–	–	4.4	4.20	22.7
25 Apr 0031	20:11	P	51	0.841	1.319	0.340	62m	–	14.1	14.04	-11.7
19 Oct 0031	03:13	P	56	-0.872	1.311	0.235	56m	–	1.7	1.48	8.5
14 Apr 0032	09:05	T–	61	0.102	2.701	1.670	112m	51m	13.4	13.37	-8.7
7 Oct 0032	12:47	T+	66	-0.130	2.643	1.627	108m	48m	1.0	0.78	5.0
3 Apr 0033	14:47	P	71	-0.679	1.671	0.586	86m	–	12.7	12.69	-5.2
27 Sep 0033	03:49	P	76	0.560	1.837	0.855	89m	–	0.3	0.11	1.3

Key: The date and universal time (UT) of the instant of greatest eclipse are found in the first two columns. The eclipse type is given (T = Total, P = Partial, N = Penumbral) along with the Saros series. Gamma is the distance of the moon's center from the shadow axis of earth at greatest eclipse (in earth radii). The penumbral and umbral magnitudes (Pen. mag. and Umb. mag.) of the eclipse are defined as the fractions of the moon's diameter obscured by each shadow at greatest eclipse. The semi-durations (S.D.) of the partial and total phases of the eclipse are given to the nearest minute. Finally, the Greenwich Sidereal Time (GST) at 00:00 UT, along with the moon's geocentric right ascension (RA) and declination (Dec) at greatest eclipse complete each record.

Thus, for A.D. 33, Date UT is April 3, greatest eclipse is 14.47, type is penumbral 71, Saros is - 0.677, Gamma, in the next column, is -0.679, Pen. mag. is 1.671, Umb. mag. is 0.586, S.D. partial phase is 86m, GST is 12.7, Moon RA is 12.69, and Moon Dec. is -5.2. Add hours on for the Near East (visible in Jerusalem *c.* 18.20—Humphreys and Waddington, p. 347).

Source: Fred Espenak, *Lunar Eclipses: 0001 to 0100,* NASA/Goddard Space Flight Center, Greenbelt, Maryland 20771 USA.

first century. Data from astronomy limit the dates for Christ's death to A.D. 27, 30, 33 and 36. These data include the positioning of the Passover, which was relative to the phases of the moon, and the references to a lunar eclipse just after Christ's death. Of this range of dates, A.D. 27 is the least likely and A.D. 33 the most likely. Humphreys and Waddington argue that a lunar eclipse that occurred on Friday, April 3, A.D. 33, is a strong pointer to that year as the date of Christ's death.[6] They also offer the suggestion that the darkening of the sun, referred to in Gospel accounts, could be accounted for by a khamsin dust storm (a hot wind that occurs for a period of around fifty days in the nearby Judean desert in March, April and May). Interestingly, a messianic section of one of the *Sibylline Oracles,* probably written after the first century, refers to the darkening effect of what may be a dust storm: "And straightway dust is carried from heaven to earth, and all the brightness of the sun fails at midday from the heavens."[7]

In terms of the period of Jesus' teaching and healing in Galilee, Samaria, Perea and the Jerusalem area, the years A.D. 27 and 36 can be ruled out. The year A.D. 30 presents problems in that the period is squeezed into one year, given that John the Baptist became active in Tiberius's fifteenth year, A.D. 29. A.D. 33 fits much better into the scale of events.

The Roman political context also points strongly to A.D. 33. It provides causal conditions that explain the otherwise puzzling actions and decisions of Pilate. Philo and Josephus agree in representing Pilate as vicious, strong-minded and greedy. In the Gospel accounts, however, Pilate appears to be pliable to the pressures of the civic and temple authorities in Jerusalem. The Gospel accounts nevertheless still place him directly responsible for the death of Christ. The uncharacteristic behavior of the prefect makes perfect sense in the political context of A.D. 33, but not of A.D. 30. He is in a vulnerable position because of the danger of being linked with the fallen Sejanus (see "Tiberius and the Shadow of Sejanus," pp. 73-82), who had probably appointed him. He had also had the very recent humiliation of withdrawing, on Tiberius's direct command, votive shields he had placed in Jerusalem in the autumn of the previous year. This action, along with an earlier provocation of the Jews, had earned him the enmity of Herod Antipas. His sending of Jesus to Antipas for trial is plausible as a symbolic gesture intended to renew friendship between the two governors and to avoid a further damning complaint from Antipas to the emperor. The report in the Gospels that Pilate and Antipas were friends after this gesture fits with an A.D. 33 date, but not one based on A.D. 30, as the two were in serious conflict in A.D. 32.

Mapping out the chronology of Paul relies on collating insights from three sets of information, though here we are only concerned with his very early career, up to a point where he is still a young and zealous Pharisee, fresh from sitting at the feet of his distinguished teacher, Gamaliel. These sets of data are the book of Acts, the letters Paul wrote, and people and events in the wider world.

The narrative of the origins and development of the early church in Acts follows a historical sequence. For information about Paul, the first marker is the stoning of Stephen, when Paul, still as Saul, is a young man—which suggests a birth date of between A.D. 5 and 15. Subsequent markers are his conversion, stay in Damascus, escape over the city wall, first visit as a Christian to Jerusalem and so on.

A careful examination of information in Paul's letters provides a sequence that generally correlates well with that in Acts. Because of the amount of interpretation involved, scholars disagree about the purport of information in individual letters. The letters, in particular Galatians 1—2, suggest a sequence of events that includes his conversion, sojourn in Arabia, return to Damascus, then, after three years (either after his conversion or his return to Damascus), his visit to Jerusalem, which, a letter reveals, lasted fifteen days. Other periods of time are indicated for various events.

Several events in the wider world provide possible coordinates for the timing of events in Paul's life. Most concern later events, but one is quite close in time to A.D. 33. In one of his letters Paul refers to King Aretas guarding Damascus (2 Corinthians 11:32-33). There are gray areas about when exactly Aretas died and when he took control of Damascus. This information may indicate that Paul's escape from Damascus happened between A.D. 37 and 38-40, or that it took place before A.D. 38-40. In collaboration with other information it is a useful datum, however.

Such information as this, carefully weighed and collated, allows scholars to conclude that Paul was likely to have been converted between A.D. 34 and 35, after which he spent three years in Arabia and Damascus. His first visit to Jerusalem as a Christian convert was in A.D. 37, the year of Tiberius's death. Subsequent events in Paul's life can be posited in a similar way.[8]

CHRONOLOGY OF THE PERIOD

(44 B.C. TO A.D. 70)

B.C.

753   traditional date of Rome's founding

44   assassination of Julius Caesar

30   suicides of Anthony and Cleopatra
       Egypt taken over by Roman rule

27   Octavian named Princeps and assumes the name of Augustus

23   publication of first three books of Horace's *Odes*

20   (or 19) birth of Herod Antipas; Herod begins constructing the temple
       in Jerusalem, starting with the inner sanctuary

19   death of Virgil

15   Tiberius and Drusus defeat Alpine tribes of Vindelicia and Raetia and
       reach the Danube

14?   birth of Agrippina the Elder

9   death of Drusus near the Elbe

8   death of poet Horace

8/7   (late 8 or early 7): Herod Antipas goes to Rome for education

6   Tiberius retires to Rhodes

4   January (or December 5 B.C.)—birth of Jesus Christ
       March 12/13—eclipse of the moon (seen as omen of Herod's death)
       March/April—death of Herod the Great
       mid-July—first trial over the will of Herod the Great
       July/August—end of revolt in Palestine
       October/November—second trial over will and Augustus's decision

3   Antipas returns to Palestine
       ?return of infant Jesus and parents from refuge in Egypt
       rebuilding of Sepphoris begins (rebuilt 3 B.C. to A.D. 8-10)

2   Augustus banishes his daughter Julia, Tiberius's second wife, for
       adultery

A.D.

4   Tiberius adopted by Augustus and sent by him to command the imperial armies

5   Paul (Saul) born in Tarsus in Cilicia around this time

6   Judea made a province

8   banishment of Ovid

         Herod Antipas completes rebuilding of Sepphoris (8-10 B.C.)

9   the Varian disaster—Publius Quintilius Varus loses three legions in Germania to Arminius

12   birth of Gaius Caligula

14   August 19—death of Augustus; accession of Tiberius

         Sejanus becomes a praetorian prefect

15   around this time Paul (Saul) begins studying in Jerusalem under Rabbi Gamaliel, grandson of Rabbi Gamaliel the Elder

16   Germanicus's campaign to advance to the Elbe in the north is curtailed by Tiberius

17   severe earthquake in Asia Minor

         death of historian Livy

         death of the poet Ovid, in exile

18   Joseph Caiaphas becomes high priest in Jerusalem

19   Jews expelled from Rome

         death of Germanicus at Antioch

         birth of Tiberius Gemellus, grandson of Tiberius

20   death of Tiberius's first wife, Vipsania

21   Tiberius retires for a period to Campania

23   death of Drusus, son of Tiberius

         Sejanus concentrates the praetorian guard in one camp

         foundation of city of Tiberias in Palestine, built by Herod Antipas

25   eastern Han Dynasty founded in China (which lasted until 220); Buddhism introduced to China during this dynasty

26   Tiberius leaves Rome, never returning

         Pilate starts governing Judea

         December 2—Pilate removes offensive standards from Jerusalem

27   Tiberius retires to Capreae, having left Rome the previous year, at Sejanus's suggestion

28   revolt of the Frisii in the north over taxation

29   (or late 28) beginning of the mission of John the Baptist

Antipas goes to Rome, marries Herodias (or 30), befriends Agrippa
about this time

death of the empress-mother Livia at 86

influenced by Sejanus, Tiberius denounces Agrippina and her son
Nero, and they are banished by the Senate

summer/autumn—baptism of Jesus, aged 32, by John, and beginning
of his ministry

30   Agrippina's son Drusus imprisoned

publication of Velleius Paterculus's *History*

(or 31) Herod imprisons John the Baptist

(April 7) Jesus' first Passover

31   Sejanus joint consul with Tiberius

(April 25) Jesus' second Passover

suspicious at last of Sejanus, in September Tiberius summons Gaius
(Caligula) to Capreae for his safety

death of Nero

(or 32) Antipas executes John

October 18—Tiberius appoints Macro as praetorian prefect as Sejanus is dramatically denounced and executed

October 21-28—Jesus at the Feast of Tabernacles, Jerusalem

Tiberius issues instructions to provincial governors to protect Jews
under their administration

32   Tiberius suffers some kind of nervous breakdown as extent of Sejanus's treachery becomes known

(or 33) Aulus Avilius Flaccus becomes prefect of Egypt after death of
freedman Hiberius

April 13/14, Passover—Pilate massacres a number of Galileans, creating tension with Herod Antipas

Feast of Tabernacles—incident of the votive shields introduced by Pilate; Jesus at the feast

(or early spring 33) winter—Tiberius orders Pilate to remove shields

December 18—Jesus at the Feast of Dedication (Hanukkah)

33   see pp. 231-33 for the detailed chronology of this year

34   Tetrarchy of Philip incorporated into Syria

Paul (Saul) persecutes the church in Jerusalem

Paul (Saul) is converted en route to Damascus, after seeing Jesus in
a vision

35 Paul in Damascus and Arabia Petrea (the region with Petra as its capital)

Lucius Vitellius becomes legate of Syria

Tiberius makes Gemellus and Gaius (Caligula) his joint heirs

35-36 Rome's conflict with the Parthians

36 summer/autumn—Antipas negotiates for a peace treaty between Rome and Parthia

autumn—Lucius Vitellius's first visit to Jerusalem

Pilate dismissed to Rome by Lucius Vitellius after his massacre of Samaritans on Mt. Gerizim

autumn—Aretas's war against Antipas and Antipas's defeat

37 Paul's first visit to Jerusalem as a Christian, meeting Peter and James; he later returns to his home region in Cilicia

Macro and Gaius Caligula may have precipitated Tiberius's death on March 16

accession of Gaius Caligula; he is consul with Claudius

Passover—Lucius Vitellius visits Jerusalem and restores the high priestly vestments to the custody of the Jews; deposes Joseph Caiaphas and appoints Jonathan

Pentecost—Lucius Vitellius revisits Jerusalem and deposes Jonathan in favor of Theophilus

38 death of Drusilla

Anti-Jewish disturbances in Alexandria

the church, now established in Antioch, begins its outreach to non-Jews

c. August—Agrippa returns to Palestine

39 summer—Antipas deposed and exiled with Herodias to southern Gaul

39/40 Jewish embassy to Rome from Alexandria, led by Philo

41 Herod Agrippa receives Judea and Samaria

assassination of Gaius (Caligula) and accession of Claudius; Jewish disturbances in Rome, leading to suppression, including a ban on assembly

Seneca exiled to Corsica

42 Herod Agrippa's persecution of the church around this time

43 expedition to Britannia

44   martyrdom of James, John's brother
        spring—arrest and deliverance of Peter
        early March, death of Herod Agrippa
47   Barnabas finds Paul in Tarsus and brings him to Antioch
48   Paul makes a second visit to Jerusalem with famine relief and dis-
        cusses the issue of Gentile Christians with the leaders of the church
        there
49   Paul writes his letter to the Galatians; Jerusalem apostolic council
        around this time agrees that male Gentile converts need not be cir-
        cumcised
        Claudius expels the Jews from Rome, leading to Priscilla and Aquila,
        important Christian believers, moving to Corinth
50   Paul in Corinth
54   death of Claudius and accession of Nero
56   (or 57) Paul writes his letter to the Romans from Corinth, before his
        visit to Rome
58   Paul imprisoned in Caesarea Maritima and eventually appeals to Caesar
60   Paul reaches Rome and is under house arrest for two years
61   revolt of Boudicca in Britannia
62   James the Just, brother of Jesus, stoned to death in Jerusalem by sen-
        tences of the high priest Ananus and the Sanhedrin, in the absence
        of the Roman governor, Albinus (successor to Festus)
63   completion of building of temple in Jerusalem, begun by Herod the
        Great
64   autumn/winter (or spring 65)—first Roman persecution of Christians
        and execution of Peter; in 64 or 65 Paul in rearrested in the after-
        math of the fire of Rome and Nero's oppression; after imprison-
        ment, perhaps in Mamertine Prison, and writing his Pastoral Letters,
        Paul is eventually executed
66   major revolt in Palestine starts around May, touched off by a riot be-
        tween Greeks and Jews in Caesarea Maritima
69   "The year of the four emperors"; Vespasian becomes emperor
70   the fall of Jerusalem and destruction of the temple

CHRONOLOGY OF A.D. 33

GENERAL EVENTS

The Roman World

- renewal of the grant of powers that in A.D. 13 made Tiberius and Augustus equal in imperium
- large numbers of people killed for connection, real or imaginary, with Sejanus
- birth of Gaius Rubellius Plautus
- Tiberius orders the death of up to twenty of Sejanus's imprisoned followers, including boys and women, their bodies exposed on the Gemonian Steps
- marriage of Agrippina's and Germanicus's daughters, Drusilla and Livilla
- marriage of Julia, sister of Gemellus
- tenth anniversary of death of Drusus, Tiberius's son by first wife, Vipsania
- Galba becomes a consul in Rome (later emperor in the "year of four emperors"); Tiberius (versed in astrology) prophesies Galba's brief principate
- Tiberius averts financial crisis due to a currency shortage by establishing an interest-free loan fund
- shortage of bread in Rome, so Tiberius imports as much grain as he can from provinces—he reminds the citizens that it was more than Augustus ever supplied
- Sextus Marius, richest man in Spain, is executed for his wealth—thrown from the Tarpeian Rock in Rome, traditional place from which traitors were hurled
- death of Drusus Caesar, brother of Gaius Caligula and Nero Caesar, son of Agrippina the Elder, adoptive grandson of his paternal great-uncle,

Tiberius; he starves to death in prison in Palatine, for eight days gnawing the stuffing of his mattress

- Gaius Asinus Gallus starves to death, hated by Tiberius because he married Vipsania, his former wife
- death of Marcus Aemillius Lepidus, born A.D. 6
- death of Munatia Plancina, enemy of Agrippina the Elder (widow of Gnaeus Calpurnius Piso, one-time governor of Syria)
- death of Marcus Cocceius Nerva, a slow suicide by starvation, in response to calamities at Rome
- marriage of Julia, daughter of Drusus and widow of Nero Caesar, to Gaius Rubellius Blandus (near end of year)
- in the last days of the year, death of Lucius Aelius Lamia, city prefect— he has a state funeral

The Provinces of Judea and Syria

- by A.D. 32/33 Agrippa has moved to Syria from Tiberias in Galilee
- Tiberius orders Pilate to remove votive shields from Jerusalem in the early spring
- Peter and John heal a disabled man and are taken before the Sanhedrin
- the Jerusalem followers of Jesus adopt a voluntary communitarianism; there is cheating by Ananias and Sapphira
- first administrators, including Stephen, chosen by the Jerusalem church
- ?killing of Stephen, the first church martyr

Beyond the Empire

- Tengnoupal, eastern India—Pakhangha establishes a dynasty that lasts until integration with the Indian union in 1947
- end of reign of Luwaang Punshiba, Meithei King of Manipur

Specific Dates

- March 19, total solar eclipse (southern hemisphere)
- Saturday, March 28 (Nisan 8), Jesus arrives in Bethany
- Sunday, March 29 (Nisan 9), crowds come to see Jesus, who makes his triumphal entry into Jerusalem

- Monday, March 30 (Nisan 10), Jesus curses the fig tree and cleanses the temple

- Tuesday, March 31 (Nisan 11), Jesus is involved in controversy at the temple and speaks of its destruction

- Wednesday, April 1 (Nisan 12), quiet day. Jesus warns the disciples of his imminent death by crucifixion. Judas goes to the authorities to arrange the arrest of Jesus

- Thursday, April 2 (Nisan 13), Jesus' last supper, farewell teaching, betrayal and arrest

- Friday, April 3 (Nisan 14), in early hours, Jesus tried by high priest; trials by Pilate and Antipas follow; Jesus' crucifixion and burial; suicide of Judas Iscariot, betrayer of Jesus

- lunar eclipse at sundown

- Sunday, April 5 (Nisan 16), beginning of the resurrection appearances

- Thursday, May 14 (Iyyar 25), ascension of Jesus

- Sunday, May 24 (Sivan 6), Day of Pentecost (Shavuot)

- August 31, twenty-first birthday of Gaius Caligula, after which he is allowed to hold a quaestorship, giving him access to the Senate; he marries Julia Claudia, an arranged marriage to link him to a powerful family; he and Gemellus clearly signaled as Tiberius's successors by now

- October 18, death of Agrippina the Elder by starvation on the island of Pandateria

ACKNOWLEDGMENTS

IN RESEARCHING AND WRITING THIS BOOK I have drawn upon the work of historical, classical and biblical scholars past and present and from many countries. This is an immensely rich, diverse and staggeringly extensive body of work—I feel as if I have only paddled in a great sea.

In particular, I must express my gratitude to Dr. Bruce Winter of Tyndale House, Cambridge, and for the use of the college library. He exemplifies all that the college stands for and gave me some important orientation in exploring this vast subject. By the nature of my self-imposed task, I have had to find my own way to a great extent and must take responsibility for any errors of fact or interpretation.

My editor at Sutton Publishing, Christopher Feeney, has been of huge importance to me with his judicious comments on the various stages of the work. Thanks are also due to my editors for the American edition, Cindy Bunch and Drew Blankman, and the team at IVP. A special thanks also to Bow Watkinson for preparing the maps.

The meticulous mapping of nineteenth-century cartographers of the Palestine Exploration Fund helped me to get a feel for the landscapes of some of the most momentous events in A.D. 33—such detail has been lost in subsequent urbanization.

Throughout, the encouragement of the Leicester Writers' Club, Rod, Chris, Gwyneth, Liz, Terri and many others, as well as that of Cindy Zudys, Sarah Manning and Christopher Catherwood, has been an important sustenance.

NOTES

Prologue: Two Kings, Two Kingdoms

[1]This vignette is based on the perhaps jaundiced portrait of Tiberius in Tacitus, Suetonius and Dio Cassius. The spilling of the wine is my invention, as is the incident of the snake, but they are typical of the way that unusual experiences could be interpreted as portents. The contents of Tiberius's dream are drawn from the imagery of the temptation of Christ. The Prince of Darkness is not noted for his originality and may have tried the same temptations on more than one occasion. I thought it preferable to use first-century imagery rather than try to invent imagery from the limited perspective of the third millennium.

[2]Who may belong to the period before Capreae—the source is not specific (Suetonius *Tiberius* 56, in *De Vita Caesarum,* trans. J. C. Rolfe, Loeb Classical Library [Cambridge, Mass.: Harvard University Press, 1920]).

[3]See Howard H. Scullard, *From the Gracchi to Nero: A History of Rome from 133 B.C. to A.D. 68* (London: Routledge, 1982), pp. 275-78, 280-83.

[4]This vignette is based on the account in the Gospel of John 10:22-42.

[5]Acts 5:36; Josephus *Antiquities of the Jews* 20.5.1, in *The Works of Flavius Josephus,* trans. W. Whiston (London: Routledge, n.d.).

[6]Josephus *Antiquities* 20.5.1.

[7]1 Maccabees 4:36-59; 2 Maccabees 10:1-8; Josephus *Antiquities* 12.316-26. The Judaism of Jesus' time is explored further in chap. 6.

[8]Alfred Edersheim, *The Temple: Its Ministry and Services as They Were at the Time of Jesus Christ* (London: James Clarke, 1959), pp. 333-34.

[9]Rodney A. Whitacre, *John* (Downers Grove, Ill.: InterVarsity Press, 1999), p. 268.

[10]See Oskar Skarsaune, *In the Shadow of the Temple: Jewish Influences on Early Christianity* (Downers Grove, Ill.: InterVarsity Press, 2002).

[11]See the reflections of the writer of the New Testament letter to the Hebrews (9:24).

[12]George Steiner, "Grave Jubilation: Auerbach's Mimesis Remains a Monument, and a Gift," *Times Literary Supplement* 5242 (2003).

Chapter 1: Papyri and Puzzles

[1]"The Origin of the Christian Codex," *Zeitschrift für Papyrologie und Epigraphik* 102 (1994): 263-68. Scrolls are still employed ceremonially in worship in synagogues.

[2]The term *Q* stands for the German "Quelle" (source).

[3]Richard Burridge, *Four Gospels, One Jesus? A Symbolic Reading* (London: SPCK, 1994), p. 7; see also Richard A. Burridge, *What Are the Gospels? A Comparison with Graeco-Roman Biography* (Cambridge: Cambridge University Press, 1992); and Helen Elsom, "The New Testament and Greco-Roman Writing," in *The Literary Guide to the Bible,* ed. Robert Alter and Frank Kermode (London: Collins, 1987).

[4]Particularly see N. T. Wright's portrayal of the rendering of the Jewish story in the various Gospels in the New Testament: *The New Testament and the People of God* (London: SPCK, 1992), pp. 371-417.

[5]Ibid., p. 381.

Chapter 2: Tiberius and the Eastern Empire

[1]Suetonius *Tiberius* 40.

[2]Ibid., p. 60.

[3]Though the murder of Drusus by Sejanus and Livilla is not certain, Tiberius became convinced of it when presented with evidence in A.D. 31.

[4]Some historians dispute a "reign of terror." See Howard H. Scullard, *From the Gracchi to Nero: A History of Rome from 133 B.C. to A.D. 68* (London: Routledge, 1982), pp. 280-83.

[5]Barbara Levick, *Tiberius the Politician,* rev. ed. (London: Routledge, 1999), p. 221; Philo *On the Embassy to Gaius* 7, in *The Works of Philo,* trans. C. D. Yonge (Peabody, Mass.: Hendrickson, 1993).

[6]Levick, *Tiberius,* p. 17.

[7]See Tacitus *The Annals of Imperial Rome,* trans. Michael Grant (London: Penguin, 1959), 4.58.1; Suetonius *Tiberius,* in *De Vita,* 56, see 70.

[8]The papyrus is in the John Rylands Library, Manchester. The fragment contains John 18:31-33 from the New Testament, and on its reverse, John 18:37-38.

[9]What we know of Pilate's life comes from Josephus (*Antiquities of the Jews* 18.2.2; 18.3.1-3; 18.4.1-2; *Jewish Wars* 2.9.2-4), Philo of Alexandria (*On the Embassy to Gaius* 38), Tacitus (*Annals* 15.44), the 1961 praefectus inscription from Caesarea, and the New Testament (the Gospels; Acts 3:13; 4:27; 13:28; 1 Tim 6:13). Information on Pilate from much later church tradition and apocryphal literature is unreliable.

[10]Josephus *Antiquities of the Jews* 15.9.6.

[11]Ibid.

[12]See Wolfgang Reinhardt, "The Population Size of Jerusalem and the Numerical Growth of the Jerusalem Church," in *The Book of Acts in Its First Century Setting:* vol. 4, *Palestinian Setting,* ed. Richard Bauckham (Grand Rapids: Eerdmans, 1995).

[13]Josephus *Antiquities of the Jews* 18.3.2; *Jewish Wars* 2.9.4.

[14]Not enough information has been preserved to link this incident over the aqueduct with the massacre of the Galileans, so it is not possible to locate the year of its occurrence.

[15]Philo *On the Embassy to Gaius* 38.

[16]As Tiberius was petitioned directly, and not via Sejanus, who filtered correspondence with the emperor, the incident clearly happened after the execution of Sejanus in October, A.D. 31. It would have been a very different story if he had still been alive.

[17]Levick, *Tiberius the Politician,* p. 137. She relates this desire to please to John 19:12 in the New Testament, where Pilate is accused of not being a friend of Caesar's by the city authorities (see p. 110).

[18]The source for this section is Harold W. Hoehner, *Herod Antipas: A Contemporary of Jesus Christ* (Grand Rapids: Zondervan, 1980).

[19]Josephus *Antiquities* 18.5.2.

[20]Ibid.

[21]Alfred Edersheim, *The Temple: Its Ministry and Services as They Were at the Time of Jesus Christ* (London: James Clarke, 1959), pp. 23ff.

[22]Josephus *Antiquities of the Jews* 18.4.3; 18.2.2

[23]Craig A. Evans, "Caiaphas Ossuary," in *Dictionary of New Testament Background,* ed. Craig A. Evans and Stanley E. Porter (Downers Grove, Ill.: InterVarsity Press, 2000), pp. 179-80.

[24]Alfred Edersheim, *Life and Times of Jesus the Messiah* (London: Longmans, Green, 1883), 1.263-64.

[25]Pliny the Elder, *The Natural History* (London: John Bostock, H. T. Riley, Taylor and Francis, 1855), 5.6.9ff.

[26]Josephus *Jewish Wars* 4.10.5.

[27]Strabo *The Geography of Strabo,* Loeb Classical Library 49-50, trans. H. L. Jones (Cambridge, Mass.: Harvard University Press, 1917-1923), 17.1.8.

[28]The notorious slaughter of the innocents is disputed by many scholars because the event is not mentioned outside the Gospel of Matthew. It is likely, however, that the number of infants in a small habitation such as Bethlehem and its district would be few, and hence the event was not historically notable. The slaughter fits with other recorded acts of Herod.

[29]Josephus *Antiquities* 14.10.1.

[30]J. M. Roberts, *History of Europe* (London: Penguin, 1996), p. 62.

[31]It was not until the second century A.D. that there were major insurgences—e.g., a revolt in 115-117 among Jewish inhabitants of Alexandria as a result of animosity between Jews and Greeks.

[32]On Egypt and Alexandria see James Jankowski, *Egypt: A Short History* (Oxford: One World, 2000).

[33]See Kevin Shillington, *History of Africa* (London: Macmillan, 1989).

[34]The canon of Scripture known to Philo was that represented in the Septuagint translation from Hebrew to Greek. Philo wrote mainly on the books of Moses (Genesis, Exodus, Leviticus, Numbers and Deuteronomy), using an allegorical method of interpretation that was hugely influential on the development of Christian theology.

[35]Philo *Concerning the World,* in *The Works of Philo,* vol. 7, trans. C. D. Yonge (Peabody, Mass.: Hendrickson, 1993).

[36]Philo *On Providence,* in *The Works of Philo,* trans. C. D. Yonge (Peabody, Mass.: Hendrickson, 1993), 2.64.

[37]Philo *The Special Laws,* in *The Works of Philo,* trans. C. D. Yonge (Peabody, Mass.: Hendrickson, 1993), 3:1-3.

[38]Philo took up the Greek translation of Wisdom (Logos) in the Septuagint, used in the beautiful section of Proverbs 8. There, Wisdom, the creative "Word" of God, is a blueprint of creation. This Hebrew concept accorded well with what the philosophers call "Middle Platonism" and its attempts to solve the problem of the one and the many, universals and particulars, by using a mediating concept. Philo's solution to the problem was a powerful and influential synthesis of Scripture and Greek Platonism. Christianity's solution was its doctrine of the Trinity and divine incarnation, fundamentally Hebrew and scriptural rather than Hellenistic.

[39]Philo *Who Is the Heir of Divine Things,* in *The Works of Philo,* trans. C. D. Yonge (Peabody, Mass.: Hendrickson, 1993), 42:205.

[40]It is not known if John read Philo or came across the concept elsewhere.

[41]Geza Vermes, *The Passion* (London: Penguin, 2005), p. 12.

[42]See John A. T. Robinson, *Redating the New Testament* (Philadelphia: Westminster Press, 1976).

Chapter 3: The Road of Courage

[1]The vignette is based upon John 11.

[2]I assume the traditional view that the apostle John was author of the Gospel, to be identified with "the disciple whom Jesus loved," mentioned several times in the Gospel. Some scholars doubt this, especially of course those who date the Gospel very late in the first century or even into the second (such as Geza Vermes). The debate is by no means closed.

Chapter 4: Tiberius and the Shadow of Sejanus

[1]Dio Cassius *Roman History,* trans. E. Cary, Loeb Classical Library (Cambridge, Mass.: Harvard University Press, 1927), 7.57.19.

[2]Tacitus *Annals of Tacitus* 4.8.10, trans. Alfred J. Church and William J. Brodribb (New York: Macmillan, 1891).

[3]Ibid., 4.59.

[4]Dio Cassius *Roman History,* 7.58.5-6.

[5]Ibid., 7.58.10.

[6]Seneca *Tranquillity of the Mind,* trans. W. B. Langsdorf (New York: Putnam, 1900), c. 11.

[7]Tacitus *Annals* 5.9.

[8]Dio Cassius *Roman History,* 7.58.11.

[9]C. Velleius Paterculus *Roman History* 2.131.

[10]Tacitus *The Annals of Imperial Rome* 6, trans. Michael Grant (London: Penguin, 1959), p. 204.

[11]Dio Cassius *Roman History,* 7.58.22.

[12]Ibid., pp. 58, 14, 16, 15.

[13]Tacitus *Annals of Imperial Rome,* p. 207.

[14]Ibid., p. 202.

[15]Dio Cassius *Roman History,* 7.58.21.

[16]Ibid.

[17]The future emperor would be born at Narnia, in Umbria, the place from which C. S. Lewis took the name for his famous children's stories.

[18]Tacitus *Annals* 6.20.

Chapter 5: Darkness at Noon

[1]W. H. Schoff, lists India's main exports as precious stones, pearls, tortoise shells, ivory, pepper, spikenard, malabathrum and silk and other textiles. For these the Romans traded tin, lead, copper, glass, realgar (a red pigment), orpiment (a gold pigment), antimony and wine, or they paid in gold coins (*The Periplus of the Erythraean Sea: Travel and Trade in the Indian Ocean by a Merchant of the First Century,* trans. and ed. W. H. Schoff (New York: Longmans, Green, and Co., 1912).

[2]It took a paradigm shift to grasp the role of suffering even though, as Jesus is recorded as pointing out, it was rooted in the Old Testament suffering Servant spoken of by Isaiah and the smitten Shepherd of Zechariah (Isaiah 53; Zechariah 13)—see R. T. France, *Jesus and the Old Testament* (London: Tyndale, 1971), p. 103ff.

[3]In Michael Grant, *The Jews in the Roman World* (London: Weidenfeld & Nicolson, 1973), p. 110.

[4]It is not clear from the narratives whether there was one animal or two.

[5]That was a second siege that Sepphoris had suffered. See James F. Strange, "Sepphoris," University of South Florida, <www.bibleinterp.com/articles/sepphoris.htm>.

[6]According to the early church historian Eusebius, Jerusalem Christians were warned in a prophecy, taking refuge in Pella, a town across the River Jordan (*History of the Church* 3.5.3, trans. G. A. Williamson [London: Penguin, 1989]).

[7]Mark A. Noll, *Turning Points: Decisive Moments in the History of Christianity* (Grand Rapids: Baker Academic, 1997), p. 27.

[8]F. F. Bruce, *The Spreading Flame: The Rise and Progress of Christianity from Its First Beginnings to the Conversion of the English* (Grand Rapids: Eerdmans, 1958), pp. 157-58.

[9]Sulpicius Severus, quoted in ibid., p. 156.

[10]Craig A. Evans, "The Destruction of Jerusalem," in *Dictionary of New Testament Background,* ed. Craig A. Evans and Stanley E. Porter (Downers Grove, Ill.: InterVarsity Press, 2000), pp. 273-80. Evans lists some of the predictions of destruction of Jerusalem: "The curtain of the temple will be torn," according to the *Testament of Levi.* The *Testament of Levi* foretells the destruction of a corrupt priesthood. The *Testament of Judah* predicts destruction by siege and fire, followed by captivity. The *Sibylline Oracles* seem to predict the siege of Jerusalem. The removal of the Jerusalem priestly establishment is anticipated by the men of the Renewed Cove-

nant at Qumran, which was an important center of the Essene sect. The demise of Jerusalem and the temple is foretold by the author of the *Lives of the Prophets in Jonah and Habakkuk*. The historian Josephus tells us that he himself predicted the city's destruction. Josephus also mentions a Jesus ben Ananias who foretold the end of the city and the temple. In addition, there are rabbinic traditions that claim that some rabbis, particularly Zadok and Yohanan ben Zakkai, made similar predictions. Most of these traditions, Evans points out, drew on the vocabulary and imagery of Israel's earlier prophets when they prophesied the first destruction of Jerusalem and the temple.

[11]Not all at this time expected this kind of Messiah (see chap. 6).

[12]F. W. Farrar, *The Life of Christ* (London: Cassell, 1903), p. 539.

[13]Some scholars believe that the Gospels document only one cleansing.

[14]Grant, *Jews in the Roman World,* p. 109.

[15]See E. P. Sanders, *The Historical Figure of Jesus* (London: Penguin, 1993); Geza Vermes, *The Passion* (London: Penguin, 2005); Craig L. Blomberg, *Jesus and the Gospels* (Nashville: Broadman & Holman, 1997).

[16]The Gospel accounts are not clear about whether this was a Passover meal taken early, or some kind of pre-Passover meal. In either event, Jesus redefined the meal, and Christian followers afterward called it "the Lord's Supper," "the Lord" being a familiar designation for Jesus among them.

[17]See Paul's use of "the Lord's Supper" in his New Testament letter 1 Corinthians 11:17-26, written approximately A.D. 53-55.

[18]See New Testament scholar John Wenham's *Easter Enigma* (Exeter, U.K.: Paternoster, 1984), pp. 47-49.

[19]A fair amount of forest has been used up discussing the identity of the "disciple whom Jesus loved." Dan Brown in the bestselling *The Da Vinci Code* thinks it is Mary Magdalene, whom he sees as the queen and wife of Christ. Scholars have posited various members of the twelve disciples or even Lazarus. A good exercise is to rule out who it is not, from descriptions of various disciples in the Gospel accounts during the Last Supper. John is a strong candidate for this close friend of Jesus. See the interesting discussion by D. A. Carson on authorship in his *The Gospel According to John* (Grand Rapids: Eerdmans, 1991), pp. 68-81.

[20]Sanders, *Historical Figure of Jesus,* pp. 274-76.

[21]Erich Auerbach, *Mimesis: The Representation of Reality in Western Literature* (Princeton, N.J.: Princeton University Press, 1968), pp. 42-43.

[22]The issue of what power the Jewish council had to pronounce and carry out the death sentence on religious grounds is complex. There is some evidence that the Jewish leaders had some limited power to carry out death sentences. The tractate *Sanhedrin,* in the Mishnah, gives various regulations for the different types of execution. There was a warning inscription on the inner sanctuary of the temple, threatening death to any foreigner. Stephen was later put to death following a session of the Jewish Sanhedrin. See J. D. Douglas and N. Hillyer, "The trial of Jesus," in *The Illustrated Bible Dictionary,* 3 vols. (Leicester, U.K.: Inter-Varsity Press, 1980).

[23]Philo *On Flaccus,* in *The Works of Philo,* vol. 6, trans. C. D. Yonge (Peabody, Mass.: Hendrickson, 1993).

[24]Geza Vermes is rather skeptical of such an amnesty, on the grounds that it was "unlikely." It is striking, however, that all the four Gospel accounts record it. As we know so little about the period, Vermes's argument is not strong. Roman governors had extensive discretionary powers (*The Passion* [London: Penguin, 2005], pp. 59-62).

[25]Colin J. Humphreys and W. Graeme Waddington, "Dating the Crucifixion," *Nature* 306 (1983): 743-46; Colin J. Humphreys and W. Graeme Waddington, "The Jewish Calendar, a Lunar Eclipse and the Date of Christ's Crucifixion," *Tyndale Bulletin* 43, no. 2 (1993): 331-51.

[26]The accounts vary in their use of calendars, using either Jewish reckoning (where, as with the Greeks, the day begins at sundown) or Roman (like ours, beginning at midnight).

[27]Some scholars believe the Gospel was written too late to be by the apostle.

[28]This reconstruction of the burial is largely based on that of John Wenham's *Easter Enigma.* There have been many other attempts, including Geza Vermes's *The Passion*—written in the aftermath of Mel Gibson's hit film *The Passion of the Christ* (2004).

Chapter 6: The Glory of the Temple

[1]Each of these titles has been the subject of complex and lengthy scholarly debate (see, e.g., I. Howard Marshall, "Son of Man," in *Dictionary of Jesus and the Gospels,* ed. Joel B. Green, Scott McKnight and I. Howard Marshall [Downers Grove, Ill.: InterVarsity Press, 1992]; Richard J. Bauckham, "The Son of Man: 'A Man in my Position' or 'Someone,' " *Journal for the Study of the New Testament* 2 [1985]: 23-33; Chrys C. Caragounis, *The Son of Man* [Tübingen, Germany: J. C. B. Mohr, 1986]; Maurice Casey, *Son of Man* [London: SPCK, 1979]; James D. G. Dunn, *Christology in the Making* [Philadelphia: Westminster Press, 1980]; Seyoon Kim, *The Son of Man as the Son of God* [Grand Rapids: Eerdmans, 1983]; Barnabas Lindars, *Jesus Son of Man* [Grand Rapids: Eerdmans, 1983]; Heinz Eduard Tödt, *The Son of Man in the Synoptic Tradition* [Philadelphia: Westminster Press, 1965]; Geza Vermes, *Jesus the Jew* [Philadelphia: Fortress Press, 1981]). In this chapter my main focus will be on the title "Messiah."

[2]D. A. Hagner, "Jewish Christianity," in *Dictionary of the Later New Testament and Its Developments,* ed. Ralph P. Martin and Peter H. Davids (Downers Grove, Ill.: InterVarsity Press, 1997), pp. 579-87.

[3]The relationship between the Essenes and the community at Qumran is still debated by scholars.

[4]Bruce Chilton, "Judaism," in *Dictionary of Jesus and the Gospels,* ed. Joel B. Green, Scott McKnight and I. Howard Marshall (Downers Grove, Ill.: InterVarsity Press, 1992), p. 404.

[5]Tacitus *The Annals of Imperial Rome* 15, trans. Michael Grant (London: Penguin, 1959), p. 354.

[6]Variant reading: "his learning was outstanding."

[7]Shlomo Pines, *An Arabic Version of Testimonium Flavianum and Its Implications* (Jerusalem: Israel Academy, 1971), quoted in Oskar Skarsaune, *In the Shadow of the Temple* (Downers Grove, Ill.: InterVarsity Press, 2002), p. 151.

[8]Admittedly, the book of Revelation was written comparatively late (around A.D. 90), and therefore, in the opinion of some scholars, it reflects later developments of Christian thought. The fact, however, that this book is steeped in the Scriptures of Judaism counts against the influence of Greek thought. Furthermore, temple imagery is present throughout many New Testament letters, written well before A.D. 70, e.g., in particular, the book of Hebrews.

Chapter 7: Fifty Days

[1]J. M. Roberts, *History of Europe* (London: Penguin, 1996), p. 61.

[2]Ibid., p. 63.

[3]Bribes were a common institutional oiling in the Roman world at this time.

[4]Claudius, quoted in E. M. Blaiklock, *The Century of the New Testament* (London: Inter-Varsity Fellowship, 1962), p. 42, from C. K. Barrett, *The New Testament Background: Selected Documents* (London: SPCK, 1957), p. 15.

[5]Tacitus is more accurate about Christ and his death in *Annals;* see pp. 206-7.

[6]Blaiklock, *Century of the New Testament,* pp. 41-43.

[7]E.g., at the momentous Council of Nicea.

Chapter 8: The Western Empire

[1]F. B. Marsh, *The Reign of Tiberius* (London: Oxford University Press, 1931), p. 210.

[2]Ibid., p. 211.

[3]Anne Ross, *Everyday Life of the Pagan Celts* (London: Transworld Publishers, 1972), p. 202.

[4]Tacitus *The Agricola and Germania,* trans. A. J. Church and W. J. Brodribb (London: Macmillan, 1877).

[5]Marshall B. Davidson, *A Concise History of France* (London: Cassell, 1972).

[6]Julius Caesar *The Conquest of Gaul* 16, Caesar's Commentaries, trans. W. A. Macdevitt, Everyman's Library 702, first published in this edition, 1915.

[7]Winston Churchill, *The Birth of a Nation* (London: Cassell, 1974), pp. x, xi.

[8]Jeremy Black, *A New History of England* (Stroud: Sutton, 2000).

[9]The use of Blake's poem "Jerusalem" in Women's Institute meetings is portrayed in the popular film *Calendar Girls* (2003).

[10]Robert Lacey, *Great Tales from English History* (London: Little, Brown, 2003).

Chapter 9: Past the Boundaries of Empire

[1]*Periplus* 64-65.

[2]John Keay, *A History of India* (New York: Grove, 2000), p. 101.

[3]Luoyang retains this name to this day.

[4]Corinne Debaine-Francfort, *The Search for Ancient China* (London: Thames & Hudson, 1999).

Chapter 10: Beyond the Ends of the Earth

[1]Arnold Toynbee, *Mankind and Mother Earth: A Narrative History of the World* (New York: Oxford University Press, 1976), pp. 302-5.

[2]Some believe that humans arrived over a more recent land bridge.

[3]See for example the Arizona State University site "Teotihuacán: The City of Gods," <http://archaeology.la.asu.edu/teo>.

[4]For more on Johan Reinhard's work see "Johan Reinhard's Journeys," <www.mountain.org/reinhard>.

Chapter 11: Simon Peter

[1]Many scholars believe that these elements in the narratives were a later invention, reflecting an extensive development of Christian thought. Such a view is usually associated with a late dating of the four Gospels, with none of the authors being eyewitness apostles or drawing upon eyewitness accounts. Many other scholars have earlier dates for the Gospels, with authors who were contemporaries of Jesus or eyewitness apostles.

[2]Luke of course was not writing dispassionate history—he was telling the story of the birth of the church and its remarkable expansion up to the time just before the death of the apostles Paul and Peter. For a theological-historical study centered on the coming of the Holy Spirit, see Charles Williams, *The Descent of the Dove,* a book which deeply influenced the poet W. H. Auden as he was writing his poem "New Year Letter."

[3]See, for example, the six-volume study *The Book of Acts in Its First Century Setting,* ed. Bruce W. Winter (Grand Rapids: Eerdmans, 1993-2004).

[4]See Craig A. Evans and P. R. Trebilco, "Diaspora Judaism," *Dictionary of New Testament Background,* ed. Craig A. Evans and Stanley E. Porter (Downers Grove, Ill.: InterVarsity Press, 2000), pp. 281-96.

[5]The number of pilgrims at such a feast could swell the population to hundreds of thousands. See Wolfgang Reinhardt, "The Population Size of Jerusalem and the Numerical Growth of the Jerusalem Church," in *The Book of Acts in its First Century Setting,* vol. 4; *Palestinian Setting,* ed. Richard Bauckham (Grand Rapids: Eerdmans, 1995), pp. 237-65.

[6]See Richard A. Burridge, *What Are the Gospels? A Comparison with Graeco-Roman Biography* (Cambridge: Cambridge University Press, 1992), p. 10.

[7]This mob would have been only a tiny fraction of the population of Jerusalem at the time, swelled as the city and its environs were by hundreds of thousands of pilgrims. Those in later centuries who used the action of this mob as a basis for anti-Semitism were grossly wrong to do so.

[8]See J. A. Weatherly, "Anti-Semitism," in *Dictionary of Jesus and the Gospels,* ed. Joel B. Green, Scott McKnight and I. Howard Marshall (Downers Grove, Ill.: InterVarsity Press, 1992), pp. 13-17.

[9]On this large number see Reinhardt, "Population Size of Jerusalem," pp. 237-65.

[10]Robin Lane Fox, *Pagans and Christians* (New York: Alfred A. Knopf, 1989), p. 89; Bradley Blue, "Acts and the House Church," in *The Book of Acts in its First Century*

Setting, vol. 2: *Graeco-Roman Setting,* ed. W. J. Gill and Conrad Gempf (Grand Rapids: Eerdmans, 1994), pp. 119-222.

[11]Josephus *Antiquities of the Jews* 20.9.1. The phrase, early in this passage, "who was called Christ" could be a later Christian interpolation, though it is possible that Josephus was simply recording a historic fact—that his followers called Jesus "the Messiah."

Chapter 12: Agrippina

[1]William Smith, *A Classical Dictionary of Greek and Roman Biography, Mythology and Geography,* 4th ed., ed. G. E. Marindin (London: John Murray, 1894).

[2]Tacitus *Annals* 1.

[3]Ibid., 2.

[4]Ibid., 4.53.

[5]Ibid., 4.54.

[6]Ibid., 5.3.

[7]Ibid., 6.24.

[8]Suetonius *Tiberius* 53; Tacitus *Annals* 6.25.

[9]Tacitus *Annals* 6.25.

[10]Ibid., 6.27.

Chapter 13: New Conflict in Jerusalem

[1]See F. F. Bruce, *The Acts of the Apostles,* 3rd ed. (Grand Rapids: Eerdmans, 1990), pp. 176-77.

[2]Ibid., p. 188.

[3]Philo *On Providence,* in *The Works of Philo,* trans. C. D. Yonge (Peabody, Mass.: Hendrickson, 1993), 2.64.

[4]Mishnah *Sanhedrin* 6.3-4, quoted in Bruce, *Acts of the Apostles,* p. 212.

Chapter 14: What Happened Next?

[1]Josephus *Antiquities of the Jews* 18.4.1, in *The Works of Josephus,* quoted in William K. Klingaman, *The First Century* (New York: HarperCollins, 1991), p. 207.

[2]See Anne Wroe, *Pontius Pilate: The Biography of an Invented Man* (London: Jonathan Cape, 1999).

[3]Tacitus *Annals* 15.

[4]Tacitus *The Annals of Imperial Rome,* trans. Michael Grant (London: Penguin, 1959), pp. 257-59.

[5]Martial *Epigrams,* Loeb Classical Library, trans. W. C. A. Ker (Cambridge, Mass.: Harvard University Press, 1919), 4.13; 11.54.

[6]Some contemporary scholars see some plausibility in the identification of Mary of Bethany and Mary Magdalene, e.g., John Wenham, in *Easter Enigma* (Exeter, U.K.: Paternoster, 1984).

[7]Philo *On the Embassy to Gaius,* in *The Works of Philo,* trans. C. D. Yonge (Peabody, Mass.: Hendrickson, 1993), 18.121-12, 124-25.

[8]Philo *On Flaccus,* in *The Works of Philo,* trans. C. D. Yonge (Peabody, Mass.: Hendrickson, 1993), 21.185-56, 188-89, 191.

[9]Tacitus, *Annals* 6.

[10]Dio Cassius *Roman History* 58.27.1; Pliny, "The Phoenix," in *The Natural History* 10. At this time there was not the radical separation of the mythical and the factual that is common today. We can get a hint of this old consciousness by reflecting on the equator, which is imaginary and yet is located at a definite place on the earth that is crossed by aircraft and ships.

[11]Barbara Levick, *Tiberius the Politician,* rev. ed. (London: Routledge, 1999), p. 206.

Dating A.D. 33

[1]Josephus *Antiquities of the Jews* 17.6.4.

[2]Ibid., 15.11.1; 15.10.3.

[3]Dio Cassius *Roman History* 54.7.4-6.

[4]Josephus *Antiquities of the Jews* 15.11.6.

[5]For the implications of the fourth Passover, see Harold Hoehner, "Chronology," in *Dictionary of Jesus and the Gospels,* ed. Joel B. Green, Scott McKnight and I. Howard Marshall (Downers Grove, Ill.: InterVarsity Press, 1992). It is interesting that Luke at one point also seems to imply a number of visits by Jesus and his disciples to Jerusalem, in Luke 22:39-40 (cf. John 18:2).

[6]Colin J. Humphreys and W. Graeme Waddington, "The Jewish Calendar, a Lunar Eclipse and the Date of Christ's Crucifixion," *Tyndale Bulletin* 43, no. 2 (1993): 331-51.

[7]*Sibylline Oracles* 3.800-802, in *The Apocrypha and Pseudepigrapha of the Old Testament,* ed. R. H. Charles (Oxford: Clarendon Press, 1913), 2:392.

[8]See L. C. A. Alexander, "Chronology of Paul," in *Dictionary of Paul and His Letters,* ed. Gerald F. Hawthorne, Ralph P. Martin and Daniel G. Reid (Downers Grove, Ill.: InterVarsity Press, 1993), pp. 115-123; Harold Hoehner, *Herod Antipas: A Contemporary of Jesus Christ* (Grand Rapids: Zondervan, 1980), pp. 39, 257, 315-16, 350; Hoehner, "Chronology," pp. 118-22; Stanley E. Porter, "Chronology, New Testament," in *Dictionary of New Testament Background,* ed. Craig A. Evans and Stanley E. Porter (Downers Grove, Ill.: InterVarsity Press, 2000), pp. 201-8.

BIBLIOGRAPHY

Aland, Kurt, ed.. *Synopsis of the Four Gospels*. New York: United Bible Societies, 1985

Alexander, L. C. A. "Chronology of Paul." In *Dictionary of Paul and His Letters,* edited by Gerald F. Hawthorne, Ralph P. Martin and Daniel G. Reid. Downers Grove, Ill.: InterVarsity Press, 1993.

Alter, Robert, and Frank Kermode, eds. *The Literary Guide to the Bible*. London: Collins, 1987.

Atlas of Ancient and Classical Geography. London: J. M. Dent, 1907.

Auerbach, Erich. *Mimesis: The Representation of Reality in Western Literature*. Princeton, N.J.: Princeton University Press, 1968

Backhouse, Robert. *The Jerusalem Temple*. London: Candle Books, 2002.

Bamm, Peter. *The Kingdoms of Christ: The Story of the Early Church*. London: Thames and Hudson, 1961.

Bauckam, Richard J. "The Son of Man, 'A Man in My Position' or 'Someone.' " *Journal for the Study of the New Testament* 2 (1985).

Bishop, Jim. *The Day Christ Died*. London: Weidenfeld & Nicolson, 1957.

Black, Jeremy. *A New History of England*. Stroud, U.K.: Sutton, 2000.

Black, Jeremy., ed. *Atlas of World History*. London: Dorling Kindersley, 1999.

Blaiklock, E. M. *The Acts of the Apostles: A Historical Commentary*. Tyndale New Testament Commentaries. London: Tyndale Press, 1959.

———. *The Century of the New Testament*. London: Inter-Varsity Fellowship, 1962.

———. *The World of the New Testament*. London: Ark Publishing, 1981.

Blomberg, Craig L. *The Historical Reliability of John's Gospel*. Downers Grove, Ill.: InterVarsity Press, 2001.

———. *Jesus and the Gospels*. Leicester, U.K.: Apollos, 1997.

Blue, Bradley. "Acts and the House Church." In *The Book of Acts in its First Century Setting*. Vol. 2, *Graeco-Roman Setting,* edited by D. W. J. Gill and Conrad Gempf. Grand Rapids: Eerdmans, 1994.

Boardman, John, Jasper Griffin and Oswyn Murray. *The Oxford History of the Classical World*. Oxford: Oxford University Press, 1986.

Bouquet, A. C. *Everyday Life in New Testament Times*. London: Batsford, 1953.

Brown, Dan. *The Da Vinci Code*. New York: Doubleday, 2003.

Bruce, F. F. *The Acts of the Apostles: Greek Text with Introduction and Commentary.* 3rd ed. Grand Rapids: Eerdmans, 1990.

————. *The New Testament Documents: Are They Reliable?* 6th ed. Downers Grove, Ill.: InterVarsity Press, 2003.

————. *The Spreading Flame: The Rise and Progress of Christianity from its First Beginnings to the Conversion of the English.* Grand Rapids: Eerdmans, 1958.

Burridge, Richard A. *Four Gospels, One Jesus? A Symbolic Reading.* London: SPCK, 1994.

————. *What Are the Gospels? A Comparison with Graeco-Roman Biography.* Cambridge: Cambridge University Press, 1992.

Caragounis, Chrys C. *The Son of Man.* Tübingen: J. C. B. Mohr, 1986.

Carcopino, Jerome. *Daily Life in Ancient Rome.* London: Penguin, 1991.

Carson, D. A. *The Gospel According to John.* Grand Rapids: Eerdmans, 1991.

————. *Jesus and His Friends: An Exposition of John 14—17.* Carlisle, U.K.: Paternoster Press, 1995.

Casey, Maurice. *Son of Man.* London: SPCK, 1979.

Chadwick, Henry. *The Early Church.* London: Penguin, 1967.

Chilton, Bruce. "Judaism." In *Dictionary of Jesus and the Gospels,* edited by Joel B. Green, Scott McKnight and I. Howard Marshall. Downers Grove, Ill.: InterVarsity Press, 1992.

Chilton, Bruce, and Jacob Neusner. *Judaism in the New Testament: Practices and Beliefs.* New York, Routledge, 1995.

Chisholm, Kitty, and John Ferguson. *Rome: The Augustan Age—A Source Book.* Oxford: Oxford University Press, 1981.

Churchill, Winston. *The Birth of a Nation.* London: Cassell, 1974.

Crofts, F. W. *The Four Gospels in One Story.* London: Longmans, 1949.

Culver, Robert D. *The Earthly Career of Jesus, the Christ: A Life in Chronological, Geographical and Social Context.* Fearn, Ross-shire, U.K.: Mentor, 2002.

Daniel, Orville E. *A Harmony of the Four Gospels.* 2nd ed. Grand Rapids: Baker, 1996.

Davidson, Marshall B. *A Concise History of France.* London: Cassell, 1972.

Dio Cassius. *Dio's Roman History.* Loeb Classical Library. Translated by E. Cary. 9 vols. Cambridge, Mass.: Harvard University Press, 1914-1927.

Douglas, J. D. and N. Hillyer. *The Illustrated Bible Dictionary.* 3 vols. Leicester, U.K.: Inter-Varsity Press, 1980.

Dunn, James D. G. *Christology in the Making.* Philadelphia: Westminster Press, 1980.

Edersheim, Alfred. *Life and Times of Jesus the Messiah.* London: Longmans, Green, 1883.

————. *The Temple: Its Ministry and Services as They Were at the Time of Jesus Christ.* London: James Clarke, 1959.

Edwards, James R. *The Gospel According to Mark.* Grand Rapids: Eerdmans, 2002.

Ellis, Peter B. *The Celtic Empire: The First Millenium of Celtic History 1000 BC-AD 51.* London: Robinson, 1990.

Elsom, Helen. "The New Testament and Greco-Roman Writing." In *The Literary Guide to the Bible,* edited by Robert Alter and Frank Kermode. London: Collins, 1987.

Eluère, C. *The Celts: First Masters of Europe*. London: Thames & Hudson, 1993.

Eusebius. *The History of the Church,* translated by G. A. Williamson. London: Penguin, 1989.

Evans, Craig A. "Caiaphas Ossuary." In *Dictionary of New Testament Background,* edited by Craig A. Evans and Stanley E. Porter. Downers Grove, Ill.: InterVarsity Press, 2000.

Evans, Craig A., and P. R. Trebilco. "Diaspora Judaism." In *Dictionary of New Testament Background,* edited by Craig A. Evans and Stanley E. Porter. Downers Grove, Ill.: InterVarsity Press, 2000.

Farrar, Frederic W. *The Life of Christ*. London: Cassell, 1903.

Fox, R. L. *Pagans and Christians*. New York: Alfred A. Knopf, 1989.

France, R. T. *Jesus and the Old Testament*. London: Tyndale, 1971.

———. *Matthew*. Tyndale New Testament Commentaries. Grand Rapids: Eerdmans, 1985.

Freedman, David N., ed. *Eerdmans Dictionary of the Bible*. Grand Rapids: Eerdmans, 2000.

Gill, David W. J., and Conrad Gempf, eds. *The Book of Acts in Its First-Century Setting*. Vol. 2, *Graeco-Roman Setting*. Grand Rapids: Eerdmans, 1994.

Grabbe, Lester L. *An Introduction to First Century Judaism: Jewish Religion and History in the Second Temple Period*. Edinburgh: T & T Clark, 1996.

Grant, Michael. *Roman Myths*. London: Penguin, 1973.

———. *The Jews in the Roman World*. London: Weidenfeld & Nicolson, 1973.

Graves, Robert I. *Claudius*. London: Vintage, 1999.

Grimal, Pierre. *The Civilization of Rome*. London: George Allen & Unwin, 1963.

Guelich, Robert A., and Craig A. Evans. "The Destruction of Jerusalem." In *Dictionary of New Testament Background,* edited by Craig A. Evans and Stanley E. Porter. Downers Grove, Ill.: InterVarsity Press, 2000.

Hagner, Donald A. "Jewish Christianity." In *Dictionary of the Later New Testament and Its Developments,* edited by Ralph P. Martin and Peter H. Davids. Downers Grove, Ill.: InterVarsity Press, 1997.

Hoehner, Harold W. "Chronology." In *Dictionary of Jesus and the Gospels,* edited by Joel B. Green, Scott McKnight and I. Howard Marshall. Downers Grove, Ill.: InterVarsity Press, 1992.

———. *Herod Antipas: A Contemporary of Jesus Christ*. Grand Rapids: Zondervan, 1980.

Humphreys, Colin J., and W. Graeme Waddington. "Dating the Crucifixion." *Nature* 306 (1983).

———. "The Jewish Calendar, a Lunar Eclipse and the Date of Christ's Crucifixion." *Tyndale Bulletin* 43, no. 2 (1993).

James, M. R. *The Apocryphal New Testament*. Oxford: Clarendon, 1955.

Jankowski, James. *Egypt: A Short History*. Oxford: One World, 2000.

Josephus. *The Works of Flavius Josephus*. Translated by W. Whiston. London: George Routledge, n.d.

Julius Caesar. *The Conquest of Gaul*. Caesar's Commentaries, translated by W. A. Macdevitt. Everyman's Library, 1915.

Juvenal. *The Sixteen Satires*. Translated by Peter Green. London: Penguin, 1974.

Keay, John. *A History of India*. New York: Grove Books, 2000.

Keener, Craig S. *Matthew*. IVP New Testament Commentaries. Downers Grove, Ill.: InterVarsity Press, 1997.

Kent, Charles F. *The Makers and Teachers of Judaism: From the Fall of Jerusalem to the Death of Herod the Great*. London: Hodder & Stoughton, 1911.

Kim, Seyoon. *"The 'Son of Man' " as the Son of God*. Grand Rapids: Eerdmans, 1983.

Kinder, Hermann, and Werner Hilgemann. *The Penguin Atlas of World History*. Vol. 1, *From the Beginning to the Eve of the French Revolution*. London: Penguin, 1978.

Klingaman, William K. *The First Century*. New York: HarperCollins, 1991.

Lacey, Robert. *Great Tales from English History*. London: Little, Brown, 2003.

Larkin, William J. *Acts*. IVP New Testament Commentaries. Downers Grove, Ill.: InterVarsity Press, 1995.

Levick, Barbara. *Tiberius the Politician*. Rev. ed. London: Routledge, 1999.

Lindars, Barnabas. *Jesus Son of Man*. Grand Rapids: Eerdmans, 1983.

Marsh, Frank B. *The Reign of Tiberius*. London: Oxford University Press, 1931.

Marshall, I. Howard. "Son of Man." In *Dictionary of Jesus and the Gospels,* edited by Joel B. Green, Scott McKnight and I. Howard Marshall. Downers Grove, Ill.: InterVarsity Press, 1992.

———. *Acts*. Tyndale New Testament Commentaries. Grand Rapids: Eerdmans, 1980.

McEvedy, Colin. *The New Penguin Atlas of Ancient History*. London: Penguin, 2002

Moltmann-Wendel, Elisabeth. *The Women Around Jesus,* translated by John Bowden. New York: Crossroad, 1997.

Monson, J. *Student Map Manual: Historical Geography of the Bible Lands*. Jerusalem: Pictorial Archive, 1979.

Morison, Frank. *Who Moved the Stone?* Grand Rapids: Zondervan, 1987.

Morris, Leon. *Luke*. Tyndale New Testament Commentaries. Rev. ed. Grand Rapids: Eerdmans, 1988.

Morton, H. V. *In the Steps of the Master*. London: Rich & Cowan, 1934.

Murphy-O'Connor, Jerome. *The Holy Land: An Oxford Archaeological Guide from Earliest Times to 1700*. 4th ed. Oxford: Oxford University Press, 1998.

Noll, Mark A. *Turning Points: Decisive Moments in the History of Christianity*. Grand Rapids: Baker, 2000.

Paterculus, Velleius. *The Roman History*. Loeb Classical Library. Translated by F. W. Shipley. Cambridge, Mass.: Harvard University Press, 1924.

Petronius. *The Satyricon,* translated by P. G. Walsh. Oxford: Oxford University Press, 1999.

Philo. *The Works of Philo,* translated by C. D. Yonge. Peabody, Mass.: Hendrickson, 1993.

Pines, Shlomo. *An Arabic Version of Testimonium Flavianum and Its Implications*.

Jerusalem: Israel Academy, 1971.

Pliny the Elder. *The Natural History*. Bohn's Classical Library. Translated by J. Bostock and H. T. Riley. London: H. G. Bohn, 1855.

Porter, Stanley E. "Chronology, New Testament." In *Dictionary of New Testament Background,* edited by Craig A. Evans and Stanley E. Porter. Downers Grove, Ill.: InterVarsity Press, 2000.

Pritchard, James B. *The Times Atlas of the Bible*. London: Times Books, 1987.

Pryor, Francis. *Britain BC: Life in Britain and Ireland Before the Romans*. London: HarperCollins, 2003.

Reinhardt, Wolfgang. "The Population Size of Jerusalem and the Numerical Growth of the Jerusalem Church." In *The Book of Acts in its First Century Setting*. Vol. 4: *Palestinian Setting,* edited by Richard Bauckham. Grand Rapids: Eerdmans, 1995.

Roberts, J. M. *History of Europe*. London: Penguin, 1996.

Robinson, John A. T. *Redating the New Testament*. Philadelphia: Westminster Press, 1976.

Rogerson, John. *Chronicles of the Bible Lands*. London: Angus, 2003.

Ross, Anne. *Everyday Life of the Pagan Celts*. London: Transworld Publishers, 1972.

Sanders, E. P. *The Historical Figure of Jesus*. New York: Penguin, 1996.

Scarre, Christopher. *Past Worlds: The Times Atlas of Archaeology*. London: Times Books, 1991.

Schoff, W. H., trans. and ed. *The Periplus of the Erythraean Sea: Travel and Trade in the Indian Ocean by a Merchant of the First Century*. New York: Longmans, Green, and Co., 1912.

Scullard, H. H. *From the Gracchi to Nero: A History of Rome from 133 B.C. to A.D. 68*. 5th ed. New York: Routledge, 1982.

Shillington, Kevin. *History of Africa*. London: Macmillan, 1989.

Skarsaune, Oskar. *In the Shadow of the Temple: Jewish Influences on Early Christianity*. Downers Grove, Ill.: InterVarsity Press, 2002.

Skeat, T. C. "The Origin of the Christian Codex." *Zeitschrift für Papyrologie und Epigraphik* 102 (1994).

Smith, George A. *The Historical Geography of the Holy Land*. London: Collins, 1966.

Smith, William. *A Classical Dictionary of Greek and Roman Biography, Mythology and Geography*. 4th ed. Edited by G. E. Marindin. London: John Murray, 1894.

Stanton, Graham. *Gospel Truth? Today's Quest for Jesus of Nazareth*. London: Fount, 1997.

Stein, Robert H. *The Synoptic Problem*. Grand Rapids: Baker, 1994.

Steiner, George. "Grave Jubilation: Auerbach's Mimesis Remains a Monument, and a Gift." *Times Literary Supplement* 5242 (2003).

Strabo. *The Geography of Strabo*. Loeb Classical Library 49-50. Translated by H. L. Jones. Cambridge, Mass.: Harvard University Press, 1917-1923.

Strange, James F. "Sepphoris." University of South Florida, <www.bibleinterp.com/articles/sepphoris.htm>.

Suetonius. *De Vita Caesarum*. 2 vols. Loeb Classical Library. Translated by J. C. Rolfel Cambridge, Mass.: Harvard University Press, 1920.

————. *The Twelve Caesars.* Translated by R. Graves. London: Penguin, 1989.

Tacitus. *The Agricola and Germania,* translated by A. J. Church and W. J. Brodribb. London: Macmillan, 1877.

————. *The Annals of Imperial Rome,* translated by Michael Grant. London: Penguin, 1959.

————. *Annals of Tacitus.* Translated by A. J. Church and W. J. Brodribb. New York: Macmillan, 1891.

————. *The Histories.* Translated by K. Wellesley. London: Penguin, 1975.

Tatian. *Diatessaron* <http://members.aol.com/GospelofTatian>.

Theissen, Gerd. *The Shadow of the Galilean.* London: SCM Press, 1987.

Thirlwall, Thomas. *Diatessaron, or the History of Our Lord Jesus Christ Compiled from the Four Gospels.* 2nd ed. London: n.p. 1804.

Tödt, Heinz Eduard. *The Son of Man in the Synoptic Tradition.* Philadelphia: Westminster Press, 1965.

Toynbee, Arnold. *Mankind and Mother Earth: A Narrative History of the World.* New York: Oxford University Press, 1976.

Vermes, Geza. *Jesus the Jew.* Philadelphia: Fortress Press, 1981.

————. *The Passion.* London: Penguin, 2005.

Walker, Peter. *Jesus and His World.* Downers Grove, Ill.: InterVarsity Press, 2003.

Weatherhead, Leslie D. *It Happened in Palestine.* London: Hodder & Stoughton, 1936.

Weatherly, J. A. "Anti-Semitism." In *Dictionary of Jesus and the Gospels,* edited by Joel B. Green, Scott McKnight and I. Howard Marshall. Downers Grove, Ill.: InterVarsity Press, 1992.

Wells, Colin. *The Roman Empire.* 2nd ed. London: HarperCollins, 1992.

Wenham, John. *Easter Enigma.* Exeter: Paternoster, 1984.

Wheeler, Mortimer. *Rome Beyond the Imperial Frontiers.* London: Penguin, 1955.

Whitacre, Rodney A. *John.* IVP New Testament Commentary. Downers Grove, Ill.: InterVarsity Press, 1999.

Wilson, Ian. *Jesus: The Evidence.* London: Pan Books, 1984.

Winter, Bruce W., and Andrew D. Clarke. *The Book of Acts in Its First-Century Setting.* Vol. 1, *Ancient Literary Setting.* Grand Rapids: Eerdmans, 1993.

Witherington, Ben, III. *The Gospel Code: Novel Claims About Jesus, Mary Magdalene and Da Vinci.* Downers Grove, Ill.: InterVarsity Press, 2004.

————. *The Paul Quest: The Renewed Search for the Jew of Tarsus.* Downers Grove, Ill.: InterVarsity Press, 1998.

Wright, N. T. *The New Testament and the People of God.* London: SPCK, 1992.

Wroe, Ann. *Pontius Pilate: The Biography of an Invented Man.* London: Jonathan Cape, 1999.

Index

Acts, book of, 170, 172-3, 198, 200

Agrippa I, Herod, 91, 104, 110, 180, 205, 207, 229-30

Agrippina the Elder, 21, 59, 75, 136, 181-89, 228

Alexandria, 18, 55-60

Ammathus (Hammath), 50

anachronism
    in Geza Vermes, 97
    in Gospels, 31, 97, 100, 171

Ananias, 176, 193

Ananus, 178, 230

Annas, 54, 55, 68, 104-5, 106, 180

Antony, Mark, 57, 226

Antioch, 120, 184, 209, 210

Antiochus Epiphanes, 116

Antipas, Herod, 45, 46, 48-53, 104, 109, 207, 223, 224

anti-Semitism, 48, 173-74, 213, 243

Antonia, 75, 78, 205

Antonia, Fortress of, 15, 26, 45, 53, 102, 107

Apicata, 60, 74, 77

Aretas, King of Arabia Petraea, 51, 183, 207, 225

Arikamedu, 155

Arimathea, Joseph of, 68, 107, 112, 113, 212

Ashoka, 156

assizes in Palestine , 45, 94, 102

astrology, 22, 80, 82, 148

Auerbach, Erich, 105-6

Augustus, emperor, 28, 40, 41, 42, 52, 58, 78, 160, 187

"Avenue of the Dead," 163

Bactria, 23, 140, 143, 145, 146, 155, 158, 159

Barnabas, 178, 194, 210

Belgic tribe, 151

Bethany, 14, 16, 24, 65-66, 69, 85, 86, 87, 88, 89, 96, 97-98, 103, 140

biography, first century, 30, 32-34, 173

Boudicca, 147, 152, 208

Britannia, 145, 150-53, 207-8

Bruce, F. F., 91, 199

Buddhism, 156-57, 158, 161

Bultmann, Rudolf, 97

Burridge, Richard, 33

Caesarea Maritima, 12, 13, 22, 43-48, 110, 212

Caiaphas, 53-55, 68, 96, 100, 106-7, 178, 194-95

Caligula. *See* Gaius "Caligula"

Camulodunum (Colchester), 9, 136

Candace, Queen, 59

Capri (Capreae), 10, 11, 21-24, 40-43, 75, 76, 205

Caratacus, 152, 208

Cassius Dio. *See* Dio Cassius

Catuvellauni, 152

causality, historical, 31, 88-89, 125-26, 172, 224-25

Celts, 39, 145, 148-50, 151-52, 208, 211

Chilton, Bruce, 118

China, 18, 30, 58, 154, 155-56, 158-60, 208-9

chronology, 226-30
    dating, 219-25

Churchill, Winston S., 150

Chuza, 50, 69, 109

Claudia Rufina, 208

Claudius, emperor, 40, 104, 127, 149, 152, 181, 208

Cleopas, 104, 112, 131

codex, 30, 43-44, 213

Colchester (Camulodunum), 151, 152

communitarianism, early, 175-76

Confucianism, 156

Cornelius, 44

crucifixion, 96, 104, 110-11, 113, 131, 141, 173, 178

Cunobelinus, 152, 207

Damascus, 129, 210, 225

Defoe, Daniel, 34

deities (polytheistic), 39, 41, 56, 58, 59, 158
    Apedemek, 59
    Isis, 160
    Jupiter, 24, 41, 78, 158, 184
    Mars, 78
    Mithras, 44
    Osiris, 58
    Serapis, 56
    Vesta, 78
    Zeus Soter, 56

denial of Jesus by Peter, 101, 104-5, 125, 133

destruction of Jerusalem temple, 27, 32, 66, 68, 90-92, 95-96, 106, 115, 122, 211

Diaspora, 23, 57, 68, 91, 122, 171-72, 196-97

Didache, 175

Dio Cassius, 23, 30, 35, 43, 74, 75-76, 79-80, 81, 152, 221

dragon, 159, 160
Druids, 148, 149, 154
Drusus, son of Germanicus, 75, 79, 82, 181, 182, 187, 188
Drusus, son of Tiberius, 22, 74, 77, 82, 184, 185, 236
dust storm on April 3, 112, 224
eclipse, lunar, 112-13, 173, 220, 223-24
Egypt, 22, 29, 39, 55-62, 89, 101-2, 151, 171, 186, 213, 214-15
Emmaus, 129,131, 153, 169-70
Ephesus, 173, 211-12
eschatology, 66-67, 95-96, 120, 122-23, 134
Espenak, Fred, 223
Evans, Craig A., 91-92, 218, 239-40
Farrar, A. W., 92
Felix (Claudius Felix Antonius), 44, 212
fiction and the Gospels, 32-33, 62, 101, 105-6, 243
Flaccus, Aulus Avilius , 22, 59, 212-13, 214
France. *See* Gaul
Gaius "Caligula" (Gaius Julius Caesar Germanicus), 23, 28, 40, 60, 76, 82, 104, 181, 188-89, 205, 207, 213-14
Galatia, 9, 147, 171, 211
Galba, Servius Sulpicius, 23, 82
Galilee, Galileans, 45, 46, 69, 70, 88, 92, 95, 96, 104, 109, 115, 133, 177
Galilee, Lake (Sea) of, 49, 132-33
Gallus, Gaius Asinus, 79, 185, 187
Gamaliel, 118, 119, 195-96, 225

Gandhara, 160
Gaul, 2, 9, 22, 39, 40, 145, 148-50, 152, 183, 206
Gemellus, Tiberius, 59, 82, 188, 189
Gemoniae (Gemonian Steps), 77, 79
genres, ancient literary, 30, 32-34, 57, 105-6, 172-73
geoglyphs, 165-66
Gerizim, Mount, 206
Germania, 22, 39, 43, 145, 148-49, 181, 182-83
Germanicus Julius Caesar, 43, 80, 181, 182-85, 186, 188
Gethsemane, 97, 99, 102, 103, 112
Gnostic Gospels, 212-13
Gondopharnes, 156-57
Gospels, 30-35, 90-91, 98, 101, 125, 173, 212-13, 221-22, 224
Grant, Michael, 89, 92
Great Fire of Rome, 91, 206-7
Guangwudi, 159-60, 208-9
Guptas, 157
Hagner, Donald A., 116
Hammath (Ammathus), 50
Han dynasty of China, 18, 154, 158-62, 163, 208-9
Hasmodean Palace, 15, 53, 141
Hellenization, 32-34, 39-40, 49-50, 56, 66, 67, 160, 172, 174, 196-97
Hengistbury, 151
Herod. *See* Antipas; Agrippa; Philip; Herod the Great
Herod the Great, 44-45, 48, 52, 54, 56, 196, 237
Herodias, 51, 52, 207
Hillel, 118
Hinduism, 157
Hinnom Valley, 53

Hispania (Spain), 9, 22, 138, 145, 172
Hoehner, Harold, 219
Holinshed, Raphael, 152-53
Holy Spirit, 123, 134, 169-71, 177, 195
    Comforter, 169
    Helper, 169
Humphreys, Colin, 219, 223-24
Iceni, 151, 208
Idumea, 45
India, 57, 58, 87, 132, 135, 154-55, 156-58, 160, 239
Indo Bactrians, 156
James, brother of Jesus, 121, 124, 128-29, 131, 133, 175, 178, 211
James, brother of John, 69, 91, 95, 100, 103, 104, 133, 177, 209
Jericho, 53, 66, 69, 70, 132
Jerusalem, 14, 15, 24 -28, 45-48, 53-55, 62, 88, 90-92, 98, 139, 141, 175, 239
Jesus Christ, 24-28, 65-70, 85-114, 120-23, 125-34
    ascension, 169, 171
    betrayal, 87-88, 103, 112, 222
    blasphemy, crime of, 26, 27, 88-89, 106-7, 198-200
    burial, 87, 113, 124, 129-30, 137, 138
    cursing of the fig tree, 93, 94, 222
    divinity, claim to, 26, 27, 62, 88, 96, 106-7, 121, 169
    farewell, 94, 97
    five hundred, appear-ance to the, 128-29
    great commission, 132-33, 210
    Last Supper, 101-2, 123, 222

miracles, 30, 66, 68, 220
parables, 25, 93, 95, 125
prophecy of destruction
of Jerusalem and tem-
ple, 90-92, 95-96, 106,
239-40
resurrection, 33, 34, 112,
124, 125-26, 127-28,
129-31, 210, 215
trial, 44, 87, 106, 107-9,
133, 207
triumphal entry into
Jerusalem, 89-92
Jewish festivals
Dedication (Hanukkah),
24-28, 67, 69, 228
Passover, 46, 58, 70, 87,
88, 92, 96, 97-104, 108,
112, 113, 129, 132
Pentecost, 170-71, 174-
77, 197-98, 209
Tabernacles, 40, 46-47
Joanna, 50, 69, 109, 112,
113, 124, 129-30, 212
Joel, book of, 173
John, 54, 67-68, 90, 98, 99,
103, 104, 112, 113, 125,
130, 133, 177, 178, 238,
240
John Mark. See Mark
John the Baptist, 50-52, 69-
70, 93, 98, 102, 134, 220-
21, 223
Jonson, Ben, 77
Jordan, River, 27, 53, 69,
129, 132
Josephus, Flavius, 26, 27,
30, 35, 44-45, 46, 51-52,
53, 54, 56, 118, 119, 120-
21, 180, 206, 220, 221,
224, 244
Judaea, 22, 24, 26, 39, 43,
44, 45, 46, 57, 104, 109,
133, 223
Judaism, 27-28, 44, 61, 62,
91, 115-23, 133, 158, 174,
196-97

circumcision, 200, 210
Essenes, 117, 118, 119
Hasmodeans, 116-17
Hebrews, 32, 196, 198-
99
Hellenists, 198, 199
Herodians, 95
high priest and chief
priests, 25, 48, 54-55,
68, 92, 94, 96, 104,
106, 118, 178, 194-95
Messiah, messiahs, 25,
26-27, 31, 66, 67, 87,
90, 92, 96, 100, 102,
106, 107, 115, 120-22,
134
Pharisees, 55, 67, 90, 95,
108, 115, 117, 118,
120, 122, 193, 195
proselytes, 94, 172, 174,
200
Rabbinic Judaism, 61,
98, 115, 117, 118, 119
sacrificial system, 27, 46,
92, 93, 101-2, 122-23
Sadducees, 66, 67, 95,
118-19, 193, 195
scribes, 25, 29, 94, 95,
106, 109, 118, 119, 193
Sanhedrin (Sanhedrim),
49, 67-68, 106, 107,
119, 178, 195-96, 198,
240
synagogue, 27, 44, 50,
58, 106, 118, 172, 174,
175, 196, 197
Wisdom (logos, Word) in
Philo, 61-62
Judas Iscariot, 86, 87-88, 96,
99-100, 101, 102, 103, 112,
125, 134
Julia Claudia, 82, 188
Julia, daughter of Drusus,
188
Julia, second wife of
Tiberius, 42, 182, 187
Julia Severa, 174

Julias. See Livias
Kama Sutra, 157
Keay, John, 157
Kerala, 157
khamsin (dust storm), 224
Kidron valley, 15, 26, 53, 90,
102, 141
"King of the Jews," 34, 104,
108, 111
Korea, 154, 159
Kushans, 161
Lazarus, 65-68, 69, 70, 85,
86, 88, 103, 124, 140, 212,
240
Lentulus Gaetulicus, 146
Levick, Barbara, 48, 215,
237
Lin-Hsiu (Lin-Xiu), 159, 208-
9
Livia, 41-42, 49, 75, 188
Livias (Julias), 49
Livilla, 43, 74, 75, 76, 77-78,
82
Logos, 61-62, 238
Luke, 30, 32, 34, 90-91, 99,
109, 116, 125, 155, 170,
172, 175-77, 193, 194, 195,
196, 198, 200, 220, 221
lunar eclipse, 112, 173, 219,
220, 202-3
Luoyang, 18, 158, 159-60,
163, 208-9
Maccabaeus, Judas, 27, 116-
17
Maccabees, book of the,
118
Machaerus, 51, 52
Macro, Naevius Sertorius,
76, 205
Magdala, 69
Manaen, 50
Mareotis, Lake, 18, 55
Mark, 32, 90-91, 94, 98-99,
125, 127, 132, 176, 194
Martha, 65-67, 69, 85, 88,
124, 212
Mary Magdalene, 69, 70,

104, 112, 113, 124, 129,
240, 244
Mary, mother of Jesus, 56,
112, 124
Mary, of Bethany, 65, 66,
69, 85-87, 88, 124, 154,
212, 244
Mary, wife of Cleopas, 112,
113, 124, 129, 130
Matthew, 30, 32, 52, 91, 113,
125, 127, 221
Matthias, 128, 134,
Meithei, 157
Meroe, 58-59
Mesoamerica, 163-64
Mesopotamia, 57, 160, 174
Mexico, 163-64
Misenum, 10, 21, 41, 78
Mishnah, 119, 199-200
Mississipi River, 163
Mithraism, 44
Moche, 7, 164-65
Moesia, 9, 145
Moon, Pyramid of the, 163-
64
Mount of Olives, 17, 53, 88,
89, 93, 95, 99, 102, 124,
135, 141
Nag Hammadi codices, 212-
13
Narnia, 239
Nathaniel, 133
Nazareth, 25, 49, 91, 92,
111, 151, 173
Nazca, 7, 165-66
Nazca lines, 165
Nero Caesar (son of
Agrippina), 75, 181, 186
Nero, emperor, 28, 40, 69,
73, 92, 170, 206-7, 210, 212
Nerva, 80-81
Nicodemus, 68, 107, 108,
112, 113, 119, 212
Nile, River, 55, 56, 58, 59
obsidian, 164
Ohio River, 163
Orissa, 156

ossuaries, 54-55, 67
Oxus River, 158
Pakhangha, 157
Pandateria, 10, 21, 42, 59,
82, 181, 182, 187, 189
Pandy, 157
papyrus, 29-30, 33, 59
Paris (Lutetia), 145
Parthia, 9, 23, 53, 132, 154,
158, 160, 171, 174, 175,
183, 207
Paterculus, C. Velleius, 78
Paul (Saul), 44, 68-69, 116,
118, 119, 128-29, 158, 171,
194, 197, 199, 200-201,
210-12, 220, 225
Pepys, Samuel, 34
Perea, 45, 48, 49, 51, 52, 69
Periplus Maris Erythraei,
155
Peru, 164, 165
Peter, 54, 90, 94-95, 98, 100,
101, 103, 104, 105, 112,
125, 128, 129, 130, 131,
133, 169-78, 193, 195, 200,
206, 212
Petra, 207
Petronius's *Satyricon*, 32
Philip, Herod, 51-52, 69
Philo (Philo Judaeus), 23,
33, 43, 46-47, 59-62, 109-
10, 172, 199, 206, 212,
213-14, 237
phoenix, 22, 89, 214-15, 245
Pilate (Pontius Pilatus), 22-
24, 40, 43-48, 94, 97, 102-
3, 104, 107-11, 113-14,
120, 121, 127, 173, 177,
206-7, 223, 224-25
Piso, Gnaeus Calpurnius,
183-85
Plancina, Munatia, 183-85,
Plato, 57, 60, 61, 62, 172,
213, 238
Pliny the Elder (Gaius
Plinius Secundus), 55,
154, 215

Pompeii, 10, 137, 194
Pondicherry, 155
Pontian islands, 189
portents, 23, 75-76, 109,
110, 111-12, 159, 160, 214-
15. *See also* prophecy
Porter, Stanley, 219
Praetorian guard, 42, 74, 75,
76, 78, 184, 205
Prasutagus, 152
prophecy, prophet 34, 50-
51, 52, 68, 90-92, 93, 95-
96, 120, 122, 162, 170,
173, 190, 239-40. *See also*
portents
Provence, 149
Psalms, book of, 102, 106,
175
Ptolemies, 39, 56, 57-58, 116
Ptolemy (Claudius
Ptolemaeus), 55, 155
Pudens, Aulus, 208
"Q," 32, 125
Qumran, 117, 122, 178. *See*
Judaism, Essenes
"reign of terror" after
Sejanus, 43, 78, 79-80
Reinhard, Johan, 165
Revelation, book of, 32, 51,
123, 242
Rhakotis, 18, 56
Rhine, River, 148, 150, 184,
185
Rhodes, 23, 42, 82
Roberts, J. M., 126
Robinson, John A. T., 62
Romanisation, 39-40, 49, 54,
145-46, 149
Rylands Library Manchester,
31
Salome, daughter of
Herodias, 51,
Salome, mother of James,
69, 113, 129
Samaria, Samaritans, 44, 45,
70, 134, 206, 224
Samaritan woman, 108

Sanders, E. P., 97, 101
Sangam period, 157
Sapphira, 176, 193
Saul. See Paul
scrolls, 29-30, 33, 176. See
   also Codex
Sejanus, 23, 24, 35, 42, 43,
   48, 50, 73-82, 104, 110,
   148, 181, 185, 186-87, 188,
   236-37
Sejanus: His Fall, 77
Seleucids, 39, 116, 160
Seneca the Younger (Lucius
   Annaeus Seneca), 43, 77
Sepphoris, 48-49, 91, 196
Septuagint, 56-57, 237
Severus, Sulpicius, 91
Sextus Marius, 79
Shakespeare, William, 77,
   152-53
Shammai, 118
Sibylline Oracles, 224
Silk Road, 8, 154, 160
Simon the Leper, 86
Skeat, T. C., 30
South America, 162, 164-66
Spain. See Hispania
spikenard, 85-87, 154
Sri Lanka, 160
Stanton, Graham, 30
Steiner, George, 28
Stephen, 197-202, 210, 225
Strabo, 56, 146
Suetonius (Gaius Suetonius
   Tranquillus), 23, 30, 35,
   40, 42, 43, 75, 79, 80, 89,
   97, 102, 127, 185, 187, 188
Sun Pyramid, 163
Susanna, 69, 70, 113, 129,
   212

"Synoptic" Gospels, 32, 66,
   90-91, 101, 120, 125
Syria, 9, 22, 24, 39, 49, 160,
   183, 185, 206, 221
Tacitus, Cornelius, 23, 26,
   30, 34-35, 43, 73, 74-75,
   77, 79, 80, 82, 89, 91, 97,
   102, 120, 148, 182, 183,
   185-86, 187, 188, 189, 214-
   15, 219
Talmud, 55, 117
Tarsus, 210
temple in Jerusalem, 24-28,
   45, 46, 53, 68, 91-92, 106,
   115-23, 172, 174, 175
   court of the Gentiles, 15,
      25, 27, 92
   destruction of, 90-92,
      95-96, 106, 239-40
   inner sanctuary, 221
   Solomon's Portico, 15,
      25, 193
Temple of the Moon, 164
Temple of the Sun, 164
Teotihuacán, 139, 163-64
Theophilus, 172-73
Theudas, 27, 195-96
Thomas, 131, 132, 133, 156-
   57
Thrasyllus, 22-23, 82
Tiber River, 77, 80
Tiberias, 14, 49-50
Tiberius, 21-24, 28 , 31, 34-
   35, 40-43, 46-48, 50, 52,
   58, 59, 73-82, 104, 107-8,
   110, 136, 145, 148, 181-82,
   183, 184, 185-89, 205-6,
   207, 220-21, 224
Togodumnus, 152, 208
travel writing, 155

Trinovantes, 153, 154, 208
Trung Nhi, 209
Trung Tac, 209
Upanishads, 157
Upper Room, Jerusalem, 98-
   99, 101, 124-25, 132, 134,
   170, 174, 176
Vatsyayana, 157
Vedas, 157
Ventotene, 187
Vercingetorix, 149
Vermes, Geza, 62, 97, 100,
   241
Vespasian (Titus Flavius
   Vespasianus), 230
Vesuvius, 21, 41, 55
Viet Nam (Nam Viet), 159,
   209
Villa Jovis, 10, 11, 21-24, 41-
   43, 78, 205
Vipsania, first wife of
   Tiberius, 42, 79, 187
Virgil (Publius Vergilius
   Maro), 146
Vitellius, Lucius, 206, 214
votive shields, incident of,
   22, 46-48, 104, 107-8, 110,
   206
Waddington, W. G., 219,
   224
Wang Mang, 159
Way, followers of the, 171,
   174, 193
Wenham, John, 241, 244
Wheathampstead, 151
Word (Logos), 61-62
Wright, N. T., 33-34
Year of Four Emperors, 230
Yellow River, 160, 209
Zebedee, 112

Sanders, E. P., 97, 101

Sangam period, 157

Sapphira, 176, 193

Saul. See Paul

scrolls, 29-30, 33, 176. See also Codex

Sejanus, 23, 24, 35, 42, 43, 48, 50, 73-82, 104, 110, 148, 181, 185, 186-87, 188, 236-37

Sejanus: His Fall, 77

Seleucids, 39, 116, 160

Seneca the Younger (Lucius Annaeus Seneca), 43, 77

Sepphoris, 48-49, 91, 196

Septuagint, 56-57, 237

Severus, Sulpicius, 91

Sextus Marius, 79

Shakespeare, William, 77, 152-53

Shammai, 118

Sibylline Oracles, 224

Silk Road, 8, 154, 160

Simon the Leper, 86

Skeat, T. C., 30

South America, 162, 164-66

Spain. See Hispania

spikenard, 85-87, 154

Sri Lanka, 160

Stanton, Graham, 30

Steiner, George, 28

Stephen, 197-202, 210, 225

Strabo, 56, 146

Suetonius (Gaius Suetonius Tranquillus), 23, 30, 35, 40, 42, 43, 75, 79, 80, 89, 97, 102, 127, 185, 187, 188

Sun Pyramid, 163

Susanna, 69, 70, 113, 129, 212

"Synoptic" Gospels, 32, 66, 90-91, 101, 120, 125

Syria, 9, 22, 24, 39, 49, 160, 183, 185, 206, 221

Tacitus, Cornelius, 23, 26, 30, 34-35, 43, 73, 74-75, 77, 79, 80, 82, 89, 91, 97, 102, 120, 148, 182, 183, 185-86, 187, 188, 189, 214-15, 219

Talmud, 55, 117

Tarsus, 210

temple in Jerusalem, 24-28, 45, 46, 53, 68, 91-92, 106, 115-23, 172, 174, 175

    court of the Gentiles, 15, 25, 27, 92

    destruction of, 90-92, 95-96, 106, 239-40

    inner sanctuary, 221

    Solomon's Portico, 15, 25, 193

Temple of the Moon, 164

Temple of the Sun, 164

Teotihuacán, 139, 163-64

Theophilus, 172-73

Theudas, 27, 195-96

Thomas, 131, 132, 133, 156-57

Thrasyllus, 22-23, 82

Tiber River, 77, 80

Tiberias, 14, 49-50

Tiberius, 21-24, 28 , 31, 34-35, 40-43, 46-48, 50, 52, 58, 59, 73-82, 104, 107-8, 110, 136, 145, 148, 181-82, 183, 184, 185-89, 205-6, 207, 220-21, 224

Togodumnus, 152, 208

travel writing, 155

Trinovantes, 153, 154, 208

Trung Nhi, 209

Trung Tac, 209

Upanishads, 157

Upper Room, Jerusalem, 98-99, 101, 124-25, 132, 134, 170, 174, 176

Vatsyayana, 157

Vedas, 157

Ventotene, 187

Vercingetorix, 149

Vermes, Geza, 62, 97, 100, 241

Vespasian (Titus Flavius Vespasianus), 230

Vesuvius, 21, 41, 55

Viet Nam (Nam Viet), 159, 209

Villa Jovis, 10, 11, 21-24, 41-43, 78, 205

Vipsania, first wife of Tiberius, 42, 79, 187

Virgil (Publius Vergilius Maro), 146

Vitellius, Lucius, 206, 214

votive shields, incident of, 22, 46-48, 104, 107-8, 110, 206

Waddington, W. G., 219, 224

Wang Mang, 159

Way, followers of the, 171, 174, 193

Wenham, John, 241, 244

Wheathampstead, 151

Word (Logos), 61-62

Wright, N. T., 33-34

Year of Four Emperors, 230

Yellow River, 160, 209

Zebedee, 112

104, 112, 113, 124, 129, 240, 244

Mary, mother of Jesus, 56, 112, 124

Mary, of Bethany, 65, 66, 69, 85-87, 88, 124, 154, 212, 244

Mary, wife of Cleopas, 112, 113, 124, 129, 130

Matthew, 30, 32, 52, 91, 113, 125, 127, 221

Matthias, 128, 134,

Meithei, 157

Meroe, 58-59

Mesoamerica, 163-64

Mesopotamia, 57, 160, 174

Mexico, 163-64

Misenum, 10, 21, 41, 78

Mishnah, 119, 199-200

Mississipi River, 163

Mithraism, 44

Moche, 7, 164-65

Moesia, 9, 145

Moon, Pyramid of the, 163-64

Mount of Olives, 17, 53, 88, 89, 93, 95, 99, 102, 124, 135, 141

Nag Hammadi codices, 212-13

Narnia, 239

Nathaniel, 133

Nazareth, 25, 49, 91, 92, 111, 151, 173

Nazca, 7, 165-66

Nazca lines, 165

Nero Caesar (son of Agrippina), 75, 181, 186

Nero, emperor, 28, 40, 69, 73, 92, 170, 206-7, 210, 212

Nerva, 80-81

Nicodemus, 68, 107, 108, 112, 113, 119, 212

Nile, River, 55, 56, 58, 59

obsidian, 164

Ohio River, 163

Orissa, 156

ossuaries, 54-55, 67

Oxus River, 158

Pakhangha, 157

Pandateria, 10, 21, 42, 59, 82, 181, 182, 187, 189

Pandy, 157

papyrus, 29-30, 33, 59

Paris (Lutetia), 145

Parthia, 9, 23, 53, 132, 154, 158, 160, 171, 174, 175, 183, 207

Paterculus, C. Velleius, 78

Paul (Saul), 44, 68-69, 116, 118, 119, 128-29, 158, 171, 194, 197, 199, 200-201, 210-12, 220, 225

Pepys, Samuel, 34

Perea, 45, 48, 49, 51, 52, 69

Periplus Maris Erythraei, 155

Peru, 164, 165

Peter, 54, 90, 94-95, 98, 100, 101, 103, 104, 105, 112, 125, 128, 129, 130, 131, 133, 169-78, 193, 195, 200, 206, 212

Petra, 207

Petronius's *Satyricon*, 32

Philip, Herod, 51-52, 69

Philo (Philo Judaeus), 23, 33, 43, 46-47, 59-62, 109-10, 172, 199, 206, 212, 213-14, 237

phoenix, 22, 89, 214-15, 245

Pilate (Pontius Pilatus), 22-24, 40, 43-48, 94, 97, 102-3, 104, 107-11, 113-14, 120, 121, 127, 173, 177, 206-7, 223, 224-25

Piso, Gnaeus Calpurnius, 183-85

Plancina, Munatia, 183-85,

Plato, 57, 60, 61, 62, 172, 213, 238

Pliny the Elder (Gaius Plinius Secundus), 55, 154, 215

Pompeii, 10, 137, 194

Pondicherry, 155

Pontian islands, 189

portents, 23, 75-76, 109, 110, 111-12, 159, 160, 214-15. *See also* prophecy

Porter, Stanley, 219

Praetorian guard, 42, 74, 75, 76, 78, 184, 205

Prasutagus, 152

prophecy, prophet 34, 50-51, 52, 68, 90-92, 93, 95-96, 120, 122, 162, 170, 173, 190, 239-40. *See also* portents

Provence, 149

Psalms, book of, 102, 106, 175

Ptolemies, 39, 56, 57-58, 116

Ptolemy (Claudius Ptolemaeus), 55, 155

Pudens, Aulus, 208

"Q," 32, 125

Qumran, 117, 122, 178. *See* Judaism, Essenes

"reign of terror" after Sejanus, 43, 78, 79-80

Reinhard, Johan, 165

Revelation, book of, 32, 51, 123, 242

Rhakotis, 18, 56

Rhine, River, 148, 150, 184, 185

Rhodes, 23, 42, 82

Roberts, J. M., 126

Robinson, John A. T., 62

Romanisation, 39-40, 49, 54, 145-46, 149

Rylands Library Manchester, 31

Salome, daughter of Herodias, 51,

Salome, mother of James, 69, 113, 129

Samaria, Samaritans, 44, 45, 70, 134, 206, 224

Samaritan woman, 108